New Casebooks

FRANKENSTEIN

MARY SHELLEY

EDITED BY FRED BOTTING

First published 1995 by
MACMILLAN PRESS LTD
Houndmills, Basingstoke, Hampshire RG21 2XS
and London
Companies and representatives
throughout the world

ISBN 0–333–59958–6 hardcover
ISBN 0–333–59959–4 paperback

A catalogue record for this book is available
from the British Library

10 9 8 7 6 5 4 3
04 03 02 01 00 99 98

Printed in Malaysia

New Casebooks

FRANKENSTEIN

NEW CASEBOOKS

PUBLISHED

Antony and Cleopatra
Hamlet
King Lear
Macbeth
The Merchant of Venice
A Midsummer Night's Dream
Shakespeare's History Plays: Richard II to Henry V
Shakespeare on Film
Shakespeare's Tragedies
Twelfth Night

Feminist Theatre and Theory
Waiting for Godot and Endgame

Bleak House
Wilkie Collins
Joseph Conrad
David Copperfield and Hard Times
Emma
E. M. Forster
Frankenstein
Great Expectations
Jane Eyre
Mansfield Park and Persuasion
Middlemarch
Mrs Dalloway and To the Lighthouse
George Orwell
Sense and Sensibility and Pride and Prejudice
Sons and Lovers
Tess of the d'Urbervilles
Toni Morrison
Tristram Shandy
The Turn of the Screw and What Maisie Knew
Villette
Wuthering Heights

William Blake
Chaucer
Coleridge, Keats and Shelley
John Donne
Seamus Heaney
Philip Larkin
Victorian Women Poets
Wordsworth

Postcolonial Literatures

Further titles are in preparation

New Casebooks Series
Series Standing Order
ISBN 0–333–71702–3 hardcover
ISBN 0–333–69345–0 paperback
(outside North America only)

You can receive future titles in this series as they are published by placing a standing order. Please contact your bookseller or, in case of difficulty, write to us at the address below with your name and address, the title of the series and the ISBN quoted above.

Customer Services Department, Macmillan Distribution Ltd
Houndmills, Basingstoke, Hampshire RG21 6XS, England

Contents

Introduction

FRED BOTTING

> And now, once again, I bid my hideous progeny go forth and prosper.
>
> (Mary Shelley, 1831 Introduction to *Frankenstein*)

I CRITICISM AND MONSTROSITY

Frankenstein is a product of criticism, not a work of literature. This is not to condemn the novel as undeserving of the attention, appreciation and admiration usually accorded literary works, but to highlight how 'literature' has lost many of its former associations with timeless and ultimate value. Indeed, what passes for literature has undergone a major process of revision in the last quarter of a century, having reached the point where it no longer signifies objects meriting virtually sacred devotion but *'a particular manner of reading and deciphering signs'*.[1] The publication of a collection of essays such as this on *Frankenstein* testifies to the changes that have already occurred in literary and critical theory and practice, marking a shift of focus in which literary and popular fiction is studied in relation to a network of other writings from political, historical and cultural spheres. Subject, in recent decades, to increasing and serious academic appraisals from various critical perspectives, *Frankenstein*'s place on courses, if not within the once established and now contested literary tradition, seems assured, an index of the function of criticism in the production of literature.

Since, and even before, its creation *Frankenstein* has been inscribed in critical relations. On its publication in 1818 the novel was received in less than approving terms by critics perturbed by its lack of morality and piety as well as its apparent affiliation with the radical political positions that came to prominence and notoriety in the revolutionary polemics of the 1790s. Published anonymously and dedicated to a renowned radical, William Godwin, the novel's political stance seemed clear enough.[2] Conservative anxieties were no doubt exacerbated, as Paul O'Flinn suggests (essay 1), by the unrest and attempted uprisings linked to Luddite machine-breaking in the same decade in which the novel was published. An aesthetic concern, itself entangled throughout the eighteenth century with moral and political issues, was also manifested in the novel's critical reception: *Frankenstein* betrayed many of the dark and gloomy hallmarks of Gothic fiction. The genre was popular, proper critical judgement of the time rather hysterically asserted, for the wrong reasons: it inculcated an appetite for sensational and terrifying events, exciting and magical adventures and extravagant, over-indulged emotions, rather than cultivating moral and virtuous understanding on the part of readers. The Introduction to the revised 1831 edition of *Frankenstein* acknowledges this tradition when it states the intention of awakening 'thrilling horror ... to curdle the blood, and quicken the beatings of the heart'.[3]

The occasion for the composition of *Frankenstein*, the author's 1831 Introduction maintains, was itself Gothic in setting and inspiration. During a stormy summer in 1816 beside Lake Leman in Switzerland, Byron, Mary and Percy Shelley, Claire Clairmont, Mary's stepsister, and Dr William Polidori, Byron's physician, regularly gathered at Byron's villa. One evening they amused themselves by reading from a collection of German Gothic tales. Byron proposed a ghost story competition. The clear winner was Mary Shelley. Her success was deserved: the 1831 Introduction details the effort that went into the process of composition as well as the influences upon it. The effect of the account of the novel's composition is to shift the significance of *Frankenstein* from a Gothic framework to one imbued with concerns that would come under the general heading of 'Romanticism', though the term, in 1816, had still to be invented. In this framework it is the Introduction's and the novel's concern with imagination, creative authority and the principle of life that form the main interest of critics. These issues also establish an important connection between poetic and scientific theories. The discussions of philosophical doctrine and scientific experiments between Byron and Percy Shelley were far from idle. As Anne Mellor (essay 5) argues in her account of the work of leading scientists of the time, Humphrey Davy, Erasmus Darwin and Luigi Galvani, ideas of the human creative imagination were bound up with desires to control and understand the newly discovered secret of natural life – electricity – and were subjects of great interest to Romantic writers, Percy Shelley in particular.

The 1831 Introduction is also important for its provision of an authorised interpretative context for the novel. Describing the images of monstrous creation that possess her in a state of waking reverie, Mary Shelley comments 'frightful it must be; for supremely frightful would be the effect of any human endeavour to mock the stupendous mechanism of the Creator of the World' (p. 9). Frankenstein's act, it seems, is transgressive, an act of presumption against the sacred and inviolable laws of God and nature. For many critics, Shelley's comment constitutes the clearest and most direct statement of the story's moral, making 'virtually explicit its expression of Faustian guilt and retribution'.[4] The statement, however, is not as straightforward as it seems. Like the 1831 Introduction as a whole, which has become a site of critical contestation as to its accuracy, motives and significance,[5] the apparently authorised moral is not necessarily an endorsement of a Christian theology.[6] Given Romantic identifications with Prometheus, who, according to Ovid's *Metamorphoses*, created the world and human life, and also the novel's subtitle, it would be unwise to validate an exclusively Christian frame of reference. Moreover, the idea of Frankenstein's presumption did not originate in the 1831 Introduction.

On Friday 29 August 1823, having only recently returned to England from Italy, where she had been since *Frankenstein*'s publication, Mary Shelley went to see a successful stage version of her novel. She commented favourably on the production in a letter to Leigh Hunt, her approval supplemented, no doubt, by the pleasant surprise attendant on discovering her novel's success: 'but lo and behold! I found myself famous'.[7] The title of the play was *Presumption: or The Fate of Frankenstein*. Not only did the production retitle and rewrite the novel, supplying it with a moral and starting the popular tradition of silencing the monster and foregrounding, like the 1831 Introduction, the process of sensational creation, it also signalled *Frankenstein*'s transformation into a modern myth, a myth sustained in popular rather than literary culture. By 1826, fifteen different melodramatic or burlesque productions of the novel had been staged. Throughout the nineteenth century popular 'Frankensteins', referring as much to the monster as the creator, appeared in many different forms: caricatures of the period used the monster to represent many demands for social and political reform, reanimating anxious associations with the mobs of the revolutionary period.[8] The 1831 Introduction and the dramatic versions also provide later films with one of their most striking scenes: the Introduction's brief mention of 'the working of some powerful engine' that generates life in the monster also generates the elaborate machinery of electrical circuitry and technical creation that is powerfully and repeatedly presented in films.

The Introduction thus serves as a significant frame for the novel in its provision of a moral and an outline of literary origins. As an engagement with popular meanings and a tacit justification of the revisions to the 1831 edition in which the identity of Mary Shelley as author is announced, it is also a work of criticism and a process of rewriting, a frame which extends rather than forecloses the discussions of the novel's meaning. Moreover, introducing a novel composed of frame narratives that, Beth Newman (essay 7) argues, disclose the work of writing in the deferral of fixed meanings and determinable origins, the 1831 inscription of authorial presence has a decidedly ambiguous status. It simultaneously offers an authorial and critical overview of the novel and furnishes it with another narrative. The Introduction thus participates in the frame structure of the novel itself, replicating, with a difference, positions from the text. In the renarration of the scene of monstrous nocturnal creation Mary Shelley's vision sees Frankenstein seeing the creature stir with life (p. 9).

To use Mary Shelley's term, the Introduction provides an 'appendage' to the novel (p. 5). It is an appendage, however, that works like a Derridean supplement since its adding of what the story lacks – origin, authority and meaning – does more than supply extra details: it supplants the novel with the new significance it provides, thus replacing, re-presenting or transforming the text with the imposition of a new frame, a frame which then grounds critical interpretations.[9] As a supplement, however, the introductory frame also opens up issues of writing and difference, inaugurating a play of meanings: when Shelley bids a benevolent farewell to the 'hideous progeny' at the end of the Introduction the reference is doubled, signifying both Frankenstein's creation and her own, *Frankenstein*. Duplicating and differentiating Shelley's position from Frankenstein's in the asymmetry of this unpossessive gesture, the introductory inscription discloses the wider movements of textuality that traverse *Frankenstein*'s narratives. It opens on to a form of textuality that appeared monstrous to critics from the eighteenth to the twentieth century.

II EIGHTEENTH-CENTURY MONSTROSITY

The connection between texts and monsters was established well before Shelley equated *Frankenstein* and monster. 'Monster' was a standard, almost technical, term of criticism in the eighteenth century and one applied to *Frankenstein* itself: one reviewer called it a 'monstrous literary abortion'. [10] The metaphor was frequently applied to Gothic novels, with none more deserving of the appellation 'monster' than M. G. Lewis's notorious *The Monk* which scandalised reviewers with its accounts of rape, murder, incest and diabolical intrigue.[11] In circulation throughout the eighteenth century, the metaphor of monstrosity applied to any literary or cultural artefact that contravened the rules of neoclassical aesthetics. Lord Kames outlined conventional rules of taste in his *Elements of Criticism*: 'every remarkable deviation from the standard makes accordingly an impression upon us of imperfection, irregularity, or disorder: it is disagreeable, and raises in us a painful emotion: monsters, exciting the curiosity of a philosopher, fail not at the same time to excite a sort of horror.'[12] Horror, pain and disgust were the proper responses to creations that failed to conform to neoclassical aesthetic ideals of unified design, harmonious composition of parts in simple regularity and proportion. Frankenstein's overwhelming feelings of horror and disgust on seeing his hideously disproportionate creation come to life display the appropriate reaction to aesthetic deformity (p. 57).

Monsters abounded in eighteenth-century writing. One critic complained at the 'flood of novels, tales, romances, and other monsters of the imagination' which encouraged 'the propagation of so depraved a taste'.[13] Emanating from France, these monsters, the critic hoped, would not survive in an English aesthetic climate. Aesthetic depravity and deformity were correlated with moral laxity. The concern about the 'lewdness and immorality' of 'this species of writing' warranted further remarks contrasting the proper, moral and instructive benefits of classical imitations of nature and common life with 'romances and novels which turn upon characters out of nature, monsters of perfection, feats of chivalry, fairy-enchantments, and the whole train of the marvellous absurd'. These fictions, moreover, 'transport the reader unprofitably into the clouds, where he is sure to find no solid footing, or into those wilds of fancy, which go for ever out of the way of human paths'.[14] In the same year another critic attacked the popularity of the 'strange monster' of romance that had been imported from France in a 'deluge of impossibility'.[15]

Hostile critics frequently cast all modern prose fiction, whether romance or novel, into a single category containing everything deemed immoral, unnatural, fanciful, absurd and unreal. The emergence of the realistic novel in the middle of the century, however, was prefaced with statements declaring direct opposition to the aesthetic and moral deformity of romances. Samuel Richardson tentatively proposed that his *Pamela* (1740) 'might possibly introduce a new species of writing' which would turn young readers away from 'the pomp and parade of romance-writing' and 'promote the cause of religion and virtue'.[16] A similar justification of realistic fiction was made by Samuel Johnson who argued that fiction should, with discrimination, imitate nature and life in order to provide useful lessons in morality.[17]

Monsters, if properly represented, could thus serve useful purposes: 'Vice', Johnson states, 'for vice is necessary to be shown, should always disgust.'[18] As figures of vice, monsters should be visible as examples of what not to do, lessons in the dangers of vicious behaviour and ideas. Barbara Freeman (essay 8) examines the Latin roots of the word 'monster' to elucidate its cautionary connotations. Chris Baldick (essay 2), following Michel Foucault, links the Latin meaning to the practice in medieval morality plays of staging vice in order to display the consequences of any deviations from the path of virtue. Monsters thus had an important function as indices of deformity. They reinforced the necessity and naturalness of the terms and values against which they were opposed and subordinated: if monsters were visible, so too were virtues. Monsters thus fulfilled a socially regulative function, one that Henry Fielding invoked in *Joseph Andrews* (1742) to distinguish his 'species of writing' from romances. Declaring that his concern was 'not men, but manners; not an individual, but a species', he outlined his project as one that held 'a glass to thousands in their closets, that they may contemplate their deformity, and endeavour to reduce it', so enabling the beneficial and private correction of faults.[19] Disclosing monstrosity or deformity in the mirror of writing regulated social attitudes and behaviour.

There was a problem, however, underlying the uses of monstrosity. Not only displaying vice in order to forestall deviancy, thereby policing enlightenment aesthetic and moral categories, monsters also disclosed the processes of differentiation entailed in the establishment of those categories in the first place. References to novels and romances as 'species of writing' and monsters drew upon natural history's modes of generic classification which categorised objects and life forms according to resemblances of type and species. Monsters constituted significant deviations from categories and norms, unnatural in their deformity. Though represented as 'out of nature', freakish aberrations in the development of species, monsters were, on a larger scale, necessary to the formation of the systems that classified them. In his account of the natural sciences of the eighteenth century, Michel Foucault argues that monsters signal the variety and diversity of nature's continuity. They enabled 'visible species' to be separated out from the ceaseless background of monstrosities that appear, glimmer, sink into the abyss, and occasionally survive'. Thus, Foucault goes on, 'the monster ensures the emergence of difference'. This difference is retrospective, involving 'the background projection of those differences and those identities that provide *taxonomia* first with structure, then with character'.[20]

Character, category and classification appear less natural in Foucault's analysis, an effect of differentiation rather than the cause. In criticism and literature monsters not only had to be visible themselves as objects of vice: their visibility, as a mark of difference, also brought to light more than the identity of virtue, disclosing a wider deviancy and difference that rendered systems of classification both unstable and artificial. As the flood of monstrous fiction increased rather than subsided in the course of the eighteenth century increasing anxiety is evident among critics, an anxiety over the effects of fiction on the stability of neoclassical structures of value. Fears about fiction's corrupting effects on the young intensified and arguments in favour of representing vice in a hideous and repulsive manner became less convincing because they depended on the assumption that the visibility of monsters was self-evident, that readers would recognise vice when they saw it. But it was not just a matter of the display of monsters: to see monsters, readers of fiction had to know what to look for, had to have already internalised the system of neoclassical values in order to know how to see, how to discriminate between virtue and vice. Perception appeared as neither natural nor empirical, but an effect of culturally constructed categories. In 1787 George Canning argued of *Tom Jones* that

> is it not also a character, in whose shades the lines of right and wrong, of propriety and misconduct, are so intimately blended, and softened into each other, as to render it too difficult for the indiscriminating eye of childhood to distinguish between rectitude and error? Are not its imperfections so nearly allied to excellence, and does not the excess of its good qualities bear so strongly an affinity to imperfection, as to require a more matured judgement, a more accurate penetration, to point out the line where virtue ends and vice begins?[21]

Fiction blurred the boundaries, crossed the lines that distinguished virtue from vice, thus rendering readers who had yet to develop proper powers of discrimination susceptible to corruption. Young, immature readers were particular subjects of critical concern, though the paternalistic and protective tones of criticism seemed to be more anxious about the preservation of the nation's taste, values and morality than individual corruption and depravity.

It is in this sense that Frankenstein's monster and *Frankenstein*'s monstrosity can be said to be effects of criticism. When Frankenstein announces the wonderful implications of his discovery of the secret of life he uses terms that resonate with eighteenth-century critical significance as well as having contemporary revolutionary and Romantic significance. Consumed by creative fervour, Frankenstein exclaims:

> Life and death appeared to me ideal bounds that I should first break through, and pour a torrent of light into our dark world. A new species would bless me as its creator and source; many happy and excellent natures would owe their being to me. No father could claim the gratitude of his child so completely as I should deserve theirs.
> (p. 54)

Paternal metaphors, as Baldick observes (essay 2), dominated the polemics of the British revolutionary debates. The totalising aspirations of the Romantic creative imagination are powerfully evident in this projection of a unity beyond all difference. In the context of romance and the novel, however, these aspirations take the form of 'monsters of the imagination', 'monsters of perfection', which in their projection of an absolute and Romantic ideal of human unity become detours along groundless flights of fancy 'which go for ever out of the way of human paths'.[22] The monstrous results of such imaginative and idealised creation are also made explicit. Indeed, it is the monster's refusal to submit to his creator's assumed power and authority, his calling Frankenstein a 'slave' (p. 167), that releases the novel's most powerful rendering of the relation between creator and creation, the dynamic of mutual, irreconcilable and reversible flight and pursuit towards the end. It manifests the subversive potential of fiction that was becoming increasingly evident in the production and consumption of romances in the eighteenth century: literature's refusal to be subordinated to moral uses and categories, a diabolical power that 'cannot be made to serve a master'.[23]

The phrases 'new species' and 'torrent of light' also allude to criticism. The latter, with its millenarian associations, suggests both a moment of apocalyptic revelation or enlightened illuminism and the deluge of romances that threatened to overwhelm the literary marketplace, blurring all boundaries, values and discriminations in an unstoppable tide of monstrous fictions. Horace Walpole's 'new species of romance', *The Castle of Otranto* (1764), was blamed for initiating a dangerous deluge of improper fictions. One critic observed with horror how 'Walpole's Ghosts' 'propagated their species with unequalled fecundity', leaving their 'spawn' in every bookshop.[24] That floods turned into dangerously unnatural and bestial modes of reproduction is significant for Frankenstein's strange procreative exercise. It was a form of propagation directly related to questions of gender. One recurrent concern about the corrupting effects of fiction was its influence on women. Romances encouraged hopeless identifications with female heroines, distracting female desires from proper feminine domestic duties and attachments: readers became 'entirely corrupted by the giddy and fantastical notions of love and gallantry' or habituated to 'loose principles and immodest practices'.[25] The dangerous corruptions of fiction were haunted by a revolutionary spectre in the way that they augured 'the complete breakdown of familial and social relations'.[26] T. J. Matthias makes explicit, and gendered, connections between fiction and political disturbance. Female writers who mix politics and fiction are seen to 'turn us wild with Gallic frenzy', inspiring distastefully unfeminine and terrifyingly revolutionary passions.[27]

Fiction destabilised the boundaries of gendered social propriety and order and overturned conventional relationships within families and also in modes of literary production. The propagation of romances and novels was associated with both female readers and writers. Hannah More noted that romances, encouraging female readers to become writers, caused a proliferation of texts and complained of 'those ever multiplying authors, that with unparalleled fecundity are overstocking the world with their quick-succeeding progeny'.[28] In the writing of *Frankenstein* Mary Shelley joins in this process of turning from reader to author in the propagation of another monster. The text, moreover, partially inscribes the figure who was the object of so much critical concern. Margaret Saville, the woman to whom *Frankenstein*, in the shape of Walton's letters, is addressed, appears as a married, middle-class and homebound woman. She represents the private reader to whom Fielding's corrective mirror of the novel was held up, but, as a result of the proliferation of romances throughout the century, whose consumption and discrimination of fiction was difficult to regulate.[29] A 'framing woman' to the novel, as Gayatri Spivak notes (essay 10), Mrs Saville occupies the uncertain space of female subjectivity. Occupying a marginal textual zone beyond the darkness and distance into which the monster disappears at the end of the novel, the female subject possesses an unknown potential, but one, in the context of female reading and writing, which harbours disturbing possibilities for male conceptions of authority. This potential is imagined by Frankenstein before he destroys the half-finished mate he has promised to create for the monster. He speculates on the desires of the female monster, on her capacity to become a 'thinking and reasoning animal' who 'might refuse to comply with a compact made before her creation' and, worse, that the monsters would reproduce 'and a race of devils would be propagated upon the earth, who might make the very existence of the species of man a condition precarious and full of terror' (p. 165). Frankenstein's fears, Peter Brooks contends (essay 4), are animated by the threat of the monstrous production of a new signifying system alien to that of man. Such a system is already embodied in the dangerous propagation of female writing.

The dangerous propagation of monsters, represented as an apocalyptic flood, constitutes a duplicitously sublime image that associates monstrosity and revolutionary threats with resistance to the authoritative figure of the father. For Frankenstein, imagining he can transcend the bounds of life and death, the 'torrent of light' signifies a sublime moment in which he is imaginarily elevated to the metaphysical position of absolute creator, father and law. The act of creation which makes this possible, however, overvaults its own aims with the production of a figure it can neither contain nor control. The monster exceeds the sublimity of paternal authority and confronts it, in the imagined shape of the female, with a spectacle of yet greater monstrosity. For Barbara Freeman (essay 8), the monster exposes a similar rupture in the framework of the Kantian sublime. In the work of an earlier theorist of the sublime, Edmund Burke, monsters exhibit a dangerously duplicitous potential. They are invoked, in his *Reflections on the Revolution in France* (1790), to display the unnatural chaos, the vicious deformity and the immoral excesses of the new French democracy in order to serve as a warning of the radical threat to English good order. In the face of French monstrosity and its sublime dissolution of all values, morals and political order, Burke stresses the need to preserve proper English traditions based on the paternal authority of the monarchy, the church, the unwritten constitution and the aristocracy.

Burke's *Reflections*, even as it attempts to reawaken an older set of English values to stem the monstrous propagation of radical ideas, tacitly recognises their time has gone. Appealing to chivalric codes of conduct, he contrasts the revolutionaries' maltreatment of the French Queen with his own reminiscences on a past visit to the old French court when 'ten thousand swords must have leaped from their scabbards to avenge even a look that threatened her with insult'. 'But', he continues, 'the age of chivalry is gone.'[30] Political polemic cedes to a nostalgia for romance. For the radical monsters that vigorously responded to Burke's polemic, his appeal to romance had distinct political overtones. In the *Rights of Man* (1791) Thomas Paine uses Burke's romantic nostalgia to criticise the *Reflections* as a work of fanciful and evocative fiction, a romance that, like the word 'Gothic' with which it was associated, signified the barbarism and irrationality of the Middle Ages. All the institutions that Burke defends, the monarchy and aristocracy in particular, are attacked as remnants of archaic feudal power. Paine dismisses the unwritten constitution of 1688 which Burke cites as the guarantee of English freedom and stability as no more than 'the vanity of governing beyond the grave' and 'the most ridiculous and insolent of all tyrannies'.[31] Like the female monster who, Frankenstein speculates, might refuse to obey laws, a 'compact', made before her creation, Paine considers it undemocratic to restrict the rights of the living by the imposition of the will of the dead. To radicals advancing the cause of reason, humanity and democracy Burke's position appeared as the Gothic antithesis to enlightened values, reinforcing social and political injustice and perpetuating inhuman practices. Mary Wollstonecraft, in her response to Burke, *A Vindication of the Rights of Men* (1790), attacks Burke's nostalgia for its want of humanity and liberalism: 'man preys on man; and you mourn for the idle tapestry that decorated a gothic pile, and the dronish bell that summoned the fat priest to prayer.'[32] A 'thinking and reasoning animal' (p. 165) to use the phrase uttered by Frankenstein of the unfinished female monster, Wollstonecraft uses the word 'Gothic' to imply everything that is antithetical to her rational humanism.

Radical replies to Burke reverse the polarity of the monster metaphor: for them, everything that Burke defends is monstrous. In his *Enquiry Concerning Political Justice* (1793) William Godwin describes the feudal system as a 'ferocious monster, devouring, wherever it came, all that the friend of humanity regards with attachment and love'. This monster is still in evidence in the 1790s in the shape of the system of titles, a sign of aristocratic power and privilege. While the feudal monster is dead, Godwin goes on, the aristocracy 'who followed in his train, and fattened upon the carcases of those he slew, have stuffed his skin, and, by exhibiting it hope still to terrify mankind into patience and pusillanimity'.[33] The stuffed monster presents an anathema to Godwin's rationalism for it indicates the persistence of relics – monarchy, aristocracy, hereditary wealth – from a dead past which, though severed from their base in feudal power, still produce imaginary, but no less potent, political effects. An illusion without basis, the stuffed monster of aristocratic power can have no reason to exist. But in the metaphor of the monster, a monster that in the fictions of the period was both attractive and terrifying, older forms of power were preserved and reproduced. This power without reason possesses the same disturbing force that emerged in eighteenth-century romances and criticism, a monstrous, passionate power of fiction, of metaphorical language whose substitutions and deviations exceeded rational control.

III TWENTIETH-CENTURY MONSTROSITY

For criticism in the twentieth century *Frankenstein* has retained its monstrosity, although the status of the monster has considerably shifted in significance. While Frankenstein's monster sailed from the darkness and distance at the end of the novel and into the glare of popular culture on stage, in cartoons and on screens, its literary and critical progress was more obscure. Even though a number of more literary novels of the nineteenth century alluded to creator and monster such acknowledgements did not warrant significant critical recognition.[34] Twentieth-century criticism still seemed to accept traditional literary hierarchies: R. Glynn Grylls, in a biography of Mary Shelley, had no hesitation in identifying the novel as 'a "period piece", of not very good date; historically interesting, but not one of the living novels of the world'.[35] The grounds for such exclusion lie in the recognition of certain structural and formal characteristics of monstrosity. Sylva Norman evaluated the novel negatively on the basis of its failure to offer a 'unifying motive'.[36] The lack of unity, meaning, moral or formal consistency defines the text as a monster. James Beattie, writing in the eighteenth century, describes the shape of textual monstrosity: 'if a work have no determinate end, it has no meaning; and if it have many ends, it will distract by its multiplicity.'[37] Grounds enough for *Frankenstein*'s exclusion from the hallowed realm of literature.

But the boundary beyond which monsters are situated becomes uncertain because monsters, in their difference, in their transgression of aesthetic limits, disclose a process of attraction and repulsion that is duplicitous: they reflect back, in the manner of the mirrors or doubles that they are, on the position that excludes them. Their flaws offer strange projections and magnifications. For Harold Bloom, *Frankenstein* achieves a degree of importance, despite and because of its monstrosity, due to the reflections it casts on Romanticism:

> I am suggesting that what makes *Frankenstein* an important book, though it is only a strong, flawed and frequently clumsy novel is that it vividly projects a version of the Romantic mythology of self, found, among other places, in Blake's *Book of Urizen*, Shelley's *Prometheus Unbound* and Byron's *Manfred*. It lacks the sophistication and imaginative complexity of such works but precisely because of that *Frankenstein* affords a unique introduction to the archetypal world of Romantics.[38]

The quotation, also, affords a unique introduction to monstrosity. For though *Frankenstein* remains in a subordinated position in terms of the privileged, literary, values – the 'sophistication' and 'imaginative complexity' of Romantic poetry – its monstrosity is peculiarly powerful. While the novel's importance is also associated with its service to the Romantic cause, it seems to be more than servile in its reflections on Romanticism. *Frankenstein* is not only the shadow to Romantic poetic substance, not only the inverse or negative to the proper and positive Romantic mythology of self. Its flaws and clumsiness, its marks of monstrosity, become crucial in the critical process of differentiating good from bad literature, in highlighting, precisely because of its darkness and its lack of sophistication and imaginative complexity, the line that announces Romantic poetry's superiority. Ironically, however, the contrast also displays how unstable the assumed values and the drawn lines can become. Literary value does not lie outside criticism or in works, but is produced in systems and processes of critical and cultural differentiation. Rather than having an external and legitimating aesthetic framework against which a particular work can be evaluated and its meaning deciphered, *Frankenstein*'s monstrosity discloses the movements associated with the deconstructive text: neither singular, nor self-evident, nor originary, textual significance is produced, 'demonstrated', in the process of reading.[39]

Nonetheless, the image of *Frankenstein* as a lesser, shadowy, negative work has underwritten many accounts of the novel. Turning on the figure of the author as the point at which some unity and meaning can be recovered for the novel, biographical criticism has reproduced literary relations in the image of familial ones. The novel's ambivalence is explained as Mary Shelley's anxiety towards her relatives. For example, her mother, Mary Wollstonecraft, is seen to influence the traumas of childbirth suggested by the novel as well as underlining feminist themes; William Godwin, as father, radical philosopher and novelist, has been identified as both a positive and a negative influence in readings of the novel's emotional and political sentiments; her husband, Percy Shelley, too, has been characterised as a politically and personally detrimental figure in Shelley's life and novel.[40] These readings stand in the shadow of monstrosity, situating Mary Shelley in an equivalently subordinate position to *Frankenstein*: as a 'child of light' or a 'moon in eclipse', she remains in the shadow of more distinguished relations.[41] The duplication of family and literary figures, however, only seems to entangle relations of generation and meaning in overdetermined networks of significance.

In the process of reading *Frankenstein* as a critique of her relations' persons, politics or aesthetic productions, a slight displacement of focus emerges. This has turned into, in criticism of the last twenty years, a significant re-evaluation, one that has reversed the polarity of positive and negative. Feminist criticism has been particularly active in fuelling this reversal of value. What were once signs of the novel's subordinate or inadequate relation to Romanticism have become positive and critical features outlining a different significance and trajectory for reading the period. Mary Poovey, for example, argues that the text performs a critique of the underlying masculine and egocentric assumptions of the Romantic imagination.[42] The similar projects, characteristics and desires of male figures in the text, as noted by Joseph Kestner (essay 3), suggest that the exclusivity, egocentricity and ambition that is presented is more than an example of an aberrant individual. For Spivak (essay 10), it is an ideological, imperialist and gendered question of individualism. In Walton's desire to conquer the Pole, in *Frankenstein*'s attempt to appropriate the secret of life and in Clerval's wish to master Oriental languages, links between masculine selfhood, imagination, knowledge, society, empire and language are established and set in opposition to figures of femininity, sexuality, mortality, motherhood and otherness. Moreover, the marked, often violent and fatal, exclusions of these figures from the action of the novel signal the pervasively patriarchal and imperialist values and practices of the historical and cultural conditions of the novel's production.

The procedures of suppression that are presented in the novel, however, do not leave one pole as the sole negative of the other, but disclose, in the course of the novel, the reversibility inherent to systems of differentiation, a reversibility loosed by Frankenstein's vain yet sovereign transgression. Frankenstein's creation of beauty produces ugliness, his benevolent intentions become destructive, his authority cedes to subservience. Walton's desire for eternal life engenders death and the voyage towards a paradise of light and knowledge ends, icebound, in a desolate sea of darkness and uncertainty. The product of Frankenstein's paternal labours delivers, not the dutiful offspring he imagined, but a rebellious Satanic force whose demands for love turn into violent energy.

The monster, however, is more than Frankenstein's mirror, more than the dark side of a Romantic imagination brought to life and misery. A sentient, rational and eloquent creature, a student of human customs, thought and literature, the monster displays a humanity that upsets the distinctions between humans and their others, distinctions which cause his exclusion from all social relations. His position, moreover, enunciates a powerful critique of the often contradictory, unjust and inhuman nature of many human institutions, characteristics and practices. The human, or, significantly, man, emerges as an irreconcilably divided being:

> Was man, indeed, at once so powerful, so virtuous, and magnificent, yet so vicious and base? He appeared at one time a mere scion of the evil principle, and at another, as all that can be conceived of as noble and godlike. To be a great and virtuous man appeared the highest honour that can befall a sensitive being; to be base and vicious, as many on record have been, appeared the lowest degradation, a condition more abject than that of the blind mole or harmless worm. For a long time I could not conceive how one can go forth to murder his fellow, or even how one man could go forth to murder his fellow, or even why there were laws and governments; but when I heard details of vice and bloodshed, my wonder ceased, and I turned away with disgust and loathing.
>
> (p. 119)

In his innocence, the monster exhibits the proper response to moral deformity in humans. But, in turning away and in being turned away from the duplicitous society of humans, he finds he has been corrupted by the very image he disavows: his subsequent violence displays the equally human characteristics that revolted him.

A similar monstrous interrogation of human institutions occurs earlier in the text, uttered by Elizabeth, Frankenstein's adoptive sister and fiancée, in response to the fate of Justine, a model of feminine servitude. Accused of the murder of Frankenstein's younger brother, she is tried and, despite her innocence, an innocence known only to Frankenstein, the monster and the reader, sentenced to death. The injustice is manifested at the level of reading. Framed by the monster, Justine is forced to condemn herself by confessing, in both a legal and a religious sense: 'my confessor', she says, 'has besieged me; he threatened and menaced, until I almost began to think that I was the monster that he said I was' (p. 87). The 'wretched mockery of a trial' and the cruelty of the confessor condemn Justine. For the reader it is the injustice and partiality of the legal and religious system that is demonstrated. The effects on Elizabeth are similarly disarming: 'misery has come home, and men appear to me as monsters thirsting for each other's blood. Yet I am certainly unjust' (p. 92). It is her certainty, however, that is at stake as a result of monstrosity. She reaches a point of sublime dissolution in which all categories become indeterminate: 'Alas! Victor, when falsehood can look so like the truth, who can assure themselves of certain happiness? I feel as if I were walking on the edge of a precipice, towards which thousands are crowding, and endeavouring to plunge me into the abyss' (p. 93). Individual identity crumbles under the weight of others, their stories, proximity and generality. Nothing seems certain or stable.

The general instability produced by the text's monstrous interrogations, the crisis of categories and distinctions, becomes, for many critics, an issue of language. Frankenstein's attempt to circumscribe maternal creativity participates, as Margaret Homans shows (essay 6), in a process of literalising cultural metaphors of femininity as the other and object of male subjectivity. The very figure of the monster confounds categories: living but composed of dead human bodily parts, an assemblage that is at once natural and artificial, the monster signifies the excess of cultural signification. Culture replaces and disturbingly replicates nature, shaping and reshaping it with language. Textuality, as Jerrold Hogle argues (essay 9), demonstrates the way otherness establishes and contests any position of human authority.

The metaphors used and generated by *Frankenstein* entail more than reversals of polarity within a restricted cultural and historical system of meaning. As they cross boundaries they disturb categories to the extent that nothing can be taken for granted, taken as read. As a metaphor for reading, however, for reading as a doubled and divergent relation of subject and object, monsters situate criticism differently in respect of texts, pasts and presents. Like the end of *Frankenstein* where the reader appears as the destination of the letters composing the text, criticism emerges in the form of reading and/as writing that returns to and departs from the novel. In the process, relations of and between literary and critical texts change in respect of the differences and proximities that emerge between the various pasts and presents of reading and writing. Another – active, intransitive and verbal – monster is glimpsed. The essays in this volume read *Frankenstein* from different positions, tracing different historical, cultural, sexual, textual and political issues in the text and in the act of reading itself, attentive to the way reading monsters.

1. Jacques Ehrmann, 'The Death of Literature', *New Literary History*, 3 (1971), 31–47, p. 43.
2. Review of *Frankenstein, Edinburgh (Scot's) Magazine* (Second Series), 2 (March 1818), pp. 249–53.
3. Mary Shelley, *Frankenstein*, ed. M. K. Joseph (Oxford, 1969), p. 8. All further references to the novel will be included in brackets in the text.
4. Marc A. Rubenstein, '"My Accursed Origin": The Search for the Mother in *Frankenstein*', *Studies in Romanticism*, 15 (1976), 165–94, p. 184.
5. See James P. Carson, 'Bringing the Author Forward: *Frankenstein* through Mary Shelley's letters', *Criticism*, 30 (1988), 431–53; John Clubbe, 'Mary Shelley as Autobiographer: the Evidence of the 1831 Introduction to *Frankenstein*', *Wordsworth Circle*, 12 (1981), 102–6.
6. See Aija Ozolins, 'Dreams and Doctrines: Dual Strands in *Frankenstein*', *Science Fiction Studies*, 2 (1975), 103–12, p. 107.
7. To Leigh Hunt, 9 September 1823, *The Letters of Mary Shelley*, ed. F. L. Jones (Norman, 1946), p. 259.
8. Stephen Earl Forry, *Hideous Progenies: Dramatizations of Frankenstein from the Nineteenth Century to the Present* (Philadelphia, 1990).
9. On the subject of supplementarity, see Jacques Derrida, *Of Grammatology*, trans. Gayarti Chakravorty Spivak (Baltimore and London, 1976), pp. 141–5.
10. Review of *The Last Man, The Literary Magnet, or Monthly Journal of Belles Lettres* (new series), 1 (1826), p. 56.
11. Review of *The Monk, British Critic*, 7 (June 1796), p. 677.
12. Henry Home, Lord Kames, *Elements of Criticism*, 11th edn (London, 1839), p. 450.
13. John Cleland, Review of *Peregrine Pickle, The Monthly Review*, IV (March 1751), in Ioan Williams (ed.), *Novel and Romance 1700–1800* (London, 1970), p. 161.
14. Ibid., p. 162.
15. William Owen, 'An Essay on the New Species of Writing' (1751), in Williams, *Novel and Romance*, p. 151.
16. Samuel Richardson, Letter to Aron Hill (1741), in *Selected Letters*, ed. John Carroll (Oxford, 1964), p. 41.
17. Samuel Johnson, *The Rambler*, 4 (1750), in *Samuel Johnson*, ed. Donald Greene (Oxford, 1984), pp. 175–9.
18. Ibid., p. 178.

19. Henry Fielding, *Joseph Andrews* (1742), ed. R. F. Brissenden (Harmondsworth, 1977), p. 30 and pp. 183–5.

20. Michel Foucault, *The Order of Things* (London, 1970), pp. 154–7.

21. George Canning, *The Microcosm* (1787), in Williams, *Novel and Romance*, p. 345.

22. Cleland, in Williams, *Novel and Romance*, p. 162.

23. Georges Bataille, 'Letter to René Char', *Yale French Studies*, 78 (1990), 31–43, p. 34.

24. T. J. Matthias, *The Pursuits of Literature*, 13th edn (London, 1805), p. 422.

25. T. Row, Letter to the *Gentleman's Magazine*, XXXVII (1767), in Williams, *Novel and Romance*, p. 272; Anon., 'Sentiments of eminent writers in Honour of the Female Sex', *Gentleman's Magazine*, LVIII (November, 1788), in Williams, *Novel and Romance*, p. 367.

26. Peter de Bolla, *The Discourse of the Sublime* (Oxford, 1989), p. 260.

27. Matthias, *Pursuits*, p. 244.

28. Hannah More, *Strictures*, I (London, 1799), pp. 188–9. In de Bolla, *Discourse*, p. 264.

29. de Bolla, *Discourse*, p. 254.

30. Edmund Burke, *Reflections on the Revolutions in France*, ed. Conor Cruise O'Brien (Harmondsworth, 1969), p. 170.

31. Thomas Paine, *The Thomas Paine Reader*, ed. Michael Foot and Isaac Kramnick (Harmondsworth, 1987), p. 228.

32. Mary Wollstonecraft, *A Vindication of the Rights of Men*, in *The Works of Mary Wollstonecraft*, vol. 5, ed. Janet Todd and Marilyn Butler (London, 1989), p. 58.

33. William Godwin, *Enquiry Concerning Political Justice*, ed. Isaac Kramnick (Harmondsworth, 1985), p. 476.

34. See Chris Baldick, *In Frankenstein's Shadow* (Oxford, 1987).

35. R. Glynn Grylls, *Mary Shelley* (London, 1938), p. 320.

36. Sylva Norman, 'Mary Wollstonecraft Shelley', in *Shelley and his Circle 1773–1822*, vol. III, ed. Kenneth Neill Cameron (London, 1970), pp. 397–422, p. 408.

37. James Beattie, *Essay on Poetry and Music, as they affect the Mind* (1776), in Williams, *Novel and Romance*, p. 252.

38. Harold Bloom, '*Frankenstein*, or the New Prometheus', *Partisan Review*, 32 (1965), 611–18, p. 613.

39. Roland Barthes, 'From Work to Text', *Image Music Text*, trans. Stephen Heath (London, 1977), pp. 155–64, p. 157.

40. See Ellen Moers, *Literary Women* (London, 1978); Rubenstein, '"Accursed Origin"'; Janet M. Todd, 'Frankenstein's Daughter: Mary Shelley and Mary Wollstonecraft', *Women and Literature*, 4 (1976), 18–27; Eileen Bigland, *Mary Shelley* (London, 1959); Katherine Richardson Powers, *The Influence of William Godwin on the Novels of Mary Shelley* (New York, 1980); Judith Weissman, 'A Reading of *Frankenstein* as the Complaint of a Political Wife', *Colby Library Quarterly*, 12 (1976), 171–80.

41. Muriel Spark, *Child of Light* (Hadleigh, Essex, 1951); Jane Dunn, *Moon in Eclipse* (New York, 1978).

42. Mary Poovey, '"My Hideous Progeny": Mary Shelley and the Feminization of Romanticism', *PMLA*, 95 (1980), 332–47.

1

Production and Reproduction: The Case of *Frankenstein*

PAUL O'FLINN

Mary Shelley's Gothic novel *Frankenstein* was published anonymously in 1818. In the same year, a couple of other novels – Peacock's *Nightmare Abbey* and Jane Austen's *Northanger Abbey* – also appeared and their derisive use of Gothic conventions suggested that the form, fashionable for fifty years, was sliding into decline and disrepute. There seemed good reason to suppose that *Frankenstein*, an adolescent's first effort at fiction, would fade from view before its print-run was sold out.

Yet several generations later Mary Shelley's monster, having resisted his creator's attempts to eliminate him in the book, is able to reproduce himself with the variety and fertility that Frankenstein had feared. Apart from steady sales in Penguin, Everyman and OUP editions, there have been over a hundred film adaptations and there have been the Charles Addams cartoons in the *New Yorker*; Frankie Stein blunders about in the pages of *Whoopee* and *Monster Fun* comics, and approximate versions of the monster glare out from chewing gum wrappers and crisp bags. In the USA he forged a chain of restaurants; in South Africa in 1955 the work was banned as indecent and objectionable.[1]

None of these facts are new and some of them are obvious to anyone walking into a newsagent's with one eye open. They are worth setting out briefly here because *Frankenstein* seems to me to be a case where some recent debates in critical theory about cultural production and reproduction might usefully be centred, a work whose history can be used to test the claims that theory makes.[2] That history demonstrates clearly the futility of a search for the 'real', 'true' meaning of a work. There is no such thing as *Frankenstein*, there are only *Frankensteins*, as the text is ceaselessly rewritten, reproduced, refilmed and redesigned. The fact that many people call the monster Frankenstein and thus confuse that pair betrays the extent of that restructuring. What I would like to offer is neither a naïve deconstructionist delight at the endless plurality of meanings the text has been able to afford nor a gesture of cultural despair at the failure of the Philistines to read the original and get it right. Instead I'd like to argue that at its moment of production *Frankenstein*, in an oblique way, was in touch with central tensions and contradictions in industrial society and only by seeing it in those terms can the prodigious efforts made over the last century and a half to alter and realign the work and its meanings be understood – a work that lacked that touch and that address could safely be left, as Marx said in another context, to the gnawing criticism of the mice.

Frankenstein is a particularly good example of three of the major ways in which alteration and realignment of this sort happens: firstly, through the operations of criticism; secondly, as a function of the shift from one medium to another; and thirdly as a result of the unfolding of history itself. The operations of criticism on this text are at present more vigorous than usual. When I was a student twenty years ago I picked up the *Pelican Guide to English Literature* to find the novel more or less wiped out in a direly condescending half-sentence as 'one of those second-rate works, written under the influence of more distinguished minds, that sometimes display in conveniently simple form the preoccupations of a coterie'.[3] *Frankenstein* may have been on TV but it wasn't on the syllabus. A generation and a lot of feminist criticism later and Mary Shelley is no longer a kind of half-witted secretary to Byron and Shelley but a woman writer whose text articulates and has been convincingly shown to articulate elements of woman's experience of patriarchy, the family and the trauma of giving birth.[4]

The second instance – the way a text's meaning alters as it moves from one medium to another – is something I'd like to look at in more detail in Sections IV and V by examining the two classic screen versions: Universal's movie directed in 1931 by James Whale and starring Boris Karloff, and Terence Fisher's picture for

Hammer Films in 1957 with Peter Cushing. Literary criticism only metaphorically rewrites texts: the words on the page remain the same but the meanings they are encouraged to release differ. But a shift of medium means the literal rewriting of a text as novel becomes script becomes film. Scope for the ideological wrenching and reversing of a work and its way of seeing is here therefore even larger; some sense of the extent such changes can reach was evident not long ago in the BBC television serial of Malcolm Bradbury's *The History Man*, a novel set in 1972 and written in 1975. Its aggrieved author complained:

> By the time [the television adaptation] appeared in 1981, instead of being a needling critique of what exists, it is a satirical attack on what has already passed – and can therefore be misused by people who want to take it over from the Right, in order to turn it into an attack on sociology, universities, radicalism, in ways I deeply resented and disapproved of. If I'd known where 1981 was leading I might have doubted whether it should be turned into a television series.[5]

Bradbury's comment leads into the third category I suggested earlier – namely the way in which the movement of history itself refocuses a text and reorders its elements. *Frankenstein*, I'd like to argue, meant certain things in 1818 but meant and could be made to mean different things in 1931 and 1957, irrespective of authorial 'intention'. Brecht noted a similar effect in the case of his play *Life of Galileo*:

> My intention was, among others, to give an unvarnished picture of a new age – a strenuous undertaking since all those around me were convinced that our own era lacked every attribute of a new age. Nothing of this aspect had changed when, years later, I began together with Charles Laughton to prepare an American version of the play. The 'atomic' age made its debut at Hiroshima in the middle of our work. Overnight the biography of the founder of the new system of physics read differently. The infernal effect of the great bomb placed the conflict between Galileo and the authorities of his day in a new, sharper light.[6]

Mary Shelley's monster, in short, is ripped apart by one or more of at least three processes in each generation and then put together again as crudely as Victor Frankenstein constructed the original in his apartment. Faced with these processes traditional literary criticism can either, with a familiar gesture, pretend not to notice and insist instead that *Frankenstein* 'spanned time' with 'timeless and universal themes' that 'live beyond literary fashion'.[7] Or it can pay attention to those changes but slip past the power and the politics that they imply, so that shifts in the work's presentation become a plain mirror of human evolution: 'the Monster ... is no longer separate, he is quite simply ourselves';[8] 'it is a magnified image of ourselves'.[9] Capitalism creates and recreates monsters; capitalist ideology then invites us to behold ourselves. I'd like to try to do something else.

I

First I'd like to argue that much of the strength in the text that continues to be released derives from certain issues in the decade of its composition, issues that the text addresses itself to in oblique, imaginative terms and that remain central and unresolved in industrial society. In that decade those issues erupted more turbulently than ever before; they were, briefly, the impact of technological developments on people's lives and the possibility of working-class revolution. Those issues fuel the Luddite disturbances of 1811–17 and the Pentridge rising of 1817.

There had been instances of machine-breaking before in British history but never with the same frequency and intensity. The size of the army marshalled to squash the Luddites – six times as big as any used previously for internal conflicts in the estimate of one historian [10] – is a measure of the extent to which the new technologies, in the first generation of the industrial revolution, threatened traditional livelihoods and provoked violent resistance. There is the same sort of new and disruptive energy evident in the Pentridge rising of June 1817, when 300 men marched towards Nottingham on the expectation of similar marches, designed to overthrow the Government, occurring across the country. The group was soon rounded up by Hussars and three of its leaders executed in November. The revolt ended in shambles and failure but its significance for E. P. Thompson is epochal – it was 'one of the first attempts in history to mount a wholly proletarian insurrection, without any middle-class support'.[11]

The composition of *Frankenstein* needs to be seen in the context of these deep changes in the nature of British society. Mary began work on the novel in June 1816 at the Maison Chapuis, Montalègre, near Geneva, where she was living with Shelley. Byron lived nearby at the Villa Diodati and the book's impetus came from Byron's challenge – 'We will each write a ghost story' – during one of their regular evening visits. The point is that as Mary set about writing her first novel she was working alongside two men who had responded publicly and politically to the Luddite crisis. Byron's magnificent maiden speech in the House of Lords in February 1812 had attacked Tory proposals to extend the death penalty for machine-breaking, denouncing a process whereby men were 'sacrificed to improvements in mechanism'. And then in January 1813, when fourteen men were executed at York for Luddite activities, Harriet Shelley had written to the radical London bookseller Thomas Hookham on Shelley's behalf: 'I see by the Papers that those poor men who were executed at York have left a great many children. Do you think a subscription would be attended to for their relief? If you think it would, pray put down our names and advertise it in the Papers.' [12] Mary and Percy returned to England from Geneva in September 1816 and Luddites were still being hanged in April 1817 as Mary made the last revisions to her manuscript. Before *Frankenstein's* publication in March 1818, Shelley reacted to the execution of the leaders of the Pentridge rising with *An Address to the People on the Death of Princess Charlotte*, a forceful political pamphlet published in November 1817 and eagerly read by Mary, as she noted in her journal. The pamphlet lamented the 'national calamity' of a country torn between abortive revolt and despotic revenge – 'the alternatives of anarchy and oppression'.[13]

What was Mary Shelley's own response to these events and reactions? To try to pass *Frankenstein* off as a conservative riposte to the politics of Godwin and Shelley, as Muriel Spark has done,[14] is to ignore the book's brave dedication to the unpopular Godwin as well as Mary's own correct anticipation that a 'courtly bookseller' like John Murray would refuse to publish it when the manuscript was offered to him.[15] (It is also, as we shall see in a moment, to ignore most of the book's contents.) Similarly, to describe her politics at the time she wrote *Frankenstein* as 'innately conservative', as Jane Dunn does,[16] is to muddle her views in middle age with those she held at eighteen – often a mistake with Romantic writers and particularly so in Mary Shelley's case. Her letters around the time of *Frankenstein* reveal a woman who shared the radicalism of Byron and Shelley. The result was a politics shaped by a passion for reform, a powerful hatred of Tory despotism with its 'grinding & pounding & hanging and taxing'[17] and a nervousness about the chance of the revolutionary violence such despotism might provoke. Thus, for example, she wrote to Shelley in September 1817 between the completion of *Frankenstein* in May and its publication the following March:

> Have you seen Cobbett's 23 No. to the Borough mongers – Why he appears to be making out a list for proscription – I actually shudder to read it – a revolution in this country would (not?) be *bloodless* if that man has any power in it... He encourages in the multitude the worst possible human passion *revenge* or as he would probably give it that abominable *Christian* name retribution.[18]

Her politics here in short are those of a radical liberal agonising in the face of the apparent alternatives of 'anarchy and oppression', to use the phrase which, as we have already seen, Shelley was to deploy six weeks later in his *Princess Charlotte* pamphlet.

That politics also addressed itself to contemporary scientific and technological developments and their social implications. Discussion and speculation at the Villa Diodati ranged across galvanism and Darwin's experiments, as Mary carefully notes in her 1831 Introduction to the novel. In the autumn of 1816, as she completed her manuscript, she read Davy's *Elements of Chemical Philosophy*.

It is out of these politics and this way of seeing that Frankenstein emerges. It is a multi-layered work; it includes odds and ends like her passing interest in recent British and Russian polar expeditions, and it is padded in parts with wads of her tourist's diary of a trip to Chamonix.[19] What I would like to show by turning to the text itself in the next two sections is that one of these layers, a layer that accounts for a lot of the story's vigorous, protean life, is an imaginative rendering of the two issues – scientific-technological developments and working-class revolt – which as we have seen asserted themselves violently in the half-dozen years preceding the text's production. It is a layer whose boundaries are drawn by the author's politics.

II

Mary Shelley's interest in scientific questions has been well documented[20] and this interest is built into the very narrative structure of her novel. Frankenstein's story is itself framed by the story of Walton, the polar explorer whom Frankenstein meets and to whom he tells his tale. Through the twin narratives of Walton and Frankenstein Mary Shelley presents two models of scientific progress. Both men are obsessed by the urge to discover and both pursue that obsession, enticed by the possibility of 'immortality and power' that success would bring. In the end the pursuit kills Frankenstein whereas Walton survives. What is the difference?

The difference is the sailors on Walton's expedition ship. Frankenstein works alone but Walton works with a crew and it is the crew who force Walton to turn back when they realise that the reckless drive through the polar ice will cost everyone's lives. Several things are worth noting at this point. Firstly, Frankenstein makes a forceful speech aimed at changing the sailors' minds by reminding them of the honour that even failure will bring and still holding out the dream of heroic success. Secondly, Walton turns back not, as has been argued, for altruistic reasons or for the sake of his sister, [21] but simply because he is forced to by the threat of mutiny, to his own fury and frustration:

> The die is cast; I have consented to return, if we are not destroyed. Thus are my hopes blasted by cowardice and indecision; I come back ignorant and disappointed. It requires more philosophy than I possess, to bear this injustice with patience.
>
> (p. 215)

And thirdly Mary Shelley takes care to distance her reader's sympathies from both Frankenstein's pleas and Walton's anger by pushing those sympathies towards the sailors. Details about the crew must inevitably be few if the text is not to become overloaded and unbalanced but nonetheless she deliberately makes space to insert near the start of the novel in Letter II an otherwise pointless anecdote designed to illustrate the 'kindliness of heart' of the ship's master. The anecdote portrays him as 'generous' and 'wholly uneducated', a man of 'integrity and dauntless courage' and 'gentleness'. The anecdote's purpose can only be to enlist reader support for the master and his crew at the sole moment when they have any part to play in the plot – namely their threat of mutiny in chapter 24, which is presented to Walton by a delegation of sailors elected by the crew.

What the text then appears to offer is straightforward contrast. Scientific development subject to some form of strong democratic control – even in the violent form of mutiny – can avert the dangers its researchers encounter and save human beings from the possibly fatal consequences of those researches. That is Walton's story. But scientific advance pursued for private motives and with no reining and directing social control or sense of social responsibility leads directly to catastrophe. That is Frankenstein's story. The text does not, contrary to Christopher Small's claim, offer us hand-wringing about some abstracted and reified 'irresponsibility of science'.[22] Rather it sees scientific development as neutral, its results tolerable or disastrous entirely depending on the circumstances in which they are produced.

Seen from this angle, the function of certain elements in the text becomes clearer – in particular those elements which emphasise the dangers of acting alone and illustrate the help that can be provided by other people. Walton's project is especially perilous because it 'hurries me out of the common pathways of man, even to the wild sea and unvisited regions I am about to explore' (p. 22) but he has to go with a crew and they save him as we have seen. From the start he is aware of the need of a colleague 'to approve or amend my plans' (p. 19) and hence his delight on meeting Frankenstein. The latter, by contrast, works deliberately alone. His move to Ingolstadt where he begins his research cuts him off from Geneva where he had 'ever been surrounded by amiable companions' (p. 45) and he stays away from them for two years. He constructs the monster 'in a solitary chamber, or rather cell, at the top of the house ... separated from all the other apartments' (p. 55), just as later he goes to 'the remotest of the Orkneys' (p. 163) to begin building the monster's mate.

Studded through the text as miniatures of its central message are moments when disaster, threatening a lone individual, is avoided by the interventions of others. The ship's master provides the solution to the tangled affairs of the young Russian Lady; Frankenstein's father rescues Caroline Beaufort from a life of beggary and she in turn pulls Elizabeth Lavenza and Justine Moritz out of similar misery. Frankenstein's life is saved when he appears to be mortally ill by the ministrations of his friend Clerval, and then there is the complex story, told by the monster, of Felix who liberates the Turk facing execution. The text's thrust on a series of levels is naïvely clear: for people together, problems can be solved; for the man alone, they can overwhelm.

III

The monster describes a crucial part of his education as follows:

> Every conversation of the cottagers now opened new wonders to me. When I listened to the instructions which Felix bestowed upon

> the Arabian, the strange system of human society was explained to me. I heard of the division of property, of immense wealth and squalid poverty; of rank, descent, and noble blood.
>
> The words induced me to turn towards myself. I learned that the possessions most esteemed by your fellow-creatures were high and unsullied descent united with riches. A man might be respected with only one of these advantages; but, without either, he was considered, except in very rare instances, as a vagabond and a slave, doomed to waste his powers for the profits of the chosen few! And what was I? Of my creation and creator I was absolutely ignorant; but I knew that I possessed no money, no friends, no kind of property.
>
> (pp. 119–20)

Looking at that passage, it is perhaps worth remembering that the first person to offer the text as a straightforward allegory of the class struggle is not some vulgar Marxist in the twentieth century but one of the book's protagonists. Read as the monster suggests, the novel argues that, just as Frankenstein's creation drives him through exhausting and unstinting conflicts to his death, so too a class called into being by the bourgeoisie and yet rejected and frustrated by it will in the end turn on that class in fury and vengeance and destroy it.

This way of seeing the work, as well as being overtly stated by the work itself, is rendered more likely if we look again for a moment at the text's context. Lee Sterrenburg has documented the extent to which the populace as a monster, bent on the destruction of the ruling class and its property, figures as a standard trope in conservative journalism in the generation after the French Revolution.[23] During the Luddite years, the monster appeared to some to be on the loose. Factories in Yorkshire were fired in January and April 1812 and in March and April in Lancashire; there were murders, attempted assassinations and executions again and again between 1812 and 1817. During the most famous attack, on Rawfolds mill in the Spen Valley in April 1812, two of the Luddites were killed and 'Vengeance for the Blood of the Innocent' appeared chalked on walls and doors in Halifax after one of the funerals.

In the midst of this crisis, Mary Shelley picks up a way of seeing – the populace as a destructive monster – provided by Tory journalism and tries to re-think it in her own radical-liberal terms. And so in the novel the monster remains a monster – alien, frightening, violent – but is drenched with middle-class sympathy and given central space in the text to exercise the primary liberal right of free speech which he uses to appeal for the reader's pity and understanding. The caricatured people-monster that haunts the dominant ideology is reproduced through Mary Shelley's politics and becomes a contradictory figure, still ugly, vengeful and terrifying but now also human and intelligent and abused.

In addition, incidents in the class struggles of the 1810s are projected into the text. The monster too turns on the De Lacey family he has worked for and, in chapter 16, burns their property to the ground. That pattern of murders and reprisals that characterise the history of the decade also constitutes much of the plot of the novel. The demand for vengeance flared on the walls of Halifax in 1812 and again and again the terms 'vengeance' and revenge' erupt in the text to describe the relations of Frankenstein and monster – on, for example, pages 92, 136, 138, 142, 145, 168, 202 and 220. It is of course precisely a violent class politics fuelled principally by 'the worst possible human passion *revenge*' that Mary wrote in fear of to Shelley, as we saw earlier in Section I, shortly before the publication of *Frankenstein*.

To see the text in these terms is not, as I have argued already, a daft left-wing distortion but a reading suggested by the text itself and one that is also apparent if we turn to the way the text was taken up in the nineteenth century. In 1848, for example, the year of revolutions and of the *Communist Manifesto*, Elizabeth Gaskell published *Mary Barton*, the first English novel with a Communist as its protagonist. Describing John Barton she writes at one point:

> And so on into the problems and mysteries of life, until, bewildered and lost, unhappy and suffering, the only feeling that remained clear and undisturbed in the tumult of his heart, was hatred to the one class, and keen sympathy with the other.
>
> But what availed his sympathy. No education had given him wisdom; and without wisdom, even love, with all its effects, too often works but harm. He acted to the best of his judgment, but it was a widely-erring judgment.
>
> The actions of the uneducated seem to me typified in those of Frankenstein, that monster of many human qualities, ungifted with a soul, a knowledge of the difference between good and evil.
>
> The people rise up to life; they irritate us, they terrify us, and we become their enemies. Then, in the sorrowful moment of our triumphant power, their eyes gaze on us with mute reproach. Why have we made them what they are; a powerful monster, yet without the inner means for peace and happiness?
>
> John Barton became a Chartist, a Communist, all that is commonly called wild and visionary.[24]

What is intriguing about this reference is that Elizabeth Gaskell obviously hasn't read the book – she confuses Frankenstein with the monster and she doesn't know that the monster has a very clear knowledge of the difference between good and evil. What she has absorbed instead and passes on is the dominant political reading of the text, the sense that the middle classes are threatened by a monster of their own making. That monster, as we have seen, was manufactured out of the violence and anxieties of the Luddite decade; a generation later, at the peak of the Chartist decade, Elizabeth Gaskell reaches into cultural mythology to find the imaginative terms for her own predicament and that of her class.

It is significant that this political reproduction of the text persists and tends to surface at times of sharpening conflict. The 1961 Supplement to the *Oxford English Dictionary* notes Sidney Webb's use in *Fabian Essays*, published in 1889 at the height of the socialist revival: 'The landlord and the capitalist are both finding that the steam engine is a Frankenstein which they had better not have raised.' And the 1972 Supplement quotes the *Daily Telegraph*, 3 May 1971: 'There are now growing indications that the Nationalists in South Africa have created a political Frankenstein which is pointing the way to a non-white political revival.' Again, in both cases, monster and Frankenstein are muddled, indicating a level in ideology at which the text itself has ceased to exist but a myth and a metaphor torn and twisted from it is being strenuously put to work.

This separating of myth and metaphor from text and constructing something entirely new in ideology begins very early. In September 1823, Mary Shelley wrote to Leigh Hunt that she found herself famous – not for her novel but for a stage adaptation of it called *Presumption, or the Fate of Frankenstein* by Richard Brinsley Peake that was having a successful run in London. The title betrays the way the work is already being realigned as one idea in the complex structure is pulled out and foregrounded, and this foregrounding is underscored by a statement on the playbills for the opening performance on 28 July at the English Opera House: 'The striking moral exhibited in this story is the fatal consequence of that presumption which attempts to penetrate, beyond prescribed depths, into the mysteries of nature.'[25] Frankenstein certainly concludes from his own experience that the pursuit of knowledge ought to be prohibited, but the text does not endorse that kind of obscurantist morality, particularly by its placing of the contrasting

Walton story. But the later, more conservative and religious Mary Shelley slides towards this position, so that we find her insisting in the 1831 Introduction: 'supremely frightful would be the effect of any human endeavour to mock the stupendous mechanism of the Creator of the world.' She herself, in fact, is among the first to nudge the text into the space occupied by the dominant ideology, and we can also see that nudging going on in some of the revisions she makes for this third 1831 edition; for example, Elizabeth Lavenza is no longer Frankenstein's cousin, so that the potentially offensive hint of incest is deleted, while the orthodox notion of the family as moral and emotional sanctuary is boosted by the addition of several passages in the early chapters idealising the domestic harmony of Frankenstein's childhood.[26] If ideology has taken hold of *Frankenstein* and remade it for its own purposes, Mary Shelley led with her own suggestions about how it might be done.

IV

What I would like to do in the rest of this article is look at the two most famous reproductions of Frankenstein in the twentieth century, namely Universal's *Frankenstein* directed in 1931 by James Whale and starring Boris Karloff as the monster, and Hammer Films' *The Curse of Frankenstein* directed by Terence Fisher with Peter Cushing as Baron Frankenstein. The constructions and the operations of ideology are complex and within the scope of an article I cannot hope to do more than gesture at what seem to me to be the implications of the content of those two versions; wider questions about, for example, the precise relationship within the movie industry between honest popular entertainment, calculated profit-seeking, capitalist propaganda and painstaking aesthetic practice must inevitably be left to one side. The more I thought about these problems and the deeper into piles of back numbers of *Screen* I got the more dense and unyielding they seemed, so it was salutory if a bit shaming to go back to Orwell for a good crude blast and a starting point:

> Broadcasting is what it is, not because there is something inherently vulgar, silly and dishonest about the whole apparatus of microphone and transmitter, but because all the broadcasting that now happens all over the world is under the control of governments or great monopoly companies which are actively interested in maintaining the

> *status quo* and therefore in preventing the common man from becoming too intelligent. Something of the same kind has happened to the cinema, which, like the radio, made its appearance during the monopoly stage of capitalism and is fantastically expensive to operate.[27]

That kind of analysis is a useful place to begin because it reminds us baldly where films come from even if it does skate over a series of important contradictions – most importantly, the tensions between the overt politics of the owners of film companies on the one hand and, on the other, both their need to make certain populist concessions in order to guarantee profits and also the politics of the hundreds of producers, directors, script-writers, make-up artists, cameramen, actors, advertisers and so on who all stand between, in this case, Hammer/Universal and the woman in the back row of the one-and-nines (we're talking about old films, remember).

That said, there seem to me to be at least three different types of shift that need to be borne in mind when looking at the gap between Mary Shelley's book and twentieth-century films: those shifts concern medium, audience and content. In the case of *Frankenstein*, the shift of medium is particularly important because it must inevitably obliterate and replace what is central to the novel's meaning and structure – namely the patterned movement through three narrators as the reader is taken by way of Walton's letters into Frankenstein's tale and on to the monster's autobiography before backing out through Frankenstein's conclusions to be left with Walton's last notes. That process cannot be filmed and so the very medium demands changes even before politics and ideology come into play.

The turning of novel into film also involves a change in the nature of the work's audience. David Punter has convincingly argued that the Gothic novel is pre-eminently a middle-class form in terms of authors and values as well as readership.[28] The films in question are middle-class in none of these senses, produced as they are by large businesses in search of mass audiences. That different site of production and area of distribution will again bear down on the work, pulling, stretching and clipping it to fit new needs and priorities.

Where this pulling, stretching and clipping appears most obviously is in the alterations in the third category mentioned earlier, namely the work's content, and I'd like to detail some of those in a moment. What needs emphasising here is that the radical change in the class nature of producer and audience hacks away at the content of the original, so that the book is reduced to no more than an approximate skeleton, fleshed out in entirely and deliberately new ways. This makes it quite different from, for example, a BBC serial of a Jane Austen novel, where some attempt is made at a reasonably faithful reproduction of the text. It is therefore a traditional critical strategy in reviewing such serials to ask questions about how 'true' to the text, how 'accurate', is the portrayal of, say, Fitzwilliam Darcy or Emma Woodhouse. It is the failure to see this difference that makes one reviewer's querulous response to the 1931 film quite laughably beside the point:

> Mary Shelley's story has artistic interest as an essay in German horrific romanticism and I think that if *Frankenstein* had been produced by a historically-minded German the result would have been much more interesting ... What is the object of taking Mary Shelley's story and then removing the whole point of it before starting to make the picture?[29]

The object, of course, is precisely to remove the whole point of it – and substitute other ones.

Other ones are necessary for several reasons – not least because there are no immutable fears in human nature to which horror stories always speak in the same terms. There is not, for all David Punter's strenuous arguing, 'some inner social and cultural dynamic which makes it necessary for those images to be kept alive';[30] rather those images need to be repeatedly broken up and reconstituted if they are to continue to touch people, which is one of the reasons why horror films that are thirty or forty years old can often seem simply boring or preposterous to a later audience.

The Universal movie was calculated quite precisely to touch the audiences of 1931. At that time Universal was not one of the front-rank Hollywood studios; its rather cautious and unimaginative policies had left it some distance adrift of the giants of the industry at the end of the 1920s, namely Famous Players, Loews and First National.[31] But a way out of the second rank seemed to offer itself with the huge box office success of Universal's *Dracula*, starring Bela Lugosi, which opened in February 1931 and soon grossed half a million dollars. In April Universal bought the rights of Peggy Webling's *Frankenstein: An Adventure in the Macabre*. The play had run in London in 1930 and its title already suggests a tilting of the work away from Mary Shelley's complex scientific and political statement towards those conventional terror terms for which *Dracula* had indicated a market. *Frankenstein*, filmed in August and September 1931, was an even bigger profit-maker than *Dracula*. Costing a quarter of a million dollars to make, it eventually earned Universal twelve million dollars, was voted one of the films of 1931 by the *New York Times* and confirmed a fashion for horror movies that was soon to include Paramount's *Dr Jekyll and Mr Hyde* and Universal's *The Murders in the Rue Morgue*.

In looking at the content of this movie I'd like to confine my comments to those three areas where the shifts from the novel seem to me most important in terms of the ideological and political re-jigging that they betray; those areas are the Walton story, the nature of the monster and the ending.

The point about the Walton story is a simple one: it's gone. It's not there in the immediate source of the movie, namely Peggy Webling's play, where its disappearance is partly prompted by the need to cram a novel into the average duration of a play. But the fact is that to take away half of Mary Shelley's statement is to change it. It was argued in Section II that the function of the Walton story within the text's meaning is to offer a different model of scientific and technological progress, one in which human survival is ensured as long as that progress is under firm and effective popular control. Remove that narrative and the work collapses into Frankenstein's experience alone which can then be presented as a universal model, replete with the sort of reactionary moralising about the dangers of meddling with the unknown and the delights of tranquillity which are implicit in that tale and made explicit at more than one point. The film can then more easily slide towards a wider statement about the perils of any kind of progress and change, feeding fears of the unknown that change brings and re-inforcing those conservative values that stand in its way.

On the question of the nature of the monster, the most important revision here concerns the creature's brain. The film adds a new episode in which an extra character called Fritz, Frankenstein's assistant, is sent to a laboratory to steal a brain for the monster. In that laboratory are two such pickled organs, in large jars boldly labelled NORMAL BRAIN and ABNORMAL BRAIN. Before the theft, the audience hears an anatomy lecture from Professor Waldman in which he draws attention to various features of the normal brain, 'the most perfect specimen', and contrasts them with the abnormal brain whose defects drive its owner to a life of 'brutality, of violence and murder' because of 'degenerate characteristics'. Its original owner was, in fact, 'a criminal'. The lecture over, Fritz creeps in, grabs the normal brain and then lets it slip so that jar and contents are smashed on the floor. He is forced to take the abnormal brain instead.

The implications for the monster and his story are immense. A central part of Mary Shelley's thesis is to insist that the monster's eventual life of violence and revenge is the direct product of his social circumstances. The monster summarizes his own life in terms that the text endorses:

> Every where I see bliss, from which I alone am irrevocably excluded. I was benevolent and good; misery made me a fiend. Make me happy, and I shall again be virtuous.
>
> (p. 100)

The film deletes this reading of the story through its insistence that the monster's behaviour is not a reaction to its experience but biologically determined, a result of nature, not nurture.

Most commentators on the film are bewildered by this change, one not found in Peggy Webling's play. It has been variously dismissed as an 'absurd and unnecessary sequence ... A cumbersome attempt at establishing motivation', 'ridiculous' and 'the main weakness'.[32] If seen from Mary Shelley's stance, these comments are true; seen in terms of the film's ideological project, they miss the point. At one level in the text, Mary Shelley was concerned to suggest, in the imaginative terms of fiction, that Luddite violence was not the result of some brute characteristics of the nascent English working class but an understandable response to intolerable treatment. The Universal film, consciously or unconsciously, destroys the grounds for such a way of seeing with its radical political implications and instead sees violence as rooted in personal deficiencies, to be viewed with horror and to be labelled, literally, ABNORMAL and so sub-human. Bashing the monster ceases to be the problem but becomes instead the only way that the problem can be met and solved. So it is that Mary Shelley is stood on her head and *Frankenstein* is forced to produce new meanings for 1931.

This upending of Mary Shelley's book and its meaning explains two other profound changes in the monster's presentation that the film introduces. In the text, the monster spends chapters 11 to 16 describing his life – a huge speech that is placed right in the centre of the novel and fills over 20 per cent of its pages. In the film the monster can't speak. Again, in the novel, the monster saves a child from drowning in chapter 16; in the film, the monster drowns a child. Both reversals are of a piece with the Abnormal Brain scene and flow from it in that both deliberately seek to suppress audience sympathy for the monster. (Hence, when in the 1935 sequel *Bride of Frankenstein* the monster did speak, Boris Karloff protested that it made him seem 'more human' so that in the second sequel *Son of Frankenstein* in 1939 he is again wordless.) The changes sharpen a re-focusing which is itself part of the shift from novel to film: reading the book, we hear the monster at eloquent length but we don't see him except vaguely, in imagination, and so reader sympathy is easily evoked; watching the film, we hear nothing from him but instead we see a shambling goon with a forehead like a brick wall and a bolt through his neck, and so audience revulsion is promptly generated. Thus the novel makes him human while the film makes him sub-human, so that in the novel his saving of the drowning child is predictable while equally predictable is his drowning of the child in the film.

The way the film ends flows directly from the drowning of the child and so brings me to the third and last piece of ideological restructuring in the Universal movie that I'd like to look at. In the novel, Frankenstein dies in his pursuit of the monster across the icy Arctic while the latter, in the final sentence, is 'borne away by the waves, and lost in the darkness and distance'. In the film, the drowning of the child provokes the villagers to pursue the brute and trap it in an old windmill which is then burnt down; a brief, single-shot coda shows a recovered Frankenstein happily reunited with his fiancée Elizabeth. The politics of the mill-burning scene are overt: as the blaze engulfs the blades they form a gigantic fiery cross that deliberately suggests the Ku Klux Klan, virulently active at the time, and so, as Tropp crudely puts it, 'points up the mob violence that does the monster in'.[33] Similarly, another observer sees the film ending 'with what Whale called "the pagan sport of a mountain manhunt", at the finale, the film's sympathies are with the monster rather than with the lynch mob'.[34]

These may have been Whale's intentions but there is a wide gap between director's aims and the movie as distributed. In Whale's original version, in the drowning scene, the girl dies because the monster innocently tries to make her float on the water like the flowers they are playing with and then searches frantically for her when she sinks. But these moments were chopped from the print of the film put out for general release: there we simply see the monster reaching out towards the girl and then cut to a grief-stricken father carrying her corpse. Child rape and murder are the obvious assumptions, so that the immediate response of the community in organising itself to eliminate the savage culprit comes across as a kind of ritual cleansing of that community, the prompt removal of an inhuman threat to civilised life which is comfortably justifiable within routine populist politics and at the same time provides the firm basis for and so receives its sanction from the conventionally romantic final scene of hero and heroine at last happy and free from danger. If Mary Shelley's monster alludes indirectly to working-class insurrection, one answer to that canvassed in the 1930s was counter-revolutionary mob violence.

Political readings of the film tend to see it either in simple reflectionist terms (Tropp, for example, regards the monster as 'a creature of the '30s shaped by shadowy forces beyond its control, wandering the countryside like some disfigured veteran or hideous tramp'[35] while another finds 'a world in which manipulations of the stock-market had recoiled on the manipulators; in which human creatures seemed to be abandoned by those who had called them in being and those who might have been thought responsible for their welfare'[36]) or as escapist – 'Large sections of the public, having difficulty in dealing with the Depression, were glad to spend some time in the company of a monster that could more easily be defeated.'[37] Readings of that sort can only be more or a lot less inspired speculation. I'd prefer to look within the film and see it as a *practice*, as an intervention in its world rather than just a picture of it or a retreat from it, a practice whose extent is marked out by the reconstruction of the text that I have indicated. Certainly it was released in the depths of the Depression, depths which can shock even when seen from Thatcherite Britain. The value of manufactured goods and services produced in the USA in 1929 had stood at 81 billion dollars and output at 119 (1923 = 100); as the film criss-crossed the nation in 1932, the value of goods and services had more than halved to 40 billion dollars and output was down to 64. There were 14 million unemployed. How the film reflects that catastrophe or seeks to escape from it is less important than what it says to it. As we saw earlier in Section III, it is historically at precisely such moments of crisis that Frankenstein's monster tends to be summoned by ideology and have its arm brutally twisted till it blurts out the statements that ideology demands. What Universal's *Frankenstein* seeks to say specifically to the mass audience at whom it is aimed concerns above all mass activity in times of crisis: where that activity might be assertive and democratic and beneficial (the Walton story), it is removed and concealed; where it is violent and insurrectionary (the monster's story), it is systematically denigrated; and where it is traditional and reactionary (the mill-burning), it is ambiguously endorsed. The extent to which the film powerfully articulates those familiar stances of the dominant ideology in the 1930s is measured by its box-office success.

V

The fact that Frankenstein's monster is most urgently hailed at times of crisis perhaps accounts for the fact that, with the jokey exception of Universal's *Abbot and Costello Meet Frankenstein* in 1948, the English-speaking movie industry left the brute alone between 1945 (Universal's *House of Dracula*) and 1957 (Hammer's *The Curse of Frankenstein*) as the long post-war boom slowly built up. The Hammer film marked the end of the lengthiest break in Frankenstein pictures in the past fifty years and was the first attempt by a British studio to reproduce the story.

The relationships between, say, *Roderick Random* and early capitalism are complex and highly mediated. The links between Hammer Films and late capitalism are less obscure; the executive producer of *The Curse of Frankenstein*, Michael Carreras, whose family founded Hammer Film Productions in 1947 and have run it for three generations, has put it simply enough: 'The best film is the one that makes money. Our job is to entertain and promote something that is really exploitable. Exploitation is the thing.'[38] Hammer's policy proceeded directly from this philosophy and has been well analysed by David Pirie.[39] It specialised in stories that were already 'pre-sold' to the public by tradition or by radio or television so that public recognition of the product was not a problem – hence early films like *P.C. 49*, *The Man in Black*, *Robin Hood* and so on. At the same time, it sought for itself an area of the market left untouched by the dimpled complacencies of Rank and Ealing Studios. These two strands of policy combined to push it towards horror films, first with *The Quatermass Experiment* in

1955, a spin-off from the 1953 BBC serial *Quatermass*. The success of both serial and film prompted Hammer to explore the genre further, and the filming of *The Curse of Frankenstein* began in November 1956.

The result was a cultural phenomenon whose scale and importance has certainly been noted but whose significance has not really been investigated. *The Curse of Frankenstein* is, it has been claimed, 'the biggest grossing film in the history of the British cinema in relation to cost'.[40] When it opened in the West End in May 1957 it at once started breaking box-office records and it did the same across the USA that summer. One consequence was that the connections that Hammer had with the American market were rapidly reinforced: in September, for example, Columbia Pictures put Hammer under contract to make three films a year and by 1968 Hammer found itself a recipient of the Queen's Award to Industry after three years in which they had brought a total of £4.5 million in dollars into Britain – this at a time, of course, when most of the rest of the British film industry was in a state of vigorous collapse. In the decade and a half after the success of *The Curse of Frankenstein* Hammer made six sequels, all starring Peter Cushing as the eponymous hero.

In looking at the first of this series, it's Cushing and the part he plays that I'd like to focus on, because it is there that the efforts of ideology in putting the myth to work for fresh purposes are most strenuous. At other points – the dropping of the Walton framework, for example – the film simply follows previous practices whose implications have been argued already. It is in the reconstruction of the protagonist that the Hammer film is distinctive, and here the director Terence Fisher was not encumbered by any sense of the original which indeed he had not read. Thus, although Fisher's script (by Jimmy Sangster) was based on the novel, the way was clear for an alignment of the material that was not inhibited by considerations of accuracy, of being 'faithful to the text', but which was free to rework the elements towards those broad Hammer policies of exploitation and money-making.

The singularity of Cushing's role has been spotted by several observers without much attempt being made to see why this should be so.[41] The fact that the film is centred on creator rather than monster in this version is signposted by the way that Boris Karloff, the monster in the Universal movie, at once became a star while Colin Clive, who was Frankenstein, remained obscure; conversely, in the

Hammer picture, it was Peter Cushing who featured in five of the six sequels whereas Christopher Lee never took the part of the monster again.

Central to the specificity of Cushing's part is the way he makes Frankenstein unambiguously the villain of the story and this shift is produced by at least three major changes in his presentation. First and most obviously there are the crimes he commits which have no basis in the text or in previous film versions: to get a brain for his creature he murders a colleague, Professor Bernstein, and later on he sets up the killing of his servant Justine to conceal the fact that he has got her pregnant from his fiancée Elizabeth. Secondly there is a marked class mutation that takes a tendency that is apparent in earlier versions several stages further. Mary Shelley's hero is a student, the son of a magistrate; in the Universal movie he becomes the son of a baron; in the Hammer film for the first time he himself is styled Baron Frankenstein and is given decadent aristocratic trappings to go with his title – he becomes, in Pirie's eyes, 'a dandy'. And then thirdly there is the change in age: Mary Shelley's youthful student is turned into Peter Cushing's middle-aged professor. The relevance of that emerges if we remember that 70 per cent of the audience for horror movies in the 1950s were aged twelve to twenty-five, a fact of which the commercially alert Hammer were well aware. A film pitched largely at adolescents could evoke hostility towards the protagonist more easily by transforming him from one of their own kind into a standard adult authority figure.

In short, the ambiguity of earlier readings of the story is removed by these revisions and we are given a Frankenstein to hate – a Frankenstein who, as Martin Tropp points out, is the real monster, a villain who ends the film facing the guillotine and straightforwardly enacting Terence Fisher's own way of seeing: 'If my films reflect my own personal view of the world ... it is in their showing of the ultimate victory of good over evil, in which I do believe.'[42] Peter Cushing's Baron Frankenstein is a lethal nutter, an archetypal mad scientist.

It is here that the break with the Universal version is sharpest. James Whale had worked specifically to avoid a mad scientist reading of the story and had written to actor Colin Clive insisting that Frankenstein is 'an intensely sane person ... a sane and lovable person'.[43] And the one moment in Whale's film when this analysis wavers – namely Frankenstein's megalomaniac cry of 'Now I know what it feels like to be God' as his creature moves for the first time – was chopped by pious censors before anybody else got to see it.

What I'd like to argue is that close to the root of this transformation in the reading and reproduction of *Frankenstein* is a shift in the structure of fears within the dominant ideology. The possibility of working-class insurrection that had concerned Mary Shelley and terrified Universal was no longer a prime source of anxiety in 1956. To take one crude statistical indicator of working-class discontent: the number of working days lost or, rather, won in strikes in Britain in the 1940s and 1950s was the lowest in the twentieth century. But on the other hand the development of atomic and hydrogen bombs created a new and dire nightmare of the risk of world destruction flowing from a single, deranged individual – a cultural neurosis that the James Bond novels and films, for instance, were to run and run again through the 1960s and beyond. To imagine a universal catastrophe initiated by one mad scientist was a fear that was simply unavailable to Mary Shelley granted the level of scientific capacities in 1818; indeed, the very word 'scientist' was not coined until 1834. *The Curse of Frankenstein*, by contrast, was made at a time when the processes of science seemed to threaten human survival. As David Pirie points out, six months before filming began, a headline in *The Times* on 21 May 1956 had read: 'Giant H-Bomb Dropped, Luminosity More Than 500 Suns.' Equally importantly, we need to remember events in the very week that filming began. The cameras turned for the first time on 19 November; two days earlier, the first Hungarian refugees had arrived in Britain driven out by the Russian tanks that smashed their revolution; a fortnight earlier, on 5 November, Anglo-French airborne troops had landed at Port Said at the depths of the fiasco of the Suez invasion.

The Curse of Frankenstein was therefore made at a unique and over-determined conjuncture in world history when, for the first time, both the technology and the crises existed to threaten the very survival of the planet. Once again Mary Shelley's novel was pulled off the shelf and ransacked for the terms of articulate cultural hysteria. In one sense, of course, the movie represents a flight from the politics of Eden and the Kremlin into a spot of escapist Gothic knockabout; but to see it and then dismiss it as no more is to wipe out a series of factors including Fisher's ideology, Hammer's business sense, American investment and contemporary critical responses,[44] all of which mark out the seriousness of the project at one level. To put it baldly, at a time of genuine and multi-layered public fears, *The Curse of Frankenstein* addressed itself to a predominantly young audience and locates the source of anxiety in a deranged individual, focuses it down to the point where its basis is seen as one man's psychological problem. Wider systematic and social readings and other possibilities (the Walton story for one) are repressed as a structure whose values go unquestioned is presented as threatened by a loony rather than as being itself at the root of instability. Responsibility for imminent catastrophe is limited to a single intellectual standing outside both ordinary lives and the political establishment, so that the film can flow from and then feed back into a populist politics and a scrubby anti-intellectualism frustrated by its own impotence. *The Curse of Frankenstein* is the curse of blocked democracy looking for a scapegoat and being sidetracked from an analysis.

VI

What I have tried to show is that there is no eternal facet of our psyche that horror stories address themselves to. The reworkings of Frankenstein's story in the last century and a half prove that if there are, in Mary Shelley's phrase in the 1831 Introduction, 'mysterious fears of our nature' to which her tale seeks to speak, those fears, like our nature itself, are produced and reproduced by the processes of history itself. Elsewhere in the same Introduction Mary Shelley insists that 'invention, it must be humbly admitted, does not consist in creating out of void, but out of chaos; the materials must, in the first place, be afforded; it can give form to dark, shapeless substances but cannot bring into being the substance itself.' To look for those materials, that chaos, that substance, elsewhere in literature alone and so to read *Frankenstein* simply as shuffling round the themes and structures of earlier Romantic and Gothic texts is to fail to account for the way the novel, ceaselessly reconstituted, vigorously survives while those other fictions are long forgotten – forgotten, indeed, even by Mary Shelley herself by 1831.[45] I suggest that the chaos and the materials were there in the struggles of the Luddite decade, just as other materials and other kinds of chaos were there first in the 1930s and then in the 1950s to produce new meanings in a process that continues. (In 1973, for example, Brian Aldiss took Mary Shelley's book apart and reconstructed it in his novel *Frankenstein Unbound* around the notion that 'man has power to invent, but not to control'.[46] This is an idea which, luckily for Walton, would have sounded daft to his crew.)

What conclusions can we draw from all this? First, surely, we need to see that here as in any text there is no 'real', 'true' reading waiting for a sharp academic to nail it down for ever in the pages of a monograph; even for its own ostensible creator, *Frankenstein* meant certain things in 1818 and began to mean other things by 1831. A historically informed criticism needs to see those meanings, not abolish them.

And then what, in the face of those meanings? S. S. Prawer concludes his study of horror movies by calling for 'standards' that will enable us to distinguish the work of the likes of James Whale from those mindlessly misusing the conventions of horror 'for the sake of profit'.[47] Such a search is likely to prove futile especially if it begins with the old assumption that somehow Universal weren't trying to make a lot of money. The standards that will distinguish between meanings – that will struggle for some and that will detect but resist others – are politically informed ones; standards that are based on a politics that knows where meanings come from and where they lead and is not afraid to fight on the grounds of that knowledge.[48]

From *Literature and History*, 9 (1983), 194–213.

NOTES

[Paul O'Flinn's essay follows the pattern of Marxist criticism in stressing the importance of specific economic and historical conditions in the determination of the text's meaning. Political and economic unrest at the time of the novel's production – attempted uprisings and Luddite machine-breaking between 1812 and 1817 – provides the basis for O'Flinn's Marxist interpretation in which material conditions shape the social and ideological meanings reproduced in the novel. In *Frankenstein*, class conflict is represented as a contradiction within the bourgeois liberalism of Victor Frankenstein's and Walton's positions, a contradiction manifested in their relations with the emergent working class, symbolised by the monster and Walton's mutinous crew. To show how textual meanings are determined by their economic and historical location, O'Flinn interprets *Frankenstein* and two film versions of the novel in terms of their very different contexts:

for the novel it is the Luddite unrest that highlights class anxieties; for the Universal film of 1931, it is the economic depression in America; for the British Hammer version it is the displacement of the atomic threat onto a mad scientist, away from the political divisions between capitalism and communism. Ed.]

1. Details from W. H. Lyles, Mary Shelley: *An Annotated Bibliography* (New York, 1975), and Peter Haining (ed.), *The Frankenstein File* (London, 1977).
2. See in particular Tony Bennett, *Formalism and Marxism* (London, 1979), chs 7, 8 and 9; Catherine Belsey, *Critical Practice* (London, 1980), chs 2 and 6; and Terry Eagleton, *Walter Benjamin: Or Towards a Revolutionary Criticism* (London, 1981), Part II, ch. 3.
3. D. W. Harding, 'The Character of Literature from Blake to Byron', in Boris Ford (ed.), *The Pelican Guide to English Literature: vol. 5 From Blake to Byron* (Harmondsworth, 1957), p. 45.
4. See, for example, Ellen Moers, *Literary Women* (London, 1977); Kate Ellis, 'Monsters in the Garden; Mary Shelley and the Bourgeois Family', in George Levine and U. C. Knoepflmacher (eds), The *Endurance of Frankenstein: Essays on Mary Shelley's Novel* (Berkeley, 1979); and Sandra M. Gilbert and Susan Gubar, *The Madwoman in the Attic: The Woman Writer and the Nineteenth-Century Literary Imagination* (Yale, 1979).
5. Quoted in Phillip Simpson, 'Presentness Precise: Notes on *The History Man*', *Screen*, 23:1 (May/June 1982), 25.
6. Bertolt Brecht, *Life of Galileo*, tr. John Willett (London, 1980), p. 125.
7. Jane Dunn, *Moon in Eclipse: A Life of Mary Shelley* (New York, 1978), pp. 131 and 134.
8. Christopher Small, *Ariel Like a Harpy: Shelley, Mary and Frankenstein* (London, 1972), p. 331.
9. Martin Tropp, *Mary Shelley's Monster* (Boston, 1976), p. 156.
10. Malcolm I. Thomis, *The Luddites: Machine-Breaking in Regency England* (Newton Abbot, 1970), p. 144.
11. E. P. Thompson, *The Making of the English Working Class* (Harmondsworth, 1968), p. 733.
12. Frederick L. Jones (ed.), *The Letters of Percy Bysshe Shelley, vol. 1: Shelley in England* (Oxford, 1964), p. 351.
13. Roger Ingpen and Walter E. Peck (eds), *The Complete Works of Percy Bysshe Shelley*: vol. VI (London, 1965), p. 81.

14. See *Child of Light: A Reassessment of Mary Wollstonecraft Shelley* (Hadleigh, Essex, 1951), ch. 11.
15. Betty T. Bennett (ed.), *The Letters of Mary Wollstonecraft Shelley*: vol. I: *'A Part of the Elect'* (Baltimore, 1980), p. 36.
16. Dunn, *Moon in Eclipse*, p. 134.
17. Bennett, *The Letters of Mary Wollstonecraft Shelley*: vol. I, p. 138.
18. Ibid., p. 49.
19. For details, see Appendix C of Mary Wollstonecraft Shelley, *Frankenstein or The Modern Prometheus*, ed. M. K. Joseph (Oxford, 1969). All subsequent references to the text are to this edition.
20. See Elizabeth Nitchie, *Mary Shelley, Author of Frankenstein* (Connecticut, 1953), pp. 26–33.
21. See, for example, Tropp, *Mary Shelley's Monster*, p. 82, and Mary Poovey, '"My Hideous Progeny": Mary Shelley and the Feminization of Romanticism', *PMLA*, 95 (May 1980), 332–47.
22. Small, *Ariel Like a Harpy*, p. 328.
23. See Lee Sterrenburg, 'Mary Shelley's Monster: Politics and Psyche in *Frankenstein*' in Levine and Knoepflmacher, *The Endurance of Frankenstein*, pp. 143–71.
24. Elizabeth Gaskell, *Mary Barton* (Harmondsworth, 1970), pp. 219–20.
25. Quoted in Appendix IV, Nitchie, 'The Stage History of *Frankenstein*', p. 221.
26. For details, see Mary Poovey, 'My Hideous Progeny'.
27. *The Collected Essays, Journalism and Letters of George Orwell: Volume II: My Country Right or Left 1940–1943*, ed. Sonia Orwell and Ian Angus (London, 1968), pp. 334–35.
28. See the concluding chapter 'Towards a Theory of the Gothic' in David Punter, *The Literature of Terror, A History of Gothic Fictions from 1765 to the Present Day* (London, 1980).
29. *New Statesman* (30 January 1932), p. 120.
30. Punter, *Literature of Terror*, p. 424.
31. Information from J. Douglas Gomery, 'Writing the History of the American Film Industry: Warner Brothers and Sound', *Screen*, 17:1 (Spring 1976). Facts about the making of the Universal *Frankenstein* in this section are derived from Haining, *The Frankenstein File*; Levine and Knoepflmacher, *The Endurance of Frankenstein*; Paul M. Jensen, *Boris Karloff and His Films* (New Jersey, 1974); and Donald F. Glut, *Classic Movie Monsters* (New Jersey, 1978).

32. See, respectively, Tropp, *Mary Shelley's Monster*, pp. 87 and 90; David Pirie, *A Heritage of Horror: The English Gothic Cinema 1946–1972* (London, 1973), p. 69; and Jensen, *Boris Karloff*, p. 30.

33. Tropp, *Mary Shelley's Monster*, p. 97.

34. Jensen, *Boris Karloff*, p. 41.

35. Tropp, *Mary Shelley's Monster*, p. 93.

36. S. S. Prawer, *Caligari's Children: The Film as Tale of Terror* (Oxford, 1980), p. 22.

37. Jensen, *Boris Karloff*, p. 44.

38. Quoted in Prawer, *Caligari's Children*, p. 241.

39. See Pirie, *A Heritage of Horror*, p. 26.

40. Allan Eyles, Robert Adkinson and Nicholas Fry (eds), *The House of Horror: The Story of Hammer Films* (London, 1973), p. 16.

41. See, for example, Pirie, *A Heritage of Horror*, pp. 69 ff.; Tropp, *Mary Shelley's Monster*, pp. 125 ff.; Donald Glut, 'Peter Cushing: Doctor Frankenstein I Presume' in Haining, *The Frankenstein File*; and Albert J. LaValley, 'The Stage and Film Children of *Frankenstein*: A Survey' in Levine and Kneopflmacher, *The Endurance of Frankenstein*, pp. 243–89.

42. Quoted in Eyles et al., *The House of Horror*, p. 15.

43. Quoted in Jensen, *Boris Karloff*, p. 35.

44. *Tribune*, for example, found the movie 'depressing' and 'degrading', and for C. A. Lejeune in *The Observer* it was 'among the half-dozen most repulsive films I have encountered'. The inadequacy of a dismissal of horror stories as merely escapist has recently been powerfully argued by Rosemary Jackson, *Fantasy: The Literature of Subversion* (London, 1981).

45. For evidence of Mary Shelley's forgetfulness of her literary sources, see James Rieger, 'Dr Polidori and the Genesis of *Frankenstein*', *Studies in English Literature*, 3 (Autumn 1963), 461–72.

46. Brian Aldiss, *Frankenstein Unbound* (London, 1982 edition), p. 77.

47. Prawer, *Caligari's Children*, p. 279.

48. My thanks are due to my English Literature colleagues in the Department of Humanities at Oxford Polytechnic who discussed and helpfully criticised an early draft of this article.

2

The Politics of Monstrosity

CHRIS BALDICK

> Vice is a monster of so frightful mien
> As, to be hated, needs but to be seen.
> (Pope, *Essay on Man*)

For the reader of Mary Shelley's novel, there is some uncertainty whether best to define the being created by Victor Frankenstein as 'monster', 'wretch', 'daemon', 'creature', or 'fiend'.[1] The myth, however, has evolved a consensus that the unnamed hominoid deserves at least the name of 'the monster'. In order to clarify the particular historical significance of the myth in its early stages, it will be worth assessing this term in its various meanings and associations. In modern usage 'monster' means something frighteningly unnatural or of huge dimensions. But in earlier usages, which persist into the nineteenth century, the word carries further connotations essential to the development of the Frankenstein myth, the essence of which is that they are not physiological but moral in their reference.

As Michel Foucault reminded us in his discussion of the public performances put on by the inmates of lunatic asylums until the early nineteenth century, a 'monster' is something or someone to be *shown*.[2] (Cf. Latin, *monstrare*; French, *montrer*; English, demonstrate.) In a world created by a reasonable God, the freak or lunatic must have a purpose: to reveal visibly the results of vice, folly, and unreason, as a warning (Latin, *monere*: to warn) to erring humanity. Theological interpretation of monsters and prodigies goes back to Augustine, who argued in his *De civitate Dei* that monsters reveal the will of God. By the time of the Reformation we find Martin Luther himself indulging in monster-interpretation, explaining the birth of a freakish 'monk-calf' as a warning from God about the corruption of Rome.[3] Not satisfied with the explicitness of this divine message, Luther and Melanchthon invented their own 'pope-ass' monster to supplement it. Popular broadsheets of this period would carry woodcuts of deformed children or animals, together with extended teratoscopic analyses of the divine message contained in these prodigious births.

It is with a similar, if more secular, sense of monstrous *display* that Shakespeare has Antony address Cleopatra, referring to her expected surrender to Octavian:

> Let him take thee
> And hoist thee up to the shouting plebeians,
> Follow his chariot, like the greatest spot
> Of all thy sex. Most monster-like be shown
> For poor'st diminutives, for dolts ...
> (*Antony and Cleopatra*, IV. xii. 33–7)

There is nothing monstrous in the modern sense about Cleopatra (whatever the length of her nose); her anticipated 'monstrosity' here will be her position in Caesar's triumphal procession as a demonstration that resistance to his power is futile. The same sense is employed in the closing scenes of *Macbeth*, as Macduff (regarded by Macbeth as the product of a monstrously unnatural birth) triumphs over the usurper, shifting on to him the stigma of monstrosity:

> Then yield thee, coward,
> And live to be the show and gaze o'the time:
> We'll have thee, as our rarer monsters are,
> Painted upon a pole, and underwrit,
> 'Here may you see the tyrant'.
> (V. viii. 23–7)

More clearly than in Cleopatra's case, the final defining tag here brings out a particular characteristic of this meaning of monstrosity: its habitual use as an illustration of a particular vice or transgression. Monstrosity, for Shakespeare, is less a matter of physiological prodigies and freaks than a way of defining moral aberrations; as Antonio remarks in *Twelfth Night*:

> In nature there's no blemish but the mind;
> None can be call'd deform'd but the unkind.
> (III. iv. 376–7)

This moral sense of monstrosity is very common in Renaissance literature generally, but to continue with Shakespearian instances alone, we find that in *Othello* Emilia characterises jealousy as a monster; Gower in the prologue and epilogue to *Pericles* refers to the 'monster envy' and 'monstrous lust'; Petruchio in *The Taming of the Shrew* complains of 'monstrous arrogance', and Gloucester in *Henry the Sixth, Part One* of 'monstrous treachery', while Holofernes in *Love's Labour's Lost* exclaims: 'O thou monster Ignorance, how deformed dost thou look.'[4] When Celia seals her promise to Rosalind by swearing 'and when I break that oath let me turn monster' (*As You Like It*, I. ii. 22), she means 'let me be displayed publicly as the very emblem of disloyalty'. In these uses, monstrosity is employed not just as an intensifier, highlighting the degree or extent of the vice, but as a special kind of superlative which indicates that the particular case has revealed the essence of the vice in question, and can be displayed as its very model and type. In Hegelian terms we can say that this usage shows degree or quantity transforming itself into quality. When the Poet in *Timon of Athens*, referring to Timon's friends, speaks of the 'The monstrous bulk of this ingratitude' (V. i. 65), he appears merely to be measuring its scale, but in fact is announcing its fully representative status as the clearest possible display of the vice – which on the stage, of course, is just what it is. The same goes for the King of France's view of Cordelia's alleged crime: 'her offence must be of such unnatural degree / That monsters it' (*King Lear*, I. i. 219–20). The monster is one who has so far transgressed the bounds of nature as to become a moral advertisement.

Timon and *Lear* highlight the most important class within this usage: the representation of ingratitude. Leaving aside the rather special case of Caliban, a literal monster and (in Prospero's eyes) ingrate, Shakespeare's most powerful and memorable representations of moral monstrosity are concentrated upon this vice. (It is not, for our purposes, important that the protagonists of these plays are blind or indiscriminate in their accusations – their sense alone concerns us.) Timon, who has 'flung in rage from this ingrateful seat / Of monstrous friends' (*Timon of Athens*, IV. ii. 45–6), is moved to exclaim:

> And yet, O! see the monstrousness of man
> When he looks out in an ungrateful shape
> (III. ii. 72–3)

The 'monster of ingratitude' (as even Time itself is described by Ulysses in *Troilus and Cressida*) is so prominent among monstrous representations of vice that, especially in cases of children's behaviour towards parents, the offence need not even be specified. So in *Lear*, Gloucester, incredulous at Edmund's accusations against Edgar, can say 'He cannot be such a monster ... to his father' (I. ii. 94–6). Lear is more specific in complaining of Goneril's 'monster ingratitude', but Albany can simply describe her behaviour as 'most monstrous' (I. v. 39; V. iii. 160). It is the vices of ingratitude, rebellion, and disobedience, particularly towards parents, that most commonly attract the appellation 'monstrous': to be a monster is to break the natural bonds of obligation towards friends and especially towards blood-relations. The crime may even be extended to cover contractual obligations: Milton writes in his *Tenure of Kings and Magistrates* that 'If I make a voluntary Covnant as with a man, to doe him good, and he prove afterward a monster to me, I should conceave a disobligement.'[5] Long before the monster of Frankenstein, monstrosity already implied rebellion, or an unexpected turning against one's parent or benefactor.

A further characteristic of the monstrous needs to be noted: it is an almost obligatory feature of the monsters in classical mythology that they should be composed of ill-assorted parts, sometimes combined from different creatures (centaurs, satyrs, the Minotaur, the Sphinx), sometimes merely multiplied to excess (Argus, the Hydra). This feature has two kinds of consequence in the history of monstrosity, one aesthetic, the other political, and both have a bearing on the Frankenstein myth. The aesthetic discussion of monstrosity does not at first proceed from the moral dimension of the concept we have discussed above, but uses instead the directly physical notion of deformity to illustrate certain problems of the relation of parts to the whole in works of art. Horace begins his *Ars Poetica* with just this problem:

> Suppose a painter chose to put a human head on a horse's neck, or to spread feathers of various colours over the limbs of several different creatures, or to make what in the upper part is a beautiful woman tail off into a hideous fish, could you help laughing when he showed you his efforts?[6]

This injunction against ridiculous and unnatural combinations became, in the Age of Reason, a sacred text within the neo-classical Rules for the decorous imitation of Nature. Transgression of

Horace's rule in fanciful and disturbing compounds of images constitutes the category of the 'grotesque', which unlike the 'picturesque' is an artificially contrived violation of Nature. The problem of wilful and unnatural assembly comes to be discussed as a major problem in the new aesthetics of Romanticism, notably in Coleridge's famous distinction between the organic fusion of parts achieved by the Imagination, and the merely mechanical combinations produced by Fancy. In Victor Frankenstein's assembly of his creature this aspect of monstrosity, too, is clearly present, and is a factor in the subsequent uses of the myth. The most important connection in which this issue presents itself is in the contribution of the image of the hybrid or hydra-monster to the political senses of monstrosity, which we should now review.

The representation of fearful transgressions in the figure of physical deformity arises as a variant of that venerable cliché of political discourse, the 'body politic'. When political discord and rebellion appear, this 'body' is said to be not just diseased, but misshapen, abortive, monstrous. Once the state is threatened to the point where it can no longer be safely identified (according to the medieval theory) with 'the King's body' – that is, with an integral and sacred whole – then the humanly recognisable form of the body politic is lost, dispersed into a chaos of dismembered and contending organs. The *OED*, under 'Monstrous', cites Starkey writing in 1538 that 'The partys in proportyon not agreyng ... make in this polityke body grete and monstrose deformyte'. Like very many of the writers who use this figure, Sir Thomas Browne in *Religio Medici* (1643) locates this 'deformyte' in the debased nature of the popular rabble, 'the multitude, that numerous piece of monstrosity, which taken asunder seeme men, and the reasonable creatures of God; but confused together, make but one great beast & a monstrosity more prodigious than Hydra'.[7] A similar image of 'the blunt monster with uncounted heads, / The still-discordant wavering multitude' appears in Shakespeare's *Henry the Fourth, Part Two* (Induction, 18). A glance at Shakespeare's more celebrated use of the body politic figure in *Coriolanus* may help to amplify the senses in which the multitude is seen as monstrous:

> Ingratitude is monstrous; and for the multitude to be ingrateful, were to make a monster of the multitude; of the which, we being members, should bring ourselves to be monstrous members.
>
> (II. iii. 9–12)

The Third Citizen's quibble here incorporates the familiar moral vice of ingratitude into the image of disorganised members, making the multitude doubly monstrous: hydra-headed and therefore irrepressible, and at the same time an ingrate, rebelling against its political parent.

In the shadow of this monster, the founding of modern political theory during the years of Revolution in the seventeenth century had to replace the integrity of the medieval 'King's body' with a fearfully inhuman substitute. This problem of the body politic and the relations of its organs is the central preoccupation of Thomas Hobbes in his *De Corpore Politico* (1640) and *Leviathan* (1651), the latter work announcing from the start its new sense of the political 'body':

> For by Art is created that great LEVIATHAN, called a COMMONWEALTH, or STATE (in latine, CIVITAS) which is but an Artificial Man; though of greater stature and strength than the Naturall ... Lastly, the *Pacts* and *Covenants* by which the parts of this Body Politique were first made, set together, and united, resemble that *Fiat*, or the *Let us make man*, pronounced by God in the Creation.[8]

There is an uneasy feeling of human responsibility involved in this conception, fully in accord with subsequent uses of 'monstrosity' since, like Horace's mermaids, the monsters both of poetic fancy and of political organisation are made not by nature but by fallible human arts. From the perception of such a gulf between nature and culture the fear that human society may itself be producing monsters emerges as early as 1697, as the *OED* records from South's *Sermons*: 'We sometimes read of Monstrous Births, but we may often see a greater Monstrosity in Educations.' This artificial man is a monster closely related to Hobbes's gigantic creature; both need to be kept in mind when we come to examine the development of the Frankenstein myth. They both reflect the dismemberment of the old body politic as incarnated in the personal authority of late feudal and absolutist rule. They signal the growing awareness, hastened in the heat of regicide and revolution, of destinies no longer continuous with nature but shaped by art, by 'policy' – the prospect in politics and in broader cultural life of the 'artificial man'. When revolution and regicide reappear on the agenda of European history, this spectre will be re-animated.

In Britain the first decade of the French Revolution witnessed the prodigious proliferation of two bodies of writing: a boom in

'Gothic' novels led by Ann Radcliffe, and a flurry of books and pamphlets provoked by Edmund Burke's *Reflections on the Revolution in France* (1790). The one is typically preoccupied with feudal forms of unlimited personal power and its tyrannical abuse: imprisonment, rape, persecution, and the victim's claustrophobia. The other is concerned with the very new 'monster' (as Burke saw it) of the French Revolution itself; with the novelty, the rationality, and the irrationality in the consciously artificial order of revolutionary France, and with the Terrors of both the new and the old regimes. Bridging these two bodies of work there is an intermediary category of writings which constitutes what Gary Kelly calls the 'Jacobin Novel'[9] – the fictional works of Robert Bage, Elizabeth Inchbald, Thomas Holcroft, Mary Wollstonecraft, and William Godwin. If the flourishing of the Gothic novel is a sure but unconscious and remote reverberation of the events in France,[10] the works of this group are more openly addressed to the social and political issues highlighted by the revolutionary process. Politico-philosophical novels (in some respects the muted British equivalents of the works of Sade), these writings bring together the terrors of the Gothic novel and the topical social criticism of *Things as They Are* – the original title of Godwin's *Adventures of Caleb Williams* (1794). It was from the area marked out by this overlapping of literary and political discourses that the Frankenstein myth was born, as a late product of the controversy generated in Britain by the French Revolution.

The controversy begins with Burke's extravagantly rhetorical attack on the French revolutionaries. What was even more shocking than Burke's apparent change of loyalties since his earlier championing of liberal causes was the ferocity of his imagery, the sheer violence of his tropes. In the *Reflections* Burke's conservative faith is tied to a powerful emotional investment in a 'natural' policy which antedates Hobbes's artificial man. Above all, he identifies the political status quo so insistently with the sanctities of familial feelings that his account becomes an Oedipal drama. 'Ingratitude to benefactors is the first of revolutionary virtues', Burke later wrote, and went on to describe the revolutionaries as 'miscreant parricides'.[11] Burke mobilises, and intensifies, a Shakespearian sense of monstrosity as rebellion against the father:

> [We] should approach to the faults of the state as to the wounds of a father, with pious awe and trembling solicitude. By this wise preju-

> dice we are taught to look with horror on those children of their country who are prompt rashly to hack that aged parent in pieces, and put him in the kettle of magicians, in hopes that by their poisonous weeds, and wild incantations, they may regenerate the paternal constitution, and renovate their father's life.[12]

Monstrous ingratitude to the father is combined here, as in *Coriolanus*, with a monstrous dismemberment, a castratory hacking which precedes the reassembly of limbs into an abortive body politic. Even before the Terror, the French Revolution is to Burke a monstrous jumble of elements, 'out of nature' (*Reflections*, p. 92), producing a 'monster of a constitution' (*Reflections*, p. 313). More important than this rehearsal of horrors is Burke's attempt to turn the events into a species of cautionary tale. His explanation of the fall of the *ancien régime* includes the following criticism of its last ministries: 'Rather too much countenance was given to the spirit of innovation, which soon was turned against those who fostered it, and ended in their ruin' (*Reflections*, p. 237). The proverbial wisdom here is not in itself original, but in its application to the understanding of the Revolution's bewildering events, it helped to formulate a very influential narrative logic. Its pattern reappears in the long quotation from the Comte de la Tour du Pin's report to the Assembly on military affairs, which was later to take on the status of a prophecy:

> *The nature of things requires*, that the army should never act but as *an instrument*. The moment that, erecting itself into a deliberative body, it shall act according to its own resolutions, the *government, be it what it may*, will immediately degenerate into a military democracy; a species of political monster, which has always ended by devouring those who have produced it.
>
> (*Reflections*, p. 333)

Burke goes on, in his own words, to complain of the municipal army of the Paris district that 'considered in a view to any coherence or connection between its parts, it seems a monster, and can hardly fail to terminate its perplexed movements in some great national calamity' (*Reflections*, p. 350).

The monster image is a powerful means of organising, understanding, and at the same time preserving the chaotic and confused nature of the revolutionary events in Burke's account. Burke had first adopted this approach in a letter to his son in October 1789, writing of 'the portentous State of France – where the Elements which compose Human Society seem all to be dissolved, and a world of Monsters to be produc'd in the place of it.'[13] After the Terror of 1793 had borne out his prophecy, the revolutionary Monster in his writings returns in even more lurid colours. Burke's *Letters on the Proposals for Peace with the Regicide Directory of France* (1796–7) repeat this kind of imagery with hysterical insistence: France is a 'monster of a state', it is 'the mother of monsters', a 'monstrous compound', and a 'cannibal republic' (*Works*, VI. 95, 127, 161, 188). In his *Letter to a Noble Lord* (1796) Burke plays upon the strong interest in scientific experiment among the radicals of his age (Paine, Franklin, and Marat, for example), attacking the French revolutionaries not just as cannibals, but as sorcerers, alchemists, and fanatical chemists. Dwelling often on stories of graves being robbed to provide materials for arms, he extends this ghoulishness into a wider accusation against the radical *philosophes* and their inhuman lust for desecration. The manufacture of saltpetre from the rubble of aristocratic houses strikes him as another such horror: 'There is nothing, on which the leaders of the republic, one and indivisible, value themselves, more than on the chemical operations by which, through science, they convert the pride of aristocracy to an instrument of its own destruction.' (*Works*, VI. 73 n.) The unfeeling *philosophes* are so fanatically devoted to scientific pride that 'they would sacrifice the whole human race to the slightest of their experiments' (*Works*, VI. 70). From this rhetorical riot of ghoulish scientists and ransacked graves looms Burke's most ominous image of the Revolution as a whole:

> ... out of the tomb of the murdered monarchy in France has arisen a vast, tremendous unformed spectre, in a far more terrifick guise than any which ever yet have overpowered the imagination, and subdued the fortitude of man.
>
> (*Works*, VI. 88)

As Conor Cruise O'Brien points out, the spectre haunting Europe in the opening sentence of *The Communist Manifesto* 'walks for the first time in the pages of Burke' (*Reflections*, p. 9), although, as we have seen, the figure has a certain tradition behind it in political metaphors of the state and the multitude.

The spate of Anti-Jacobin writings inaugurated by Burke took up the same themes, regularly depicting the Parisian mob as a monster. Augustin de Barruel, whose writings were later devoured by Percy Shelley, wrote of 'that disastrous monster Jacobin', which he believed had been 'engendered' by a conspiracy of Enlightenment intellectuals (the 'Illuminati') originating in Ingolstadt.[14] The basis of the monstrous imagery used in these diatribes is a sketchy explanation of events in France: that godless *philosophes* had consciously desecrated traditional sanctities and produced from the resulting chaos a monster which, according to mythic logic, was sure to devour its creators. As J. M. Roberts has shown in his fascinating study of the masonic and Illuminati scares of this period, conscious design and conspiracy was the only kind of causal logic available to most people at the time as an explanation for the French events. Percy Shelley himself, whose idealism stretched so far as to claim that poets were the unacknowledged legislators of the world, must have found Barruel's conspiracy theory so attractive because of the enormous influence it attributed to a determined and enlightened elite. And for all his deep commitment to traditional continuities, prejudices, and unexamined loyalties, even Burke shared the age's belief in the limitless power of conscious human will, for he concedes that 'Man' is 'in a great degree a creature of his own making' (*Reflections*, p. 189). Burke observed that self-making capacity at work on the grandest and most momentous scale: a parricidal dismemberment of the old body politic, and unprecedented reassembling of its disjointed parts, and the armed multitude conjured up by the propertied and educated classes, but no longer under their control. Burke first recognised and named the great political 'monster' of the modern age.

Burke's opponents rarely resort to such lurid figures; much of their criticism, indeed, is levelled at these extravagances of his rhetoric as well as at his arguments. But the charge of monstrosity had to be answered. In the most important of the responses to Burke, Tom Paine in *Rights of Man* attempts to turn the tables on him. Singling out Burke's phrase 'out of nature', he castigates the system of monarchy and aristocracy as itself a monstrous regime: 'It is by distortedly exalting some men, that others are distortedly debased, till the whole is out of nature.'[15] If the actions of the 'mob' appear unnatural, then the cause is to be found in the artificial exaggerations of wealth, rank, and privilege. Paine picks up on Burke's parricidal imagery and turns the accusation of unnatural child–parent relations back upon the aristocratic system itself:

> By the aristocratical law of primogenitureship, in a family of six children, five are exposed. Aristocracy has never more than *one* child.

> The rest are begotten to be devoured. They are thrown to the cannibal for prey, and the natural parent prepares the unnatural repast.
> As everything which is out of nature in man, affects, more or less, the interests of society, so does this ... To restore, therefore, parents to their children, and children to their parents – relations to each other, and man to society – and to exterminate the monster Aristocracy, root and branch – the French constitution has destroyed the law of PRIMOGENITURESHIP. Here then lies the monster; and Mr Burke, if he pleases, may write its epitaph.
> (*Rights*, p. 104)

Paine has aimed his blow astutely at the parental callousness of primogeniture, thereby establishing aristocracy as a monstrous parent to counter Burke's monster child. Burke announces the birth of the monster child Democracy, while Paine records the death of the monster parent Aristocracy.[16] The 'sort of breathing automaton' (*Rights*, p. 196) which is Monarchy is laid to rest, giving way to a remade humanity: 'the present generation will appear to the future as the Adam of a new world' (*Rights*, p. 290), declares Paine, heralding the new rational Creation.

Paine's purpose in *Rights of Man* goes beyond the desire to trade monstrous countercharge against charge. It is to identify not merely the true monster but the true *parent* of the Revolution: the aristocracy, rather than any innovators or Illuminati, is to blame for exposing not just its younger sons but its whole people to cannibalism. In the darker years of the Revolution the importance of this argument to the radical cause increases noticeably, as can be seen in a second major reply to Burke, that of Mary Wollstonecraft in her *Historical and Moral View of the Origin and Progress of the French Revolution* (1794). Wollstonecraft traces the causes of the Revolution to the negligence of the decadent and over-refined French court. The widening gulf between court luxury and popular starvation has made French life inhospitable to the 'healthy beams' of the human soul:

> But, by the habitual slothfulness of rusty intellects, or the depravity of the heart, lulled into hardness on the lascivious couch of pleasure, those heavenly beams are obscured, and man appears either an hideous monster, a devouring beast; or a spiritless reptile, without dignity or humanity.[17]

Wollstonecraft's Nonconformist distaste for court luxuries here identifies the source of monstrosity less in primogeniture than in the dehumanising callousness of a life of lascivious pleasure. To Burke's picture of the revolutionaries as a 'race of monsters', Wollstonecraft responds with a reminder of the cruelty and despotism practised by Europe's aristocratic governments:

> Sanguinary tortures, insidious poisonings, and dark assassinations, have alternately exhibited a race of monsters in human shape, the contemplation of whose ferocity chills the blood, and darkens every enlivening expectation of humanity: but we ought to observe, to reanimate the hopes of benevolence, that the perpetration of these horrid deeds has arisen from a despotism in the government, which reason is teaching us to remedy.
>
> (*View*, p. 515)

Wollstonecraft does not deny that elements of the Parisian crowd deserve to be regarded as monstrous (*View*, pp. 258, 447), but these are, in the first place, 'a set of monsters, distinct from the people' (*View*, p. 450), and moreover, their bloody actions are engendered by despotism, as retaliation. The actions of the people are compared with those of a blind elephant lashing out indiscriminately under provocation (*View*, p. 32): in these circumstances 'the retaliation of slaves is always terrible' (*View*, p. 520). Identifying, like Paine, the aristocracy as the parent of the revolutionary violence, Wollstonecraft adapts Burke's model of poetic justice to them: 'whilst despotism and superstition exist, the convulsions, which the regeneration of man occasions, will always bring forward the vices they have engendered, to devour their parents' (*View*, p. 259). Wollstonecraft is prepared to extend the same logic to the fate of the Jacobins too, in what looks more like a Burkean argument: they brought about 'public misery, involving these short-sighted men in the very ruin they had themselves produced by their mean intrigues' (*View*, p. 465–6). The inhumanity of the court or of the Montagne recoils upon itself, but Wollstonecraft insists that the same process cannot be imputed to rational innovation and enlightenment, as Burke has suggested. Wollstonecraft's purpose is to refute all attempts to use the Terror as an illustration of the consequences of political change:

> We must get entirely clear of all the notions drawn from the wild traditions of original sin: the eating of the apple, the theft of Prometheus, the opening of Pandora's box, and the other fables, too tedious to enumerate, on which priests have erected their tremendous

> structures of imposition, to persuade us, that we are naturally inclined to evil ...
>
> (*View*, p. 17)

The apparently monstrous actions of the French people show not the evils of change, but the reflected evils of government tyranny, the retaliation of slaves. It is provocation rather than innate wickedness that engenders them: 'People are rendered ferocious by misery; and misanthropy is ever the offspring of discontent' (*View*, p. 71). This is the essence of the radical explanation of the Revolution as a product of insufferable circumstances rather than of monstrous designs.

The most intellectually prestigious of the English radical responses to Burke, and to the Revolution, came from Mary Shelley's other parent, William Godwin, whose *Enquiry Concerning Political Justice* (1793) enjoyed for a while an influential stature as the theoretical cornerstone of English 'Jacobinism', inspiring the early thinking of Wordsworth, Coleridge, and Percy Shelley. Godwin's measured tones are a distinct contrast to the rhetorical extremes of Burke or even of Paine, and he rarely ventures into a figurative rendition of political principles. Indeed, Godwin takes some care to parody the colourful style of the reactionaries when introducing their hypothetical objections to his arguments.[18] One such imaginary opponent is made to assert that 'Democracy is a monstrous and unwieldy vessel, launched upon the sea of human passions, without ballast.'[19] Godwin recognises and mimics the characteristic tropes of Burkean discourse, to reply along with Paine that it is the institutions of monarchy and aristocracy that are monstrous. 'The feudal system', writes Godwin, 'was a ferocious monster, devouring, wherever it came, all that the friend of humanity regards with attachment and love' (*Enquiry*, p. 476).

Political Justice, though, is concerned less with supporting Paine's kind of direct riposte to Burke than with conducting a general critique of Government from a standpoint of rationalist anarchism. Godwin finds that Government itself, since it is a Hobbesian 'artificial man' with too many heads, is monstrous in its actions:

> A multitude of men may be feigned to be an individual, but they cannot become a real individual. The acts which go under the name of the society are really the acts now of one single person and now of another. The men who by turns usurp the name of the whole perpetu-

> ally act under the pressure of incumbrances that deprive them of their true energy. They are fettered by the prejudices, the humours, the weakness and vice of those with whom they act; and, after a thousand sacrifices to these contemptible interests, their project comes out at last, distorted in every joint, abortive and monstrous.
>
> (*Enquiry*, p. 558)

From the standpoint of Godwin's atomised individualism, the monstrosity of Government is a perversion, not of any organic 'King's body', but of the integrity of responsible individual action.

That gulf between project and abortive outcome, in which we can already read the outlines of the Frankenstein story, was a crucial discrepancy which English radicalism had to explain to itself in the 1790s. For the basic doctrine of the radical group, proclaimed in *Political Justice*, is the invincibility of Reason's progress in eliminating the injustices and superstitions of the old feudal heritage. Mary Wollstonecraft had described the principles embodied in the Declaration of the Rights of Man as 'truths, the existence of which had been eternal; and which required only to be made known to be generally acknowledged' (*View*, p. 489). The eternal truths of reason had only to be announced in order that the structures of despotism and priestcraft should fade painlessly away. It is in this conviction that Godwin devotes the fourth Book of *Political Justice* to an attack upon what he sees as the hot-headed impatience of more genuinely Jacobinical radicals like Thelwall, who advocated practical political action to secure reforms. The contemplation and propagation of Reason, Godwin felt, would suffice. And yet, in the mid-1790s, Godwin's circle was to find that the diffusion of truth and reason had encountered unforeseen obstacles: Britain, far from embracing enlightenment, was in the grip of war and reaction, with the radicals besieged by legal persecution or by 'Church and King' rioters, and the Revolution itself taking a far from rational course. How, then, could Reason so miscarry?

Mary Wollstonecraft's attempts at an answer place their emphasis on the corrupting tendency of aristocratic institutions, which debase their victims to the point either of servility or of unthinking retaliation. Her work usually looks for answers in the realm of education and reformed upbringing, while William Hazlitt was later to reflect upon the slave mentality as an explanation. Godwin's brief consideration of the abortive projects of Government begins to offer a mode of explanation far removed from the world of

Illuminati plots and conscious orchestration, which tries to account for the *inadvertent* distortion of a purpose as it is filtered through a welter of contradictory and competing pressures. The kind of monstrosity produced in such a process will no longer be the old emblem of vice or caricature of the mob, but a new and puzzling image of humanity's loss of control over its world.

Godwin's new-found sense of the obstacles to rational progress was to be presented and explored in his novel *Things as They Are, or The Adventures of Caleb Williams*. This novel is, as its title implies, very much an attempt to explain the actual conditions of British society in the 1790s; an examination of the entrenched mechanisms and wide extent of established power, in the field of what Godwin calls 'domestic tyranny'. A powerful study of persecution and fear, it embraces a range of political issues from crime and imprisonment to servitude, chivalry, honour, and of course justice. Behind its action can be detected allegories of the English Revolution, of Edmund Burke's career, and of the radical philosopher's remorse for attacking a culture to whose values he is ultimately still committed.[20] In its central incident the novel's narrator-protagonist Caleb Williams is overpowered by his ruling passion, 'a mistaken thirst of knowledge'.[21] Gripped by this epistemophilia, Caleb breaks into his master Falkland's private box, the dark secret of which is never fully disclosed. Apprehended by the proud Falkland, who is now incriminated by the glimpse at his secret, Caleb is to be pursued with the full rigour of class injustice. Falkland is able, because of his social position, to track his potential accuser across the length and breadth of the country and purchase the means of unremitting legal persecution, driving Caleb into outlawry and prison. Through Caleb's ordeal we are shown the capacity for persecution and injustice available to the English ruling class by virtue of its control over the legal machine; we are given the point of view of the complete outcast, as Caleb disguises himself successively as gipsy, Jew, and Irishman, encountering the higher morality of outlaws and convicts. The dynamic principle of the narrative is one of endless flight and ineluctable pursuit, as the roles of accuser and accused exchange between 'father' and 'son' figures. Falkland and Williams, master and servant, are recognisable examples of the 'double', locked into a guilty duel in which they constantly mirror one another. Yet the field of action expands beyond the private struggle of master and servant into the arena of 'legal despotism' (*Caleb Williams*, p. 184), to the point at which Caleb can regard 'the whole human species as so many hangmen and torturers' (*Caleb Williams*, p. 183). Caleb, like both Victor Frankenstein and his monster, has to endure the intolerable injustice of suffering for the misdeeds of another. Falkland brings about his own ruin by persisting in his persecution: Caleb had not intended to betray his master's secret, but is driven at last to take this course of revenge, the emptiness of which finally spoils his success in having Falkland convicted of murder.

Apart from its concern with curiosity and mutual destruction, *Caleb Williams* prefigures *Frankenstein* in its unsettling of stable identities and values. The unreliable first-person narrative and the undisclosed secrets place all moral certainties in a state of suspension, leaving us only a terrible power-struggle in which the injustices of contemporary society are (as in the sub-plots of *Frankenstein*) brought into the open. In the confusion of identities and moral bearings which is brought about by the mutual mirroring of Caleb and Falkland, what is lost is that clear shape of vice which traditionally distinguishes the monstrous from the human. Even Caleb himself comes to doubt whether he is morally superior to the murderer Falkland, and we find that robbers and outlaws have a surer sense of honour and justice than magistrates have. It is from this new species of politico-philosophical novel that Mary Shelley's *Frankenstein* derives many of its preoccupations, while its story of the creation of a monster emerges from her parents' debate with Burke over the great monstrosity of the modern age, the French Revolution.

Before we leave Godwin, a final point needs to be made about the place of *Political Justice* in the Frankenstein myth. There is one interpretation of *Frankenstein* which takes the figure of Victor Frankenstein to be a satirical representation of William Godwin himself. Now there are some biographical connections here in Mary Shelley's experience of parental neglect, but the principal basis for this identification, insisted upon by D. H. Lawrence,[22] is the unreliable legend of Godwin's supposed doctrine of human 'perfectibility'. According to the repeated misconception of his stated views on this question, Godwin believed that rational enlightenment would produce a new 'perfect' kind of human being. Not surprisingly, then, he is taken as the original of the similarly deluded Victor Frankenstein. But although it is true that Godwin did entertain some bizarre notions about the future possibilities open to the species, his doctrine of 'perfectibility' is in fact the precise opposite of the delusion so often attributed to him. Godwin's own explanation could hardly be clearer:

> Lastly, man is perfectible. This proposition needs some explanation.
> By perfectible, it is not meant that he is capable of being brought to perfection. But the word seems sufficiently adapted to express the faculty of being continually made better and receiving perpetual improvement; and in this sense it is here to be understood. The term perfectible, thus explained, not only does not imply the capacity of being brought to perfection, but stands in express opposition to it. If we could arrive at perfection, there would be an end to our improvement.
>
> (*Enquiry*, pp. 144–5)

The idea of absolute human perfection is, Godwin insists, 'pregnant with absurdity and contradiction' (*Enquiry*, p. 145). His quite distinct claim is that 'man' is always *im*perfect, and therefore always open to improvement, and that he has a capacity for such improvement, which (again contrary to the legend) is not an inevitable prospect, as he explains in his critique of optimism in Book IV of *Political Justice*. Godwin was of course mistaken in believing that the word 'perfectible' was sufficiently clear to convey this view; on the contrary, it has done much mischief with his reputation.

In the genuine weaknesses of Godwin's Romantic idealism, however, faint traces of a Frankensteinian mentality can be detected. The final and least convincing chapters of *Political Justice* introduce some dizzying extrapolations from the 'sublime conjecture', attributed to Benjamin Franklin, that 'the term of human life may be prolonged, and that by the immediate operation of the intellect, beyond any limits we are able to assign' (*Enquiry*, p. 776). The men of the future (given the nature of the prediction, it is hard to tell whether Godwin includes women here) 'will probably cease to propagate. The whole will be a people of men, and not of children' (*Enquiry*, p. 776). It is a chillingly disembodied extension of Godwin's often rarefied rationalism, but if it smacks of Frankensteinian irresponsibility, this is not a consistent feature of Godwin's outlook. His anarchist individualism, which prohibits marriage, procreation, and even collaborative work, is qualified by important warnings against the detachment of science from social ties: 'science and abstraction will soon become cold,' Godwin argues, 'unless they derive new attractions from ideas of society' (*Enquiry*, p. 300). Elsewhere he asserts that little good can be done by solitaries, a principle illustrated by his disciple Percy Shelley in *Alastor, or The Spirit of Solitude* (1816). This doctrine supplies the moral of *Frankenstein* too; Mary Shelley dedicated it to Godwin less because she was a dutiful daughter (her elopement lost her that title) than because Godwin was in so many ways the novel's intellectual begetter.

From Chris Baldick, *In Frankenstein's Shadow: Myth, Monstrosity and Nineteenth-century Writing* (Oxford, 1987), pp. 10–29.

NOTES

[The book from which this essay comes identifies the political meanings of the monster in the literature of the nineteenth and early twentieth centuries. In this essay Chris Baldick traces the way that the word 'monster' is far from an ideologically neutral term. He shows how, historically, aesthetic and moral uses are underscored by a political significance that is cloaked in terms of the body and the family. A figure of ugliness and vice, the monster must also be excluded from the 'body politic' as an ungrateful child rebelling against the authority of the father and the state. Historically, Baldick argues, these are the terms in which the revolution debates of the 1790s were fought. In establishing literature's location within a wider historical and political sphere, the monster metaphor indicates the importance of social bonds and values in processes of creativity and provides a critique of individualism. Ed.]

1. A simple word-tally shows 'monster', with 27 appearances, to have won by a short head from 'fiend' (25), followed by 'daemon' (18), 'creature' (16), 'wretch' (15), and 'devil' (8); 'being' (4) and 'ogre' (1) also ran.
2. Michel Foucault, *Madness and Civilization: A History of Insanity in the Age of Reason*, trans. Richard Howard (London, 1967), pp. 68–70.
3. See Lorraine J. Daston and Katherine Park, 'Unnatural Conceptions: The Study of Monsters in Sixteenth- and Seventeenth-Century France and England', *Past and Present*, XCII (1981), 20–54.
4. *Othello*, III. iv. 161; *Pericles*, Prologue, 12; V. iii. 86; *Taming of the Shrew*, IV. iii. 107; *I Henry VI*, IV. i. 61; *Love's Labour's Lost*, IV. ii. 23.
5. John Milton, *Selected Prose*, ed. C. A Patrides (Harmondsworth, 1974), p. 276.

6. Horace, 'On the Art of Poetry', trans. E. T. Dorsch, in Aristotle, Longinus, Horace, *Classical Literary Criticism* (Harmondsworth, 1965), p. 79.
7. Sir Thomas Browne, *The Major Works*, ed. C. A. Patrides (Harmondsworth, 1977), p. 134.
8. Thomas Hobbes, *Leviathan*, ed. C. B. Macpherson (Harmondsworth, 1968), pp. 81–2.
9. Gary Kelly, *The English Jacobin Novel 1780–1805* (Oxford, 1976).
10. In his 'Idée sur les romans' (1800), the Marquis de Sade wrote of the Gothic novels of Lewis and Radcliffe as 'the inevitable result of the revolutionary shocks which all of Europe has suffered'. *The 120 Days of Sodom and Other Writings*, trans. A Wainhouse and R. Seaver (New York, 1977), p. 109.
11. *The Works of the Rt Hon Edmund Burke*, 6 vols (Oxford, 1907), VI. 67, 78. Subsequent page references in the text are to this edition, abbreviated as *Works*. On Burke's Oedipal version of the Revolution, see Ronald Paulson, *Representations of Revolution (1789–1820)* (New Haven, 1983), ch. 6.
12. Edmund Burke, *Reflections on the Revolution in France, and on the Proceedings in Certain Societies in London Relative to that Event*, ed. Conor Cruise O'Brien (Harmondsworth, 1968), p. 194. Subsequent page references in the text are to this edition, abbreviated as *Reflections*.
13. *The Correspondence of Edmund Burke*, ed. Alfred Cobban and Robert A. Smith (Cambridge, 1967), VI. 30.
14. Abbé Barruel, *Memoirs Illustrating the History of Jacobinism*, trans. R. Clifford (London, 1798), III. 414; cited by Lee Sterrenburg, 'Mary Shelley's Monster: Politics and Psyche in *Frankenstein*', in *The Endurance of 'Frankenstein'*, ed. George Levine and U. C. Knoepflmacher (Berkeley, 1979), p. 156. On the Illuminati scare, see J. M. Roberts, *The Mythology of the Secret Societies* (London, 1972), ch. 5–6.
15. Thomas Paine, *Rights of Man*, ed. Henry Collins (Harmondsworth, 1969), p. 81 (cf. pp. 95, 104). Subsequent page references in the text are to this edition, abbreviated as *Rights*.
16. Paine had already challenged England's right to be regarded as a natural 'parent' in his *Common Sense* pamphlets: Americans have fled, he claims, 'not from the tender embraces of the mother, but from the cruelty of the monster'. *The Writings of Thomas Paine*, ed. Moncure David Conway, 4 vols (New York, 1894–6), I. 87.

17. Mary Wollstonecraft, *An Historical and Moral View of the Origin and Progress of the French Revolution: and the Effect it has Produced in Europe* (London, 1794), pp. 513–14. Subsequent page references in the text are to this edition, abbreviated as *View*.

18. On the politics of Godwin's style see James T. Boulton, *The Language of Politics in the Age of Wilkes and Burke* (London, 1963), ch. 11.

19. William Godwin, *Enquiry Concerning Political Justice and its Influence on Modern Morals and Happiness*, ed. Isaac Kramnick (Harmondsworth, 1976), pp. 487–8. Subsequent page references in the text are to this edition, abbreviated as *Enquiry*.

20. See Kelly, *Jacobin Novel*, ch. 4; Boulton, *Language of Politics*, ch. 11; and Kelvin Everest and Gavin Edwards, 'William Godwin's *Caleb Williams*: Truth and "Things as They Are"', in *1789: Reading Writing Revolution*, ed. Francis Barker *et al.* (Colchester, 1982), pp. 126–46.

21. William Godwin, *Caleb Williams*, ed. David McCracken (Oxford, 1970), p. 133. Subsequent page references in the text are to this edition.

22. D. H. Lawrence, *The Symbolic Meaning: The Uncollected Versions of 'Studies in Classic American Literature'*, ed. Armin Arnold (Arundel, 1962), p. 36.

3

Narcissism as Symptom and Structure: The Case of Mary Shelley's *Frankenstein*

JOSEPH KESTNER

In his essay 'Narcissism and Modern Culture', Richard Sennett presents two cases of pathological narcissism, the first of which involves hysteria:

> The doctor is presented with the involuntary expression of feeling, a demon breaking through the surface of polite order, and this naturally suggests a duality or two levels or a peculiar set of connections between what is evident and what is hidden in the mind ... The patient signals the doctor through sharp little eruptions.

On the other hand, Sennett argues, there are those 'people who evince no concrete, betraying symptom of distress, but rather report on malaise endemic to their character states: an inability to feel or to become aroused; a persistent sense of illegitimacy which is at its strongest when one is being rewarded as legitimate; a sense of being dead to the world'.[1] This second kind of narcissism manifests itself as follows:

> Every time he gets close to another person, he gets scared and has to run away. His feelings for the other are not strong enough to overcome his terror, or, he reports, he 'goes blank' at a certain point in his relations with the other person ... While making love he feels empty, bored. The manifest content of such a distress is 'I cannot feel'; the latent content, however, is that the Other, the other person

> or the outside world, is failing to arouse me. The statement of inadequacy is double-edged. I am inadequate; those who care about me, by their very caring become inadequate for my needs and not really the 'right ones'. As a result of this double-edged formula, the person caught in this bind feels that those who try to get close to him are violating him, giving him no room to breathe; and so he flees, on to the next person who is idealised as perfect until he or she begins to care.
>
> This is what clinical narcissism is about. It is egoism[2] rather than egotism, but egoism of a special kind. The world is a mirror of the self, a surface on which one's own needs are projected, needs one genuinely yearns to have fulfilled. But when another image is reflected back, outside oneself but reaching to oneself, that whole ability to desire, to imagine and to body forth one's desire is threatened, as if when two images are reflected on the mirror, the mirror itself will break.
>
> It is to this situation that the myth of Narcissus speaks. True, he is in love with his own beauty, but the myth would still make sense if he were in love with his own unhappiness ... The emotional structure of the myth is that, when one cannot distinguish between self and other and treats reality as a projection of self, one is in danger.[3]

Sennett's analysis of the Narcissus myth illustrates that there is rarely one type of individual involved in this pathology: in reality, there are two, one whose reaction evolves an hysterical 'demon', another whose symptoms induce a solipsistic, benumbed self-projection. In this consideration of the narcissistic condition, Mary Shelley's *Frankenstein; or, The Modern Prometheus* (1818) constitutes one of the greatest explorations of pathological narcissism.

Victor Frankenstein's evident longing for another, despite his close friendship with Henry Clerval and his betrothal to Elizabeth, leads to the creation of a being who becomes the Inadequate Other which is in reality Victor himself. Gérard Genette argues in his 'The Narcissus Complex': 'In itself, the reflection is an equivocal theme: the reflection is a *double*, that is to say at the same time an *other* and a *same*. This ambivalence provokes in baroque thought an inversion of significations which makes identity fantastic (*I am an other*) and otherness reassuring (*There is another world, but it is similar to this one*).' Genette further emphasises the concept noted by Sennett, the narcissist's desire to *flee* 'on to the next person who is idealised as perfect until he or she begins to care'. To Genette, the *flight* is the result of the reflection, 'two motifs already ambiguous'. Since Mary Shelley's novel employs the element of flight (Walton to the pole, Victor from the Creature, the Creature in pursuit of

Victor), *Frankenstein* embodies an additional element of the Narcissus complex:

> In this image of himself over which he bends, Narcissus does not discover in its resemblance a sufficient security. It is not the stable image of Herodias ... it is a fleeing image, an image in *flight*, because the element which carries it and constitutes it is consecrated in essence to vanishing. Water is the place of all the treacheries and all the inconstancies: in the reflection which faces him, Narcissus can neither identify himself without anxiety nor love without danger.

Victor Frankenstein's longing for the Other, then the fleeing from the Other, then the Other's pursuit of Victor, all constitute signal instances of the corollary of the narcissist's reflection, flight. As much as Mary Shelley's novel concerns 'The Modern Prometheus', it is much more involved with 'The Modern Narcissus'.

The importance of *Frankenstein* to the literature of narcissism, however, is not restricted to its content. If this were so, it would be interesting but not remarkable. Discussing further the Narcissus myth, Genette notes: 'The Self is confirmed, but under the species of the Other: the mirror image is a perfect symbol of alienation'.[4] How does this 'mirror image' become functional as a literary structure? How the literature of narcissism finds a *structure* of narcissism is the more profound and more necessary question. One must distinguish between literary works which deal with narcissism and literary works which, while dealing with narcissism, structure themselves in a narcissistic manner. What is the structural equivalent for the 'image spéculaire', the double, the mirrored narcissistic Other? Two essays, Jean Ricardou's 'The Story Within the Story' and Tzvetan Todorov's 'The Categories of Literary Narrative', provide the essential response to the structural presentation of narcissism in a literary text.

For Ricardou, it is the *mise en abyme*, the enclosure of one story within another story, which supplies this structure: by the *mise en abyme*, the narrative is 'imposing on itself in a *narcissistic* manner'.[5] As heraldry encloses one coat of arms within another, so the narrative constructed by a *mise en abyme*, an enclosed narrative challenging the primary narrative, becomes structurally a narcissistic text. A particularly crucial instance of the *mise en abyme* exists for Ricardou in the Oedipus legend, where Oedipus was himself a *mise en abyme* in his mother's womb: it is not insignificant, therefore, that Victor Frankenstein experiences oedipal dreams after creating the Creature. The *mise en abyme* assumes in Mary Shelley's *Frankenstein* the form of a *Rahmenerzählung* or 'frame narrative', where one tale encloses another. In this way it realises one of Todorov's essential structure devices as expressed in 'The Categories of Literary Narrative': 'Embedding [*enchâssement*] is the inclusion of one story inside another'.[6] Mary Shelley's attempt to find a structural corollary for her narcissistic tale exists in her use of three narratives. The first, which serves as the 'outer frame', is a series of four letters from the Arctic explorer Robert Walton to his sister Margaret Saville in England. When Frankenstein strays to Walton's ice-bound ship, he recounts to Walton, chapters 1 through 10, his story of the invention of the Creature; within his tale, chapters 11 through 16, the Creature recounts his story to Frankenstein, who recounts it to Walton. With the seventeenth chapter, the narrative becomes once again Frankenstein's to chapter 24, when Walton returns to his letters and concludes the narrative. The *mise en abyme* can be visualised thus:

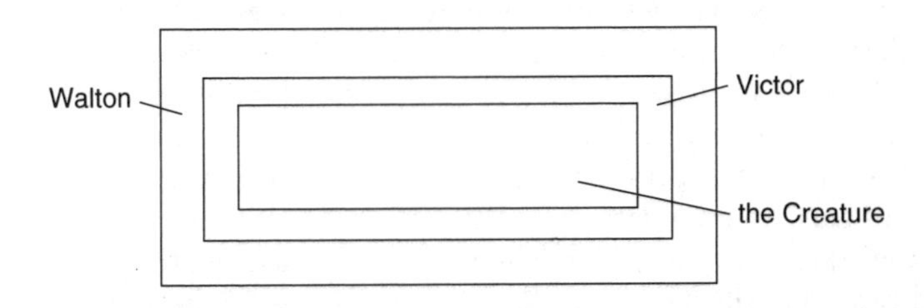

This series of embeddings or *mises en abyme* constitutes the 'image spéculaire', the structural double and series of reflections so crucial to the presentation of a story of narcissism. It is the special form of narcissistic reflection noted by Genette, 'reflection being penetrated without being dissolved: it is no longer concerned with a formal alteration or dispersion, but with a truly *substantial evanescence*'.[7] Furthermore, he continues, the reflection, while penetrated without being dispersed, paradoxically presents a surface of depth: 'the most innocent watery surface covers an abyss [*un abîme*]: transparent, it allows one to see; opaque, it suggests it all the more dangerously as it conceals it. To be on the surface is to dare the depth.' In this manner, Mary Shelley's narrative structure in *Frankenstein* employs a narcissistic *mise en abyme* to analyse a narcissistic *abîme*. 'Narcissus contemplates in the water another Narcissus who is more Narcissus than himself and this other is himself an abyss [*abîme*],'

Genette notes.[8] This triple embedding illuminates the similarities among the three protagonists – Walton, Frankenstein, the Creature – which signal their doubleness and otherness, the one the *doppelgänger* of the next, including their desire to explore, their failure to love, their loneliness, their avid reading, and their egoism. Furthermore, in his Tenth Lecture, 'Symbolism in Dreams', Freud noted that 'for the male genitals as a whole the sacred number 3 is of symbolic significance'.[9] Mary Shelley's triply-embedded *mise en abyme*, therefore, reflects the latent homosexuality and egoism that characterises the three men. While one may conceive the Creature as Sennett's hysterical narcissist, Frankenstein as the introverted narcissist, and Walton as the resolution of the two, one must remember Genette's observation, perfectly reinforced by the structural *mise en abyme*, that in narcissism 'the self is a succession of unstable states where ... nothing is constant except the instability itself':[10] each of these men embodies Otto Kernberg's definition of narcissism as 'libidinal investment of the self'.[11] Thus, *Frankenstein*, through its structure, presents a narrative of narcissistic Selves and Others.

Walton's narrative, the outer frame of these mirrors, instantly signals the narcissistic nature of his personality. Writing from St Petersburg Walton tells his sister: 'My daydreams become more fervent and vivid. I try in vain to be persuaded that the pole is the seat of frost and desolation; it ever presents itself to my imagination as the region of beauty and delight.'[12] In this passage, the pole/penis indicates that the motive for Walton's voyage is not as he contends, 'the inestimable benefit which I shall confer on all mankind to the last generation, by discovering a passage near the pole' (p. 270) but a self-love, which he expresses when he mentions his object as 'a point on which the soul may fix its intellectual eye'. In his Twenty-Sixth Lecture, Freud argues that the delusion of grandeur, such as Walton reveals, 'is the direct result of a magnification of the ego due to the drawing in of the libidinal object-cathexes – a secondary narcissism which is a return of the original early infantile one'.[13] As the first letter continues, the narcissistic nature of Walton's personality becomes obvious: he was a poet, he tells Margaret, and 'for one year lived in a Paradise of my own creation' (p. 271). While he fails in that venture, he spurns the luxury a legacy might have given him; instead, 'I preferred glory to every enticement that wealth placed in my path' (p. 271). This impression is reinforced in the second letter when Walton writes, 'I have no friend' (p. 273). To emphasise this narcissistic isolation of Walton, Mary Shelley never has the sister respond to Walton's letters, nor does the reader ever learn how they were transmitted, if sent at all.

In Letter IV, Walton recounts his taking Victor Frankenstein on board his ship, stating his finding of his narcissistic Other: 'I said in one of my letters ... that I should find no friend on the wide ocean; yet I have found a man who, before his spirit had been broken by misery, I should have been happy to have possessed as the brother of my heart' (p. 283). That Walton recognises Victor as the 'brother of my heart' suggests the homosexuality latent in his narcissism, noted by Freud's observation that homosexuals 'proceed from a narcissistic basis, and look for a young man who resembles themselves', a trait clear in the Greek myth where Narcissus is loved by the god Apollo.[14] Walton acknowledges that Victor has a 'double existence' (p. 285). With Frankenstein recognised as the Other, it is clear Walton's 'voyage' is really a process of narcissistic introversion and self-love. By the *mise en abyme*, Mary Shelley embeds Frankenstein's narrative within Walton's, the structural equivalent of the fixation on the Self/Other.

By the age of seventeen, Frankenstein tells Walton, he 'ardently desired the acquisition of knowledge' (p. 305); influenced by the works of Paracelsus, Albertus Magnus, and the instruction at the university at Ingolstadt, Victor at the age of nineteen 'succeeded in discovering the cause of generation and life; nay, more, I became myself capable of bestowing animation upon lifeless matter' (p. 312). Immediately, after declaring this power, Frankenstein tells Walton: 'I will not lead you on, unguarded and ardent as I then was, to your destruction, and infallible misery. Learn from me ... how dangerous is the acquirement of knowledge' (p. 313): thus, Walton's search for the polar route and Frankenstein's finding of the secret of life are mirror images. 'On a dreary night of November', the result occurred:

> How can I describe my emotions at this catastrophe, or how delineate the wretch whom with such infinite pains and care I had endeavoured to form? His limbs were in proportion, and I had selected his features as beautiful. Beautiful! – Great God!... The beauty of the dream vanished, and breathless horror and disgust filled my heart. (p. 318)

Freud's essay 'On Narcissism' illuminates several elements of this passage. First, it reflects the megalomania that may accompany the grandiose self-image of narcissists; Freud specifically mentions as a trait 'a technique for dealing with the external world – 'magic' – which appears to be a logical application of these grandiose premises':[15] thus Frankenstein's interest in pseudo-science like that of Paracelsus is a specific sign of his narcissism. The creation of the Creature, an ego-ideal, is further narcissistic. In the Twenty-Sixth Lecture, Freud discusses libidinal choice of object, noting one process, 'where the subject's own ego is replaced by another one that is as similar as possible'.[16] Such persons, writes Freud in 'On Narcissism', 'are plainly seeking themselves as a love-object, and are exhibiting a type of object-choice which must be termed "narcissistic"'.[17] This object-choice is distinctive; initially it has the 'beauty of the dream':

> This ideal ego is now the target of the self-love which was enjoyed in childhood by the actual ego. The subject's narcissism makes its appearance displaced on to this new ideal ego, which, like the infantile ego, finds itself possessed of every perfection that is of value ... The object ... is aggrandised and exalted in the subject's mind.[18]

In addition to the narcissistic nature of Frankenstein's megalomaniacal propensity for science and for the narcissistic fantasy of his creation, the nature of his narcissism is explored even more deeply in his dreams immediately following the creation of the Creature:

> I was disturbed by the wildest dreams. I thought I saw Elizabeth, in the bloom of health, walking in the streets of Ingolstadt. Delighted and surprised, I embraced her, but as I imprinted the first kiss on her lips, they became livid with the hue of death; her features appeared to change, and I thought that I held the corpse of my dear mother in my arms; a shroud enveloped her form, and I saw the grave-worms crawling in the folds of the flannel.
>
> (p. 319)

Upon awakening, Frankenstein 'beheld the wretch – the miserable monster whom I had created'. The narcissism of these passages is apparent: the combined reflection and the desire to flee, the simultaneous idealisation and debasement of the Other, the longing followed by rejection, the self-exaltation leading to self-disgust, the self-projection leading to self-rejection. The dream *per se* is profound: first, Frankenstein as he becomes a male-mother to his own self-image/Creature repudiates other women for the sake of the mother. In addition, the fact that the mother is dead and the Creature is a male suggests Freud's recognition that among some narcissists with homosexual tendencies 'in their later choice of love-objects they have taken as a model not their mothers but their own selves'.[19] The full implication of this dream is revealed in the events on Frankenstein's wedding night. Frankenstein observes, 'I bore a hell within me, which nothing could extinguish' (p. 351); indeed, the Creature was within Frankenstein (*I am an other*). This 'within' becomes evident when Frankenstein meets his Creature and hears his tale, in another narcissistic *mise en abyme*.

The Creature prefaces his narrative with a direct evocation of his narcissistic status vis-à-vis Frankenstein:

> 'All men hate the wretched; how, then, must I be hated, who am miserable beyond all living things! Yet you, my creator, detest and spurn me, thy creature, to whom thou art bound by ties only dissoluble by the annihilation of one of us ...'
>
> 'Remember, that I am thy creature; I ought to be thy Adam: but I am rather the fallen angel, whom thou drivest from joy for no misdeed. Everywhere I see bliss, from which I alone am irrevocably excluded. I was benevolent and good; misery made me a fiend.
>
> (pp. 363–4)

The Creature's allusion to Genesis is startling, for it suggests Freud's association of narcissistic symptoms with biblical creation when he quotes Heine's poem: 'Illness was no doubt the final cause of the whole urge to create. By creating, I [God] could recover; by creating, I became healthy'.[20] After repeated rejection, ostracism, and repudiation, the Creature finds Frankenstein's journal, which reinforces the narcissistic mirror image relationship:

> 'Every thing is related in them which bears reference to my accursed origin; the whole detail of that series of disgusting circumstances which produced it is set in view; the minutest description of my odious and loathsome person is given, in language which painted your own horrors and rendered mine indelible. I sickened as I read. "Hateful day when I received life!" I exclaimed in agony. "Accursed creator! Why did you form a monster so hideous that even *you* turned from me in disgust? God, in pity, made man beautiful and alluring, after his own image; but my form is a filthy type of yours, more horrid even from the very resemblance."'
>
> (p. 397)

His form is a 'type' of Frankenstein's, beheld in the water: 'I cherished hope, it is true; but it vanished when I *beheld my person reflected in water*' (p. 398, emphasis added). The narcissistic bond is cemented when the Creature, as had Frankenstein, observes he has 'a hell within me' (p. 403), recognising the *mise en abyme* that is his narcissistic origin: he is Frankenstein's foetus *mise en abyme*.

Although Frankenstein promises to create a female counterpart for the Creature, he fails to do so, ostensibly because of conscience. However, Freud's essay 'On Narcissism' again shows the nature of this excuse:

> Large amounts of libido of an essentially homosexual kind are drawn into the formation of the narcissistic ego ideal and find outlet and satisfaction in maintaining it. The institution of conscience was at bottom an embodiment, first of parental criticism, and subsequently of that of society ... The self-criticism of conscience coincides with the self-observation on which it is based.[21]

The narcissist, argues Freud in the Twenty-Sixth Lecture, has a peculiar kind of conscience: 'He senses an agency holding sway in his ego which measures his actual ego and each of its activities by an ideal ego that he has created for himself in the course of his development'.[22] Frankenstein's assertions about conscience are thus data of narcissism. No female self-image, furthermore, appeases the narcissistic longing for the homosexual Self/Other.

This pathology is confirmed on Frankenstein's wedding night. At the inn, prior to consummating his marriage with Elizabeth, Frankenstein records:

> I had been calm during the day; but so soon as night obscured the shapes of objects, a thousand fears arose in my mind. I was anxious and watchful, while my right hand grasped a pistol which was hidden in my bosom; every sound terrified me; but I resolved that I would sell my life dearly, and not shrink from the conflict until my own life or that of my adversary, was extinguished.
>
> Elizabeth observed my agitation for some time in timid and fearful silence, but there was something in my glance which communicated terror to her, and trembling she asked, 'What is it that agitates you, my dear Victor? What is it you fear?'
>
> 'Oh! Peace, peace, my love,' replied I; 'this night, and all will be safe; but this night is dreadful, very dreadful.'
>
> (p. 466)

Having told Elizabeth to retire, Victor suddenly hears 'a shrill and dreadful scream. It came from the room into which Elizabeth had retired. As I heard it, the whole truth rushed into my mind' (p. 467). Like Echo in the Greek myth, Elizabeth is destroyed by her

Narcissus. The whole truth of this episode is that, fearing sexual contact, Frankenstein wanted the woman dead, desiring only to love himself, latently homosexual. The narcissistic Other (the Creature), by strangling Elizabeth, intervenes to prevent the normal separation of 'ego-libido' and 'object-libido' discussed by Freud in 'On Narcissism'. Instead, Frankenstein's libido is a narcissistic auto-erotism.[23] Just as the face of the Creature had appeared when Frankenstein awakened from his dream about Elizabeth and his mother, so now does 'the face of the monster' (p. 468) grin at him through the inn window.[24] In fact, through the narcissistic Other, Frankenstein is himself grinning. The *mise en abyme*, the story within the story, proves how integral is the Creature to Frankenstein, and of Frankenstein to Walton, all 'types' of one another.

When the narrative returns to Walton's, the primary narrative, the narcissistic symptom is confirmed: 'Frankenstein discovered that I made notes concerning his history; he asked to see them, and then himself corrected and augmented them in many places' (p. 483): the men thus share the pen/penis, and the act of writing, like the act of narrating through the *mise en abyme*, becomes a narcissistic and onanistic gesture. When Frankenstein dies, Walton records: 'It is past; I am returning to England. I have lost my hopes of utility and glory; I have lost my friend' (p. 489); his flight led to his reflection. On learning of his creator's death, the Creature vanishes in the icy waste, Walton is bereft, and the *mise en abyme* concludes. The solipsism of Frankenstein and the demonism of the Creature, uniting in Walton through the *mise en abyme* /foetus narrative, reveal the nature of Walton's narcissistic 'libidinal investment of the self'.

In the literature of narcissism, Mary Shelley's *Frankenstein* is distinguished by the reciprocal strength of its content and its structure, where the *mise en abyme* structurally embodies the self-generating, self-contained narcissists of her narrative. Mary Shelley has presented symptoms of narcissism in her text which involve the reader. 'A symptom is a pain which does not explain itself. It requires an act of decoding, of reading ... Symptoms are the language of repression: they are a hermeneutic system,' writes Sennett. In a passage clearly relevant to *Frankenstein*, he writes:

> As long as non-self-referencing signals, i.e. symptoms, appear, psychic work is being done to create a within, a foreground screening a background, a surface and a beneath. The action of creating a hermeneutic system in need of decoding is the psyche.[25]

It is the achievement of *Frankenstein* that Mary Shelley ('foreground') has created by Ricardou's narcissistic *mise en abyme* the *abîme* 'within' recognised by Sennett, a 'background' (Frankenstein), a 'surface' (Walton), and a 'beneath' (the Creature). As Gérard Genette notes in 'The Narcissus complex', 'to be on the surface is to dare the depth'. The reader exists to 'decode' the 'hermeneutic system' of *Frankenstein; or, The Modern Prometheus* to realise that in its depth it is *Frankenstein; or, the Modern Narcissus.*

From *The Nature of Identity: Essays Presented to Donald E. Hayden by the Graduate Faculty of Modern Letters* (Tulsa, 1981), pp. 15–125

NOTES

[Joseph Kestner's essay combines a structural analysis of *Frankenstein*'s narrative with a Freudian interpretation of the theme of narcissism. The novel is interpreted in the manner of a case study in structural psychoanalysis rather than in terms of its literary and historical context. Citing the work of famous structuralists, Gérard Genette and Tzvetan Todorov, the essay's close analysis of the novel's structure shows how its content is reflected in its form: the frame structure, encasing the monster's story within Frankenstein's which is within Walton's, is formally equivalent to a mirror, symbolic of narcissism. Within the structure of the text narcissism is signalled by the reciprocal identifications shared by the male narrators in which they are seen to mirror each other's egoistical desires. This is interpreted in the light of Freud's accounts of narcissism as a manifestation of homoeroticism. Focusing on the novel's structural relation of form and content, the essay does not pursue the suggestive cultural and sexual implications it opens up: male desire, exclusiveness and fantasy, however, are all concerns examined in various ways by the following essays in this collection. Ed.]

1. Richard Sennett, 'Narcissism and Modern Culture' *October*, 4 (1977), 71. Sigmund Freud discussed hysteria vis-à-vis narcissism in the *Introductory Lectures on Psychoanalysis*, the Twenty-Sixth Lecture, 'Libido Theory and Narcissism', in *The Standard Edition of the Complete Psychological Works of Sigmund Freud*, trans. and ed. James Strachey (London, 1953–74), XVI, p. 428. Several good assessments of literature and its relation to psychology are the following: *Psychopathology and Literature*, ed. Leslie Y. Rabkin (San Francisco, 1966); F. L. Lucas, *Literature and Psychology* (Ann Arbor, 1957); and *Psychoanalysis and Literature*, ed. Hendrik M. Ruitenbeek (New

York, 1964); the last includes Lionel Trilling's important essay 'Freud and Literature'. A good survey of contemporary theories of narcissism is contained in the second chapter of Christopher Lasch's *The Culture of Narcissism* (New York, 1979), including discussions of hysteria, Richard Sennett, and Otto Kernberg.

2. Freud, in 'Libido Theory', distinguishes narcissism and egoism, stating, 'Narcissism ... is the libidinal complement to egoism' *Standard Edition*, XVI, p. 417.
3. Sennett, 'Narcissism', pp. 71–2.
4. Gérard Genette, 'Complexe de Narcisse', *Figures I* (Paris, 1966), pp. 21–2; translations mine.
5. Jean Ricardou, 'L'histoire dans l'histoire', *Problèmes du nouveau roman* (Paris, 1967), p. 172; trans. Joseph Kestner as 'The Story Within the Story', *James Joyce Quarterly*, 18 (1981), p. 323–38.
6. Tzvetan Todorov, 'Les catégories du récit littéraire', trans. Joseph Kestner, 'The Categories of Literary Narrative', *Papers on Language and Literature*, 16 (1980), 23.
7. Genette, 'Complexe', p. 24.
8. Ibid., p. 28.
9. Freud, 'Symbolism in Dreams', in *Standard Edition*, XV, p. 154.
10. Genette, 'Complexe', p. 26.
11. Otto Kernberg, *Borderline Conditions and Pathological Narcissism* (New York, 1975), p. 315.
12. Mary Shelley, *Frankenstein; or, The Modern Prometheus* (Baltimore, 1968), p. 269. Page numbers hereafter cited in brackets in the text. This is the 1831 text embodying the author's final revisions. In contrast to the 1818 edition, the 1831 edition contains a greater amplification of Frankenstein's childhood, considerably more information about Elizabeth and Clerval, and greater detail about the death of Justine, all of which contribute to a deeper understanding of the narcissism of the novel. The 1818 text, with an Appendix collating the variants, has been edited by James Rieger (Indianapolis, 1974).
13. Freud, *Standard Edition*, XVI, p. 424.
14. 'Three Essays on the Theory of Sexuality', *Standard Edition*, VII, p. 145. In *The Greek Myths*, I (Baltimore, 1955), Robert Graves records that the love of Apollo for Hyacinthus/Narcissus was the first instance of homosexual love between a god and a man; the mortal Thamyris also loved Hyacinthus, 'the first man who ever wooed one of his own sex', p. 78.
15. Freud, *Standard Edition*, XIV, p. 75.

16. Ibid., XVI, p. 426.
17. Ibid., XIV, p. 88.
18. Ibid., XIV, p. 94.
19. Ibid., XIV, p. 88.
20. Ibid., XIV, p. 85.
21. Ibid., XIV, p. 96.
22. Ibid., XVI, p. 429.
23. Ibid., XIV, pp. 76–7.
24. In the Tenth Lecture, Freud discusses two images crucial to the narrative of Frankenstein's wedding night, the pistol, a phallic symbol (Ibid., XV, p. 154), and the window, a body orifice (Ibid., XV, p. 158). In the narrative, Frankenstein conceals the pistol/penis from Elizabeth, repudiating contact with her and desiring connection with the narcissistic Self/Other, the Creature.
25. Sennet, 'Narcissism', p. 76.

4

What is a Monster? (According to *Frankenstein*)

PETER BROOKS

> monstrum horrendum informe ingens cui lumen ademptum
> (Virgil, *Aeneid*, 3:658)

Frankenstein, first published in 1818, concerns an exotic body with a difference, a distinct perversion from the tradition of desirable objects. The story of this ugly, larger-than-life, monstrous body raises complex questions of motherhood, fatherhood, gender, and narrative. The afterlife of the novel in the popular imagination has been intensely focused on that monstrous body, to the extent that the name 'Frankenstein' tends to evoke not the unfortunate over-reaching young scientist Victor Frankenstein but his hideous creation. This is both faithful and unfaithful to Mary Shelley's original: faithful, in that a monster indeed, even etymologically, exists to be looked at, shown off, viewed as in a circus sideshow; unfaithful, in that Shelley's novel with equal insistence directs us to issues of language in the story of the monster and his creator. In fact, the central issues of the novel are joined in the opposition of sight and speech, and it unfolds its complex narrative structure from this nexus.

That narrative structure involves framed or imbedded tales, a tale within a tale within a tale: in the outer frame, explorer Robert Walton writes to his sister Mrs Saville, and tells of meeting Frankenstein in the Arctic; in the next frame, Frankenstein recounts his life story to Walton; in the innermost tale, the monster at a crucial moment tells his tale to Frankenstein. When the monster has finished, Frankenstein resumes speaking in his own right; when he has done, Walton resumes.[1] The nested narrative structure calls attention to the presence of a listener for each speaker – of a narratee for each narrator – and to the interlocutionary relations thus established. Each act of narration in the novel implies a certain bond or contract: listen to me because ... The structure calls attention to the motives of telling; it makes each listener – and the reader – ask: Why are you telling me this? What am I supposed to do with it? As in the psychoanalytic context of storytelling, the listener is placed in a transferential relation to the narrative. As a 'subject supposed to know', the listener is called upon to 'supplement' the story (to anticipate the phrase Freud will use in the case history of Dora), to articulate and even enact the meaning of the desire it expresses in ways that may be foreclosed to the speaker. Storytelling in *Frankenstein* is far from an innocent act: narratives have designs on their narratees that must be unravelled. The issues posed by such a narrative structure may most of all concern relation, or how narrative relation relates to intersubjective relation, and the relation of relation, in both these senses, to language as the medium of telling and listening, as the medium of transmission, transaction, and transference.

These issues take on their full import only in the context of the visual. I shall start with the opening of the innermost tale – which strikingly poses the issues of the visual – and then work out to the framing structures. Following the first murders committed by the Monster – Frankenstein's brother William strangled, the family servant Justine Moritz executed as his killer through maliciously planted evidence – Frankenstein seeks solace in the Alps above Chamonix. He penetrates the 'glorious presence-chamber of imperial Nature', climbing to Montanvert and the Mer de Glace, hoping to recapture a remembered 'sublime ecstasy that gave wings to the soul and allowed it to soar from the obscure world to light and joy'.[2] His ascension takes him to a 'wonderful and stupendous scene', overlooking the Mer de Glace and facing the 'awful majesty' of Mont Blanc; his heart once again opens to joy and he exclaims, in the tones of the Ossianic bard, 'Wandering spirits, if indeed ye wander, and do not rest in your narrow beds, allow me this faint happiness, or take me, as your companion, away from the joys of life.' At this point, the vision of sublimity is both fulfilled and undone by the sight of a superhuman shape that comes bounding toward Frankenstein over the ice. The Monster appears to be – as in his original creation – both born of nature and supernatural, and as such he puts normal measurements and classifications into question. In particular, he puts into question the meaning of looking, of optics, as the faculty and the science most commonly used to judge meanings in the phenomenal world.

Frankenstein's immediate reaction to the appearance of the Monster is to tell it to go away. When the Monster persists in his claim that he has the right to a hearing from his creator, Frankenstein curses the day of the Monster's creation, and reiterates: 'Begone! Relieve me from the sight of your detested form' (p. 97). To this the Monster, in a touching gesture, responds by placing his huge hands over Frankenstein's eyes: 'Thus I relieve thee, my creator ... thus I take from thee a sight which you abhor. Still thou canst listen to me, and grant me thy compassion.' The Monster clearly understands that it is not visual relation that favours him – indeed, as we will discover when he tells his own story, his only favourable reception from a human being thus far has come from the blind de Lacey – but rather the auditory or interlocutionary, the relation of language. Thus, this first meeting of Frankenstein and his Monster since the day of his creation presents a crucial issue of the novel in the opposition of sight and language, of the hideous body and the persuasive tongue.

For the Monster is eloquent. From the first words he speaks, he shows himself to be a supreme rhetorician, who controls the antitheses and oxymorons that express the pathos of his existence: 'Remember that I am thy creature; I ought to be thy Adam, but I am rather the fallen angel, whom thou drivest from joy for no misdeed. Everywhere I see bliss, from which I alone am irrevocably excluded. I was benevolent and good; misery made me a fiend. Make me happy, and I shall again be virtuous' (pp. 95–6). When we learn of the Monster's self-education – and particularly his three master-texts, Milton's *Paradise Lost*, Plutarch's *Lives*, and Goethe's *Werther* – we will understand the prime sources of his eloquence and of the conception of the just order of things that animates his plea to his creator. But beyond the motives of his eloquence, it is important to register the simple fact of Shelley's decision to make the Monster the most eloquent creature in the novel. This hideous and deformed creature, far from expressing himself in grunts and gestures, speaks and reasons with the highest elegance, logic, and persuasiveness. As a verbal creation, he is the very opposite of the monstrous: he is a sympathetic and persuasive participant in

Western culture. All of the Monster's interlocutors – including, finally, the reader – must come to terms with this contradiction between the verbal and the visual.[3]

By persuading Frankenstein to give his creature a hearing, thus opening the innermost frame of the novel, the Monster has adumbrated what Roland Barthes would call a 'narrative contract' between narrator and narratee.[4] The narrative contract, like the psychoanalytic transference, is based on and implies the intersubjective, transindividual, cultural order of language. Language by its very nature transcends and pre-exists the individual locutor; it implies, depends on, and necessitates that network of intersubjective relations from which the Monster protests he has been excluded. That is, in becoming the narrator of his story, the Monster both dramatises his problem and provides a model for its solution, the solution implicit in the discursive interdependence of an 'I' and a 'thou' in any interlocutionary situation.[5] The Monster's words assign to Frankenstein a parental role for the first time in the novel: 'For the first time ... I felt what the duties of a creator towards his creature were' (p. 97) – a role all the more glaring in its neglect in that Frankenstein has dwelt at length on the parental love and concern lavished on him in his early years, the way he was guided by a 'silken cord' toward happiness and goodness (p. 33). By the time the Monster has completed his narrative, Frankenstein still feels horror and hatred when he looks upon this 'filthy mass that moved and talked', but he also avows: 'His words had a strange effect upon me. I compassionated him' (p. 140). After establishing this tenous link with his creator through narrative, the Monster takes the decisive step in his argument: 'My vices are the children of a forced solitude that I abhor, and my virtues will necessarily arise when I live in communion with an equal. I shall feel the affections of a sensitive being and become linked to the chain of existence and events from which I am now excluded' (pp. 140–1).

The metaphor of the chain is one that will reappear in various guises throughout the novel. It represents relation itself, including affective interpersonal relations (see the 'silken cord' of Frankenstein's childhood) and the relations between tellers and listeners – relations established through language and as language. The chain here closely resembles what Jacques Lacan calls the 'signifying chain' of language, especially language as the vehicle of desire. In the Monster's confrontation of and narrative to Frankenstein, we have a representation of the Lacanian distinction between the imaginary and the symbolic orders. The imaginary is the order of the specular, of the mirror stage, and arises from the subject's perception of itself as other; it is thus the order of deceptive relations, of ideology and fascination. The symbolic order ultimately is language itself, the systematic and transindividual order of the signifier, the cultural system or law into which individual subjects are inserted.[6] In the specular or imaginary order, the Monster will ever cease to be the 'filthy mass'. In the symbolic order, on the other hand, he can produce and project his desire in language, in relation to an interlocutor. It is, however, in the logic of Lacanian desire and the 'signifying chain' that such desire should be unappeasable, a metonymical movement that extends desire forward without reaching a goal: a goal which cannot be named, since the object of desire is unconscious. The Monster's stated object of desire is for a mate, a female creature like himself, which Frankenstein must create. But we will have occasion to ask whether this demand truly corresponds to the needs stipulated by the Monster's desire.

Before considering the Monster's demand for – and Frankenstein's temporary acquiescence to – the creation of a female monster, it is important to register the Monster's narrative of his discovery of language, its contexts and its effects. His first experience with humanity, he tells us, already demonstrated the hopelessness of the specular relation: the shepherd he discovered in a hut fled shrieking from his sight, the villagers pelted him with stones. Retreating into a hovel adjoining the de Lacey cottage, he commences his education as voyeur, observing the family through an 'almost imperceptible chink through which the eye could penetrate', seeing and himself unseen. His most important discovery is that of human language, which is presented in the context of human interaction and affect:

> 'I found that these people possessed a method of communicating their experience and feelings to one another by articulate sounds. I perceived that the words they spoke sometimes produced pleasure or pain, smiles or sadness, in the minds and countenances of the hearers. This was indeed a godlike science, and I ardently desired to become acquainted with it. But I was baffled in every attempt I made for this purpose. Their pronunciation was quick, and the words they uttered, not having any apparent connection with visible objects, I was unable to discover any clue by which I could unravel the mystery of their reference. By great application, however, and after having remained

> during the space of several revolutions of the moon in my hovel, I discovered the names that were given to some of the most familiar objects of discourse; I learned and applied the words, "fire", "milk", "bread", and "wood". I learned also the names of the cottagers themselves. The youth and his companion had each of them several names, but the old man had only one, which was "father". The girl was called "sister" or "Agatha", and the youth "Felix", "brother", or "son". I cannot describe the delight I felt when I learned the ideas appropriated to each of these sounds and was able to pronounce them. I distinguished several other words without being able as yet to understand or apply them, such as "good", "dearest", "unhappy".'
>
> (pp. 106–7)

Like so much else in the story of the Monster's education through sensation, experience, and the association of ideas, his discovery of language stands within Enlightenment debates about origins, coming in this instance close to the scenarios of Rousseau's *Essai sur l'origine des langues*, which sees language as originating not in need but in emotion.[7] As the Monster encounters it, language is tied to human love and patterns of kinship and relation, as if in confirmation of the views of an anthropologist such as Claude Lévi-Strauss, for whom the structures of kinship are the first 'writing' of a society. The Monster also discovers the proto-Saussurian notion that the linguistic sign is arbitrary, that there is no intuitable connection of a sign to its referent, and indeed that some signs ('good', 'dearest', 'unhappy') have no apparent referent. As a consequence, the Monster grasps the nature of language as a system, wherein meaning is created not as a simple movement from sign to referent but in context, dependent on the rule-governed relation of signs one to another.

Hence language presents itself as both the tool he needs to enter into relation with others, and a model of relation itself: it implies – it both depends on and makes possible – that 'chain of existence and events' from which he feels himself excluded. The 'godlike science' of language is thus explicitly a cultural compensation for a deficient nature; it offers the possibility of escape from 'monsterism', which is precisely lack of relation, apartness. Language is what he must use to experience human love. In Rousseau's terms, it is a 'supplement' to nature. The Monster tells Frankenstein: 'I easily perceived that, although I eagerly longed to discover myself to the cottagers, I ought not to make the attempt until I had first become master of their language, which knowledge might enable me to make them overlook the deformity of my figure, for with this also the contrast perpetually presented to my eyes had made me acquainted' (p. 108).

Language is richly thematised at this moment of the novel. With the arrival of Safie, we have lessons in French offered to an Arab, in the context of what we know to be a German-speaking region, the whole rendered for us in English. This well-ordered Babel calls attention to issues of communication and transmission, in somewhat the same manner as the narrative frames of the novel. The Monster learns language through overhearing, and observing, the instruction of Safie by Felix and Agatha. He learns to read – that is, he masters language in what is for Rousseau its mediate form, supplementary to the spoken word: the form in which it is most transmissible, since it does not demand presence, the specular relation, for its exchange, yet also the form in which it is potentially most deceitful, freed from immediate expressivity. The three texts which the Monster now discovers and reads – Plutarch's *Lives*, Goethe's *Werther*, and Milton's *Paradise Lost* – cover the public, the private, and the cosmic realms, and three modes of love. They constitute a kind of minimal Romantic *cyclopedia universalis*. Of the three, it is *Paradise Lost* – in the literalist reading the Monster gives it – that excite the profoundest reactions, and poses in emblematic terms the enigma of the Monster's nature. In the manner of Adam, he appears to be a unique creation, 'united by no link to any other being in existence' (p. 124). Yet, 'wretched, helpless, and alone', he is unlike Adam. 'Many times I considered Satan as the fitter emblem of my condition, for often, like him, when I viewed the bliss of my protectors, the bitter gall of envy rose within me.' In particular, the intertextual presence of *Paradise Lost* insistently poses the relation of language to the specular, especially in the implicit comparison of the Monster to Eve, in two passages in which he views himself in a mirroring pool. 'I had admired the perfect forms of my cottagers – their grace, beauty, and delicate complexions; but how was I terrified when I viewed myself in a transparent pool! At first I started back, unable to believe that it was indeed I who was reflected in the mirror; and when I became fully convinced that I was in reality the monster that I am, I was filled with the bitterest sensations of despondence and mortification' (p. 108). This echoes Eve's report of the day of her creation, in Book 4 (460–76) of *Paradise Lost*. After first awakening to life, she finds a mirroring lake:

> As I bent down to look, just opposite,
> A Shape within the wat'ry gleam appear'd
> Bending to look on me, I started back,
> It started back, but pleas'd I soon return'd,
> Pleas'd it return'd as soon with answering looks
> Of sympathy and love; there I had fixt
> Mine eyes till now, and pin'd with vain desire,
> Had not a voice thus warn'd me, What thou seest,
> What there thou seest fair Creature is thyself,
> With thee it came and goes; but follow me,
> And I will bring thee where no shadow stays
> Thy coming, and thy soft imbraces, hee
> Whose image thou art, him thou shalt enjoy
> Inseparably thine, to him shalt bear
> Multitudes like thyself, and thence be call'd
> Mother of human Race: what could I do,
> But follow straight, invisibly thus led?

The passage of course recalls Ovid's Narcissus, and anticipates Lacan's scenario of the infant's discovery of his reflected self – both same and other – at the mirror stage. Narcissism is here a temptation to which Eve, immediately enamoured of her own image, would succumb, pining 'with vain desire', were it not for the intervention of a divine voice that commands her to set aside this moment of primary narcissism in favour of sexual difference. The place 'where no shadow stays' is almost explicitly the place of the phallus, as opposed to the insubstantiality of the female's sex and the love of two female bodies. As the Miltonic scenario unfolds, Eve's first perception of Adam is not itself sufficient to move her beyond primary narcissism: Adam is 'fair indeed and tall', she says, 'yet methought less fair, / Less winning soft, less amiably mild, / Than that smooth wat'ry image; back I turn'd' (4:478–80). She would return to the 'answering looks' of the lake were it not that Adam at this point seizes her hand, and she yields to what is for Milton, in his thoroughly misogynist scenario, the explicit hegemony of the male.

Milton's story is thus about Eve's discovery of the law, which is variously the command of God, the law of sexual difference, and the rule of the phallus. In her submission to the law, she gives up desire for her own image, and for indifferentiation, with reluctance, in a prefiguration of her subsequent disobedience. The Monster, on the other hand, discovers himself as different, as violation of the law, in a scenario that mirrors and reverses Lacan's; the outer image – that in the mirror – presents the body in its lack of wholeness (at least in human terms) while the inner apprehension of the body had up until then held it to be hypothetically whole: 'At first I started back, unable to believe that it was indeed I who was reflected in the mirror.' The experience is anti-narcissistic, convincing the Monster that he is, indeed, a monster, thus in no conceivable system an object of desire. As the Monster will put it in the second passage of self-reflection, 'Increase of knowledge only discovered to me more clearly what a wretched outcast I was. I cherished hope, it is true, but it vanished when I beheld my person reflected in water or my shadow in the moonshine, even as that frail image and that inconstant shade' (p. 125). The mirror image becomes the negation of hope, severing the Monster from desire. He is simply outside the law, and thus will require a separate creation – his own Eve – in order to come under its sway. Thus his narrative plea to his creator concludes by focusing the discourse of desire on a new object to be desired, the monster woman.

The Monster's self-reflections in relation to *Paradise Lost* are succeeded by discovery of the literal story of his creation, in Frankenstein's laboratory journal, which he finds in the pocket of the coat he has worn since the day of his creation. Here, he discovers that he is the anti-image of Adam: 'God, in pity, made man beautiful and alluring, after his own image; but my form is a filthy type of yours, more horrid even from the very resemblance' (p. 125). Self-recognition as 'filthy type' completes the mirror stage of the Monster's development. He now knows he must trust wholly in the symbolic order. Having mastered language, he goes to confront the patriarch de Lacey. The 'godlike science' at first appears to achieve the desired effects: 'I am blind', de Lacey responds to the Monster's plea, 'and cannot judge of your countenance, but there is something in your words which persuades me that you are sincere' (p. 128). Sympathy is on the point of creating the Monster's first entry into the social chain, when Felix, Agatha, and Safie enter the cottage, and the Monster is brutally returned to the specular order: Agatha faints, Safie flees, and Felix violently separates the interlocutors. The Monster in consequence becomes explicitly Satanic: 'I, like the arch-fiend, bore a hell within me' (p. 130); he sets fire to what had late been his happy seat, and sets forth into the world in search of the hidden face of his creator, the *deus absconditus* who alone, now, has the power to bring him into social relation, through a second monstrous creation.

Along the way to his meeting with Frankenstein, the Monster – after being shot and wounded by a rustic whose daughter he has saved from drowning – commits his first murder, that of Frankenstein's brother William, in a scene that evokes the question of relation in the most acute ways. The Monster's first idea is to take the boy as a companion; in a common Enlightenment thought experiment, he conceives that a child is probably too young 'to have imbibed a horror of deformity' (p. 136). His error is immediately apparent: to his address of 'Child', William in return calls him 'monster! Ugly wretch! ... ogre'. But what provokes the murder is William's exclamation that his father is 'M. Frankenstein' – Victor's father also, of course, and by extrapolation the Monster's 'grandfather' – whom the Monster here calls 'my enemy'. When William lies dead at his feet, the Monster notices a miniature portrait worn around his neck: 'I took it; it was a portrait of a most lovely woman. In spite of my malignity, it softened and attracted me. For a few moments I gazed with delight on her dark eyes, fringed by deep lashes, and her lovely lips; but presently my rage returned; I remembered that I was forever deprived of the delights that such beautiful creatures could bestow and that she whose resemblance I contemplated would, in regarding me, have changed that air of divine benignity to one expressive of disgust and affright' (p. 136). This moment of scopophilic fixation, of the gaze erotically medused by its (painted) object, has a special resonance because we know (as the Monster does not) that the portrait is of William and Victor's dead mother. The novel is notable for the absence of living mothers: Felix and Agatha's mother is dead (and the word 'mother' nowhere figures in the language lesson observed by the Monster), so is Safie's, Madame Frankenstein dies after contracting scarlet fever from her adopted daughter, Elizabeth – Frankenstein's intended bride – and the Monster of course has no mother, only a 'father'. The portrait of the dead mother thus represents an essential lack or gap in existence, most particularly for the Monster, whose primal erotic experience here is directly Oedipal, but censored from the outset: the father's interdiction of the mother as erotic object to the son has never been so radical as in the case of Frankenstein and his created Monster.[8]

The Oedipal overtones of the scene become richer and more complex as we read on. Having taken the portrait, the Monster enters a barn, where he finds a sleeping woman – Justine Moritz – whom he describes as 'young, not indeed so beautiful as her whose portrait I held, but of an agreeable aspect and blooming in the loveliness of youth and health' (p. 137). In imitation of Satan whispering into the ear of the sleeping Eve in *Paradise Lost*, the Monster whispers to Justine: 'Awake, fairest, thy lover is near – he who would give his life but to obtain one look of affection from thine eyes; my beloved, awake!' But this first attempt at seduction on the Monster's part is self-censoring; when the sleeper stirs, the Monster reflects that if she awakes, she will denounce him as a murderer. As a consequence, he decides to pin the murder on her. 'Thanks to the lessons of Felix and the sanguinary laws of man, I had learned how to work mischief.' He plants the mother's portrait in the folds of her dress and flees, with the reflection: 'The crime had its source in her; be hers the punishment!' The claim is curious and excessive, since Justine is in no manner the 'source' of William's murder, which takes place before the Monster has discovered her sleeping form. In the logic of desire, if not in syntax, we must find the referent of 'her' in the mother herself. Under the (paternal) interdiction of the mother, the monster-child turns to a substitute woman, in a clear example of what Freud calls an 'anaclitic' object choice.[9] When it becomes apparent that this object choice, too, is forbidden, censored at the root, the erotic drives turn to death drives, to sadism. The stolen portrait becomes, in the manner of Rousseau's famous stolen ribbon, a token of the reversibility of drives and the inversion of love offerings into poisoned gifts.

The story of this double crime terminates the Monster's narrative. He has now only to sum up the demand to which all his story has tended: 'I am alone and miserable; man will not associate with me; but one as deformed and horrible as myself would not deny herself to me. My companion must be of the same species and have the same defects. This being you must create' (p. 137). The Monster thus attempts to state the object of his desire. In constructing his narrative appeal, he has contextualised desire, made it, or shown it to be, the very principle of narrative, in its metonymical forward movement. This movement, in Lacanian terms, corresponds to the slippage of the inaccessible signified – the object of unconscious desire – under the signifier in the signifying chain. The movement now, as so often when stories are told to a narratee, passes on the desire to the interlocutor, who is charged explicitly with finding the object of desire: of crossing the 'bar' of repression between signifier and that other occulted signifier that stands in the place of the signified of desire, in this instance by the creation of that which is supposed to signify desire. And yet, the Monster's call for a female companion, however sincere, may be only in the realm of conscious desire, may not have access – as how could it? – to what lies under the bar.

If one considers that desire (again in Lacanian terms) is born in the split between need and demand, where demand is always in excess of need (for nourishment from the breast, essentially) and is always an absolute demand for recognition, and thus desire is essentially unappeasable since it is driven by infantile scenarios of fulfilment, one wonders whether Frankenstein's provision of a female companion would really satisfy the Monster. Love depends on demand – it is the creation of speaking beings – and is in essence the demand to be heard by the other. What matters is not so much the content of the demand as the fact that it is unconditional; it expresses 'not the desire of this or that, but desire *tout court*', writes Lacan. What is finally desired by the speaker is 'the desirer in the other', that is, that the speaking subject himself be 'called to as desirable'.[10] The Monster's unconscious desire may most of all be for unconditional hearing, recognition, love from his parent. Its absolute requital could only take the form of handing over the mother, which in this case is barred not only by the law of castration but more radically still, since this mother does not exist and has never existed.

It appears that the Monster's artful activation of the symbolic order, in his narrative plea, results in a demand to his listener that, in its consciously stated desire, brings us back into the order of the imaginary – to the desire for phantasmatic satisfactions, impossible to fulfil. How can you create a mother substitute, or a relationship of the 'anaclitic' type, when there is no mother to substitute for? The radically absent body of the mother more and more appears to be the 'problem' that cannot be solved in the novel. The female monster, furthermore, is conceived quite simply as the mirror image of the Monster, with solely the sexual difference: she has no other definition than 'a female me', which suggests her place in a primal narcissism which the Monster needs to, and cannot, go beyond, however 'filthy' his mirror image. This inability to escape primal narcissism is suggested by other near-incestuous relations in the novel, particularly the marriage of Frankenstein and Elizabeth.

The female monster will never fully come into being. Frankenstein tears her nearly completed body to pieces, in another scopic scene: the Monster is watching at the window of the laboratory with a 'ghastly grin' which turns to a 'howl of devilish despair and revenge' when his promised body is denied him (p. 159). It is as if the Monster's phallic gaze at the female monster's body makes Frankenstein aware of the bodily potential of a sexed pair of monsters. Ostensibly, Frankenstein abrogates the contract he has made at the end of the Monster's narrative appeal through his reflection on the 'Eve problem': that procreation by the monsters will be simply a 'propagated curse', and that the female monster, as a secondary creation, 'might refuse to comply with a compact made before her creation' (p. 158) – she might, like Eve, disobey the paternal injunction, which in this case stipulates exile from the inhabited parts of the globe. To allow the couple to create a race of monsters would be to create a new and wholly uncontrollable signifying chain from their desire, one whose eventual outcomes 'might make the very existence of the species of man a condition precarious and full of terror'. Rather than accepting a nurturing role toward the Monster, offering him 'the small portion of happiness which was yet in my power to bestow' (p. 140) – as he has decided to do at the close of the Monster's narrative – Frankenstein performs the ultimate gesture of castration on the desiring Monster.

The destruction of the female monster negates any hope that the Monster might gain access to a 'chain of existence and events' that would offer him relation and the possibility – even the phantasmatic possibility – of satisfaction for his desire. The godlike science of language has proved deceptive: it has contextualised desire as lack, as metonymic movement in search of the meaning of desire, but it has not provided a way to overcome lack and satisfy desire – as, indeed, language never can. The Monster's error is to believe that signs in artful rhetorical patterns can produce the desired referent from one's interlocutor. His definition as monster leads him to an overvaluation of language, as that which could take him out of that specular position. Yet he is required, by the logic of desire, to attempt to make language produce another body, to return to the imaginary, the specular, and the drama of sexual difference.

The result is an exacerbated agon of desire between the Monster and Frankenstein, whereby the Monster strikes at Frankenstein, not directly, but through elements in Frankenstein's own 'chain of existence and events': after William and Justine Moritz, Frankenstein's bosom friend Henry Clerval and his bride (and also adoptive sister) Elizabeth. 'I will be with thee on thy wedding-night', the Monster tells Frankenstein after the destruction of the female monster

(p. 161), a remark that Frankenstein interprets as a direct menace to his person, thus repressing what the reader at once grasps: that the threat is to Elizabeth. On the wedding night he sends Elizabeth to the nuptial chamber alone, while he prowls about, armed with pistols, looking to engage in combat with the Monster. 'Peace, peace, my love', he says to Elizabeth; 'this night, and all will be safe; but this night is dreadful, very dreadful' (p. 185). We may read this dread as related to the quasi-incestuous nature of his union with Elizabeth. As his father has said, in sounding Frankenstein's intentions: 'You, perhaps, regard her as your sister, without any wish that she might become your wife' (p. 144). Frankenstein denies this sentiment, but we cannot help but be struck by the complication and overlapping of kinship relations in the novel (as in the family in which Mary Shelley grew up), especially because they are thrown in high relief by the Monster's own lack of relation. As the Monster once again watches from the window, the wedding night ends in a necrophilic embrace, which may be in the logic of incestuous desire: 'I rushed towards her and embraced her with ardour, but the deadly languor and coldness of the limbs told me that what I now held in my arms had ceased to be the Elizabeth whom I had loved and cherished. The murderous mark of the fiend's grasp was on her neck, and the breath had ceased to issue from her lips' (p. 186). The Monster has marked the body of Frankenstein's bride at the moment when Frankenstein's desire is on the point of consummation, in dialectical response to the destruction of his monstrous bride. The Monster has put his body in the way of Frankenstein's desire.[11]

Frankenstein's narrative from this point on tells of the struggle of his nearly transferential relation with the Monster, where each represents the lack or gap in the other. 'You are my creator, but I am your master; – obey!' (p. 160) the Monster has said to Frankenstein, in a phrase that represents the impossibility of the situation in which each becomes for the other the 'subject supposed to know' but neither can furnish satisfaction of the other's lack. Like the Monster, Frankenstein becomes explicitly Satanic: 'like the archangel who aspired to omnipotence, I am chained in an eternal hell' (p. 200). The Monster leads a chase that will take them to the lifeless polar regions, maintaining the willpower and the strength of his pursuer by leaving inscribed indications of his route and caches of food. 'Come on, my enemy; we have yet to wrestle for our lives' (p. 195) reads one inscription, nicely balancing enmity and affection.

The Monster, Frankenstein states following William's murder, is 'my own vampire, my own spirit set loose from the grave and forced to destroy all that was dear to me' (p. 74). The statement is as excessive and curious as it is accurate. It turns the Monster into a symptom, in Lacan's sense of the term – that is, a metaphor, a signifier standing for the indecipherable signifier of unconscious desire. It may ultimately speak of the sadism inherent in all intersubjective and especially familial orders of relation. In particular, it may in this novel suggest the destructive affect that inhabits the relational order of language, and particularly narrative language, in the transferential situation of telling and listening. The Monster's narrative of unrequited desire and unappeasable lack cannot produce access to the referent of desire. Instead, it passes on desire and lack, through the signifying chain of language and through the interlocutionary relation established in language, with the result that lack and desire come to inhabit the listener. As listener or narratee, once you have entered into a narrative transaction with the Monster, you are yourself tainted with monsterism: you cannot break out of the relation established by the pronouns 'I' and 'thou' once they are seen as complementary, each elusively representing the answer to the lack within oneself. The interlocutionary relation, like the transferential relation in psychoanalysis, could be dissolved only by the production of that which would answer the Monster's lack. Because this is impossible, lack is passed on through the narrative frames – which is indeed what the framing structure of the novel is all about.

Frankenstein, once he has become interlocutor to the Monster, is marked by the taint of monsterism, which he can never appease or dispel. When in turn, in the next frame (working out from the inside), Walton becomes Frankenstein's interlocutor, he, too, is marked by this taint. Walton, we note, is at the outset of the novel in a position analogous to Frankenstein's when he sets about his act of creation: he, too, is seeking for Promethean knowledge, dominion over the unknown, which in his case means exploration of the unknown polar regions. And like both Frankenstein and the Monster, he is searching for relation; he complains to his sister, Margaret Saville, that he has no one 'to participate my joy' or to 'sustain me in dejection' (p. 18). Frankenstein speaks for both of them when he says: 'I agree with you ... we are unfashioned creatures, but half made up, if one wiser, better, dearer than ourselves – such a friend ought to be – do not lend his aid to perfectionate our weak and faulty natures" (p. 27). Friendship, relation, interlocution, suggest an ideal model of the androgyne, which, as in the Platonic myth, has been split in half and now desires the missing half. But by the end Walton's hopes for both Promethean conquest and friendship lie 'blasted', as his mutinous sailors vote to turn southward and Frankenstein sinks into death (p. 204). All that remains to Walton is his epistolary narratee, his sister; and as he explains to her, being reduced to writing is no substitute for the living interlocutionary relation: writing is 'a poor medium for the communication of feeling' (p. 18). Moreover, his sister may never even receive these letters written from beyond the social world. In any event, for the reader of the novel, Mrs Saville has no more existence than a postal address, or even a dead-letter office – the place where messages end up when they have nowhere else to go. Her lack of characterised personality makes her all the more effectively stand for the reader, as the ultimate receiver of all the nested messages of the novel.

Thus it is that the taint of monsterism, as the product of the unarrestable metonymic movement of desire through the narrative signifying chain, may ultimately come to rest with the reader of the text. Like Frankenstein at the close of the Monster's act of narration, like Walton at the end of Frankenstein's narrative, we have a residue of desire and meaning left over, which we must somehow process. Perhaps it would be most accurate to say that we are left with a residue of desire *for* meaning, which we alone can realise. One could no doubt say something similar about any narrative text, especially any narrative that dramatises the fact and the process of its transmission, as 'framed tales' always do. In *Frankenstein*, the thematisation of the passing on of unresolved desire for meaning is particularly evident because the key question, the vital enigma, concerns the nature of monsterism itself. What is a monster? Reading inward from the outermost frame, the reader is led to believe that he or she is making a nearer approach to the solution to this problem; when the Monster speaks in his own person, assumes the pronoun 'I', we enter the subjectivity of monsterism. But that solves nothing, and as we read outward from the innermost frame, we come to realise that we are following the process of the passing on of this unresolved question, in an unarrestable metonymy of desire.

In closing his narrative to Walton, Frankenstein warns his interlocutor against listening to the Monster's voice: 'He is eloquent and persuasive, and once his words had even power over my heart; but trust him not ... Hear him not' (pp. 198–9). Yet when the Monster does finally appear to Walton, saying farewell to Frankenstein's corpse, Walton bids him stay, and soon his impulses to destroy the destroyer of his friend are 'suspended by a mixture of curiosity and compassion' (p. 208) – the very elements required to seal again the interlocutionary relation, to produce a new narrative transaction. It is the Monster who unknots this relation – and its possible production of a new narrative frame, a new nested box containing the Monster and Walton – when he announces that he has resolved to destroy himself. Once the other of his transferential desire has ceased to be, the only choice that remains for the Monster is self-immolation. He announces to Walton: 'Neither yours nor any man's death is needed to consummate the series of my being and accomplish that which must be done, but it requires my own' (p. 210). A moment before, he has stated that with Frankenstein's death, 'the miserable series of my being is wound to its close' (p. 207). 'Series' here is used in the sense of 'sequence' or 'order'. Conceptually, this phrase is related to the 'chain' which figures the Monster's understanding of human interrelation, and its counterparts in language and narration. Failing to enter the 'chain of existence and events', his narrative sequence has wound down to self-destruction. But the order in which he signifies cannot so easily be brought to a close, as the passing on of narrative messages, and narrative desire, may suggest.

In his peroration over Frankenstein's corpse, the Monster also claims: 'Blasted as thou wert, my agony was still superior to thine' (p. 211). While the context assigns the cause of this superior agony to the Monster's remorse, we may want to read it, more absolutely, as a statement about the fact of being a monster. That is the supreme agony, which no other problem in desire can efface. The phrase, like so much else in the novel, returns us to the question, What is a monster? The novel addresses this question in different registers. Initially, there is the creation of the Monster, which is a result of Frankenstein's illicit curiosity. He takes, in his youth, to reading such alchemical literature as Cornelius Agrippa, Paracelsus, Albertus Magnus. When his father censures such work as 'trash', he – like Dora with her volume of Mantegazza – seems to be only the more convinced that they will enable him to 'penetrate the secrets of nature' (pp. 38–9). He finds that philosophy has only partially 'unveiled the face of Nature'. 'I had gazed upon the fortifications and impediments that seemed to keep human beings from entering the citadel of nature, and rashly and ignorantly I had repined' (p. 39). Frankenstein recapitulates here the traditional imagery of nature as a woman, and proposes that truth is a difficult penetration into her body. As in the case of Dora, epistemophilia finally centres on the woman's body as the key to forbidden knowledge.

When he reaches the university at Ingolstadt, he falls under the spell of the chemistry professor Waldman, who tells him that modern scientists 'penetrate into the recesses of nature and show how she works in her hiding-places' (p. 47). This increases his desire to discover the hidden principle of life itself, to be able to bestow animation on inanimate matter – the Promethean revelation at the centre of the text, which it of course censors. He then learns how to proceed backward from death to a new life, using the 'loathsome' robbing of graves to create a new living species. 'Life and death', he recalls, 'appeared to me ideal bounds, which I should first break through, and pour a torrent of light into our dark world' (p. 52). Yet when, after two years of intense labour, he stands over his created body and sees 'the dull yellow eye of the creature open', his heart is filled with 'disgust' and he flees from his progeny.

Frankenstein's intense curiosity for forbidden knowledge, coupled with his hysterical reaction to witnessing its realisation, suggest, as the imagery of unveiling and penetration already indicated, that his epistemophilia centres on the arcana of the woman's body, specifically the mother's body in its reproductive function. The novel, as the psychoanalyst Marc A. Rubenstein has so well observed, is full of 'primal scene imagery', to the extent that 'the spirit of primal scene observation penetrates into the very structure of the novel and becomes part of a more deeply hidden search for the mother'.[12] The Freudian primal scene is an intense object of infantile curiosity which, even without actual observation by the infant, can have the status of a 'primal phantasy'. Parental copulation is of course for any individual the origin of origins, the very 'citadel of nature'. The novel suggests a fixation on the primal scene in the conjoined obsession with origins on the part of both Frankenstein and his Monster – who are both deprived of a literal mother on whom to exercise this curiosity, with the result that they must strive to create the scene – and in the intensely visual nature of the scenes created. Most pertinent here are the scenes of the Monster's creation (the moment when the Monster opens his eye produces Frankenstein's hysterical reaction, very much in the manner of the traumatic dream of Freud's 'Wolf Man'); the aborted creation of the female monster as the Monster watches at the window; and the wedding night, which recapitulates the Monster at the window, watching the nuptial bed become a bier.[13] Every time we reach one of the novel's manufactured primal scenes, something monstrous happens, and the observer is stricken, punished.[14] The very structure of the novel, as Rubenstein argues, suggests the pervasive effects of primal scene curiosity, a need to witness the forbidden moment of origin, which produces the inextinguishable taint of monsterism that gets passed on through the narrative chain.

It is significant, too, that the creation of the Monster from Frankenstein's studies in physics and chemistry, which are always on the verge of becoming metaphysics and alchemy, takes place on the borderline of nature and culture. The Monster is a product of nature – his ingredients are 100 per cent natural – yet by the process and the very fact of his creation, he is unnatural, the product of philosophical overreaching. Since he is a unique creation, without precedence or replication, he lacks cultural as well as natural context. He radicalizes the situation of Eve, who also has no 'model' – Adam is created in God's image, God is male; thus in whose image is Eve created? – and is hence a unique creation, but one that will then be replicated by half the human race. The Monster is, so to speak, postnatural and precultural. That a monster can be created within nature may stand as something of an indictment of nature itself, especially when one considers the generally ambiguous conceptual position of nature in the novel. An important thematic focus of this ambiguity is the figure of Henry Clerval, a being formed 'in the very poetry of nature', Frankenstein tells us (quoting Leigh Hunt), who is described through the citation of lines from Wordsworth's 'Tintern Abbey':

> The sounding cataract
> Haunted *him* like a passion: the tall rock,
> The mountain, and the deep and gloomy wood,
> Their colours and their forms, were then to him
> An appetite; a feeling, and a love,
> That had no need of a remoter charm,
> By thought supplied, or any interest
> Unborrow'd from the eye.

The italicised 'him' replaces the 'me' of the original. The lines are traditionally taken to represent the speaker's first, immediate, unreflective relation to nature, now lost to him but operative still in his sister Dorothy, to whom he can say that 'Nature never did betray / The heart that loved her'. Clerval loves and trusts nature, but he falls victim to the monstrous creation of his best friend and explicitly pays for Frankenstein's destruction of the Monster's mate. There is more to nature than sounding cataracts and sublime mountains: there is also one's friend's accursed curiosity, creating monsters demanding sexual satisfaction. It is in the awesome natural sublimity of the Alps, where Frankenstein has gone to seek consolation, that the Monster appears to his creator. One senses in Mary Shelley's novel a profound dissent from some of the more optimistic Romantic views of the moral principles embodied in nature – a dissent which recent readings of Wordsworth and P. B. Shelley find figured in some of their most problematic moments. Nature in *Frankenstein* appears not to be a principle at all: it is rigorously amoral, it is absence of principle.

What, then, in unprincipled nature, is a monster? A monster is that outcome or product of curiosity or epistemophilia pushed to an extreme that results – as in the story of Oedipus – in confusion, blindness, and exile. A monster is that which cannot be placed in any of the taxonomic schemes devised by the human mind to understand and to order nature. It exceeds the very basis of classification, language itself: it is an excess of signification, a strange byproduct or leftover of the process of making meaning. It is an imaginary being who comes to life in language and, once having done so, cannot be eliminated from language. Even if we want to claim that 'monster', like some of the words used by Felix and Agatha – 'dearest', 'unhappy' – has no referent, it has a signified, a conceptual meaning, a place in our knowledge of ourselves. The novel insistently thematises issues of language and rhetoric because the symbolic order of language appears to offer the Monster his only escape from the order of visual, specular, and imaginary relations, in which he is demonstrably the monster. The symbolic order compensates for a deficient nature: it promises escape from a condition of 'to-be-looked-at-ness'.

That, we may recall, is the term that Laura Mulvey applies to the 'traditional exhibitionist role' given to women in the cinema.[15] When one considers the Monster's creation in the place of the absent mother, his role and very definition as the insistent object of visual inspection, with the inevitable hysterical reaction, and his equally insistent attempt to redefine his person within the medium of language, especially narrative language as the vehicle of interpersonal relation, one may ask if the Monster is not in fact a woman who is seeking to escape from the feminine condition into recognition by the fraternity.[16] The very peculiarity of a novel about the monstrous that insistently stages its central issues in terms of language, rather than in sheerly visual terms – characteristic, for instance, of Gothic novels – would thus become doubly determined: on the thematic level, by the Monster's attempts to escape the imaginary order; and in the creative process itself, by Mary Shelley's attempts to escape the generic and cultural codes that make heroines into objects to be looked at – a fate that such heroines as Jane Eyre or Gwendolen Harleth never entirely escape. If, as Mulvey and other feminist film theoreticians have argued, the male gaze defines both the place of the female and the codes for looking at and defining her – and also the very genres that stage that looking – we may want to understand the persistent counter-visual emphasis of the Monster himself, and the contexts created around him, as an effort to deconstruct the defining and classifying power of the gaze, and to assert in its place the potential of affect created in interlocutory language – as used, notably, in the relation of love.

The Monster would thus be a woman, but a woman who would answer Freud's infamous question 'What does a woman want?' with the ostensible reply: to be a male, with a female to love. In the failure of that project, the Monster is forced to play the role of the castrating Medusa woman.[17] The novel of course never for a moment suggests that the Monster is anything but a male, and both Frankenstein and his creature assume that he is sexually functional as a male (there would otherwise be no need for Frankenstein to destroy the female monster). Yet the Monster never is given the chance to function sexually, and we are never given a glimpse of those parts of the body that would assure us that he is male. Of course we aren't: such is not part of the discourse of the novel (setting aside pornography) at the time. But this necessary cultural reticence, subjected to our retrospective critical pressure, may add a further ambiguity to the problems of definition of monster – may indeed add another dimension to that question 'What is a monster?' A monster may also be that which eludes gender definition. In this sense, *Frankenstein* would be a more radical version of that considerable body of Romantic and 'Decadent' literature – such as Théophile Gautier's *Mademoiselle de Maupin*, Henri de Latouche's

Fragoletta, Balzac's *Sarasine*, Rachilde's *Monsieur Vénus* – that uses cross-dressing and hermaphroditism to create situations of sexual ambiguity that call into question socially defined gender roles and transgress the law of castration that defines sexual difference. The Monster's demand for recognition by his father could then be read not only as desire for the absent mother but as a wish to be a sexual object for the father, in the manner of Freud's Senatspräsident Schreber.[18] Because a monster is that which calls into question all our cultural codes, including language itself, we can understand the persistent afterlife of Mary Shelley's creation, which shows us that, quite literally, once you have created a monster, whatever the ambiguities of the order of its existence, you can never get rid of it.

In this context, one might reflect on the moment when Frankenstein perceives the Monster for the first time following his flight from the scene of its creation. It comes when Frankenstein is on his way home after receiving news of William's murder. It is another of those scenes that bring into play the sublime power of nature. A storm breaks out in the Alps, a tempest 'so beautiful yet terrific' (p. 73). 'This noble war in the sky elevated my spirits; I clasped my hands and exclaimed aloud, "William, dear angel! This is thy funeral, this thy dirge!"' No sooner has he uttered these words than a flash of lightning reveals the presence of the Monster: natural sublimity once again produces the monstrous. With this revelation swiftly comes the thought that the Monster must be William's murderer. '*He* was the murderer! I could not doubt it. The mere presence of the idea was an irresistible proof of the fact' (pp. 73–4). The logic of the 'mere presence of the idea' becoming an 'irresistible proof of the fact' does not stand the test of reason. It is an excessive conclusion. Yet it is also true. The statement in fact mimes the process of creation of the Monster, who from a scientific idea becomes a bodily fact: an idea embodied.

We are always led back, in *Frankenstein*, to the peculiarity that this cultural creation, this epistemophilic product, has become part of nature – that the idea or concept of the monster, which at first has no referent in the natural world, gains one. It gains this referential status as a body. On a basic level, it is nothing but body: that which exists to be looked at, pointed to, and nothing more. You can't do anything with a monster except look at it. Like Virgil's Cyclops, it blocks out the light, including the light of reason, if reason be a matter of mental classification and rationalisation. In this manner, the Monster offers an inversion of the many scenarios, in Balzac and other novelists, in which the human body is marked or signed in order to bring it into the field of signification, so that it can be a narrative signifier. In *Frankenstein*, language is marked by the body, by the process of embodiment. We have not so much a mark on the body as the mark of the body: the capacity of language to create a body, one that in turn calls into question the language we use to classify and control bodies. In the plot of the novel, that body cannot be touched by any of the human bodies; apparently indestructible, it can be eliminated only when the Monster himself chooses to burn himself up. 'I shall ascend my funeral pile triumphantly and exult in the agony of the torturing flames' (p. 211). Note that his words are in the future tense. The Monster's death never is recorded within the novel; it never becomes matter for retrospective narration. We know it is not so easy to get rid of the monstrous body linguistically created. Mary Shelley's monster is still out there. It has taken a permanent place in our imaginary.

From Peter Brooks, *Body Work* (Harvard, 1993), pp. 199–220.

NOTES

[Peter Brooks' essay uses Lacanian psychoanalysis to examine relationships between narrative, sexuality and subjectivity, exploring the way that identity and connections between beings are constructed in language. The subject is formed by means of a specular identification with the mirror image of the body: the imaginary unity of the body that is glimpsed, as other, in the mirror also provides a sense of psychical integrity. The assumption of this imaginary unity allows the subject to position him/herself in relation to the Other, the rules and values of language and culture. Conventionally the body constitutes a sign of natural origin, but from Lacanian perspectives it is always inscribed with cultural and symbolic significance. In *Frankenstein*, however, the monster has an artificial body whose development runs counter to conventionally natural human modes of socialisation: its image is repulsive and it is only in language that an almost human identity is attained. The monster thus exceeds and undermines symbolic categories, showing how notions of nature, culture and humanity are effects of language and culture. The process of unnatural embodiment questions the way bodies are created, classified and controlled, demanding that the relationship between bodies and representation be seen and thought in different ways. Ed]

1. A diagram of the narrative structure would look like this: { [( )] }.

2. Mary Shelley, *Frankenstein*; *or*, *The Modern Prometheus* (New York, 1983), pp. 92–3. Subsequent references are to this edition, which reprints the revised text of 1831. I have also consulted the helpful critical edition by James Rieger (Indianapolis and New York, 1974), which prints the original text of 1818 (with the corrections of 1823) and indicates the variants occurring in the revised edition.

3. For the reader, the contradiction between the visual and the verbal appears also as a clash of generic expectations, between the Gothic novel and the philosophical tale: the Monster's hideous body and frightful crimes belong to the Gothic tradition, whereas his autobiographical narrative and the issues it raises suggest an eighteenth-century philosophical tale.

4. See Roland Barthes, *S/Z* (Paris, 1970), pp. 95–6. For some comments on the model of the 'narrative contract', and the need to extend it toward a more dynamic concept of narrative transaction, see Peter Brooks, 'Narrative Transaction and Transference', in *Reading for the Plot* (1984; rpt. Cambridge, Mass., 1992), pp. 216–37.

5. On these questions, see the classic essay by Emile Benveniste, 'De la subjectivité dans le langage', in *Problèmes de linguistique générale* (Paris, 1967), pp. 258–66.

6. On the Lacanian terms used here see in particular Jacques Lacan, 'Le stade du miroir' and 'L'instance de la lettre dans l'inconscient ou la raison depuis Freud', in *Ecrits* (Paris, 1966), pp. 93–100 and 493–528.

7. See Jean-Jacques Rousseau, *Essai sur l'origine des langues* (Paris, 1973), reprinted from the 1817 edition of Rousseau's works published by A. Belin. For a thorough and subtle discussion of Rousseau's presence throughout *Frankenstein*, see David Marshall, '*Frankenstein*, or Rousseau's Monster: Sympathy and Speculative Eyes', in *The Surprising Effects of Sympathy* (Chicago, 1988), pp. 178–227. Marshall's comments on the *Essai sur l'origine des langues* start from my own evocation of the pertinence of that text in a very early version of this chapter, '"Godlike Science/Unhallowed Arts": Language and Monstrosity in *Frankenstein*', *New Literary History*, 9:3 (1978), reprinted (slightly modified) in *The Endurance of Frankenstein*, ed. George Levine and U. C. Knoepflmacher (Berkeley, 1979) – but Marshall treats the subject far more fully than I did.

8. Several critics have pointed to the importance of the absence of mothers, and the search for a mother, in *Frankenstein*: see in particular Marc A. Rubenstein, '"My Accursed Origin": The Search for the Mother in *Frankenstein*', *Studies in Romanticism*, 15 (1976), 165–94; Sandra M. Gilbert and Susan Gubar, 'Horror's Twin: Mary Shelley's Monstrous

Eve', in *The Madwoman in the Attic* (New Haven, 1979), pp. 213–47; Mary Jacobus, 'Is There a Woman in This Text?' in *Reading Women: Essays in Feminist Criticism* (New York, 1986), esp. p. 101; and Margaret Homans, 'Bearing Demons: Frankenstein's Circumvention of the Maternal', in *Bearing the Word* (Chicago, 1986), pp. 100–19. On the biographical resonances of some of these issues – particularly the relation of Mary Shelley to her mother, Mary Wollstonecraft, who died shortly after giving birth to her, and her father, William Godwin, and her children, especially William – see, in addition to the studies just mentioned, Ellen Moers, 'Female Gothic', U. C. Knoepflmacher, 'Thoughts on the Aggression of Daughters', and Kate Ellis, 'Monsters in the Garden: Mary Shelley and the Bourgeois Family', all in *The Endurance of Frankenstein*. See also Barbara Johnson, 'My Monster/My Self', in *A World of Difference* (Baltimore, 1987), pp. 144–54. The fullest and most useful biography of Mary Shelley is Emily W. Sunstein, *Mary Shelley: Romance and Reality* (Boston, 1989).

9. On the 'anaclitic' or 'attachment type' (*Anlehnungstypus*) of object choice, see Freud, 'On Narcissism: An Introduction', *Standard Edition*, 14:87. The attachment is that of the sexual instincts to the ego instincts, with the result of a choice of love objects that takes the subject back to the mother.

10. 'Qu'est-ce qui est désiré? C'est le désirant dans l'autre – ce qui ne peut se faire qu'à ce que le sujet lui-même soit convoqué comme désirable. C'est ce qu'il demande dans la demande d'amour.' Lacan, *Le séminaire*, vol. 8, *Le transfert* (Paris, 1991), p. 415.

11. Note in this context the curious scenario leading to the death of Clerval: Frankenstein rows out to sea in his skiff and throws the mangled pieces of the female monster overboard; a storm comes up and blows him off course; he lands on a strange shore – it is Ireland – and is at once arrested as a murderer, and taken to see the body of his supposed victim, Clerval. Thus there is a direct exchange between the body of the female monster and that of Clerval.

12. Rubenstein, 'My Accursed Origin', p. 165.

13. In the Wolf Man's dream, 'suddenly the window opened of its own accord', and the terrified child sees the wolves sitting in a tree in front of the window, looking at him attentively. Freud's patient then interprets the window opening to mean 'My eyes suddenly opened'. See Freud, 'From the History of an Infantile Neurosis', *Standard Edition*, 17:29–47. On 'primal phantasies', see this case history and also *Introductory Lectures on Psycho-Analysis, Standard Edition*, 16:367–71. David Marshall, working from Marc Rubenstein's suggestions, gives a fine analysis of these scenes, in *The Surprising Effects of Sympathy*, pp. 222–6.

14. It is worth mentioning in this context that during the evenings of reading ghost stories in the Villa Diodati, on the shores of Lake Geneva, that brought together the Shelleys with Lord Byron, his personal physician Dr Polidori, and Claire Clairmont (Byron's mistress and Mary's stepsister) and led to the ghost story writing 'contest' that produced *Frankenstein*, P. B. Shelley had a hallucination: 'Byron repeated some verses of Coleridge's *Christabel*, of the witch's breast; when silence ensued, and Shelley, suddenly shrieking and putting his hands to his head, ran out of the room with a candle. Threw water in his face and after gave him ether. He was looking at Mrs Shelley, and suddenly thought of a woman he had heard of who had eyes instead of nipples, which taking hold of his mind, horrified him' (*The Diary of Dr John William Polidori*, ed. W. M. Rossetti [London, 1911], pp. 128–9, quoted by Rubenstein, p. 184). The woman with eyes in the place of nipples effectively sexualises vision, and turns the male's scopic fixations back on the voyeur, with hallucinatory results.

15. Laura Mulvey, 'Visual Pleasure and Narrative Cinema', in *Visual and Other Pleasures* (London, 1989), p. 19.

16. See Gilbert and Gubar, who suggest that the Monster's 'intellectual similarity to his authoress (rather than his "author")' indicates that he may be 'a female in disguise' (*The Madwoman in the Attic*, p. 237). Mary Jacobus notes the 'bizarre pun' in which Frankenstein describes the Monster as 'a mummy again endued with animation' (*Reading Women*, p. 101). Margaret Homans, citing my own argument (in my earlier essay on the novel) about the Monster's failure to gain his place in the symbolic order, states: 'I would argue that in its materiality and its failure to acquire an object of desire, the demon enters the symbolic primarily as the (dreaded) referent, not as signifier. The negative picture of the demon's materiality is a product of its female place in the symbolic, and not of any lingering in the realm of the imaginary (which Brooks, with other readers of Lacan, views as tragic)' (*Bearing the Word*, pp. 304–5, n. 18). I would agree with this to the extent that the materiality of the Monster continually vitiates his assumed place – the place he would assume – in the symbolic. But doesn't that status as dreaded referent continually throw him back into the imaginary?

17. The Monster, we have noted, is often the observer in the novel, which is the male role. When he is looked at, however, he takes on aspects of the Medusa, who turns (male) observers to stone, and who for Freud represents the terror of the female genitals to the (childish) male observer: see Freud, 'Medusa's Head', *Standard Edition*, 18:273–4. Note, in this context, Walton's reaction when he first meets the Monster: 'Never did I behold a vision so horrible as his face, of such loathsome yet appalling hideousness. I shut my eyes involuntarily' (p. 207).

18. See Freud, 'Psychoanalytic Notes upon an Autobiographical Account of a Case of Paranoia (Dementia Paranoides)' (1911), *Standard Edition*, 12:9–82.

5

A Feminist Critique of Science

ANNE K. MELLOR

From a feminist perspective, the most significant dimension of the relationship between literature and science is the degree to which both enterprises are grounded on the use of metaphor and image. The explanatory models of science, like the plots of literary works, depend on linguistic structures which are shaped by metaphor and metonymy. When Francis Bacon announced, 'I am come in very truth leading to you Nature with all her children to bind her to your service and make her your slave',[1] he identified the pursuit of modern science with the practice of sexual politics: the aggressive, virile male scientist legitimately captures and enslaves a fertile but passive female nature. Mary Shelley was one of the first to comprehend and illustrate the dangers inherent in the use of such gendered metaphors in the seventeenth-century scientific revolution.

Mary Shelley grounded her fiction of the scientist who creates a monster he cannot control upon an extensive understanding of the most recent scientific developments of her day. She thereby initiated a new literary genre, what we now call science fiction. More important, she used this knowledge both to analyse and to criticise the more dangerous implications of the scientific method and its practical results. Implicitly, she contrasted what she considered to be 'good' science – the detailed and reverent description of the workings of nature – to what she considered 'bad' science, the hubristic manipulation of the elemental forces of nature to serve man's private ends. In *Frankenstein, or the Modern Prometheus*, she illustrated the potential evils of scientific hubris and at the same time challenged the cultural biases inherent in any conception of science and the scientific method that rested on a gendered definition of nature as female. To appreciate the full significance of Mary Shelley's feminist critique of modern science, we must look first at the particular scientific research upon which her novel is based.

The works of three of the most famous scientists of the late eighteenth and early nineteenth century – Humphry Davy, Erasmus Darwin, and Luigi Galvani – together with the teachings of two of their ardent disciples, Adam Walker and Percy Shelley, were crucial to Mary Shelley's understanding of science and the scientific enterprise. While no scientist herself (her description of Victor Frankenstein's laboratory is both vague and naïve; apparently Victor does all his experiments in a small attic room by the light of a single candle), Mary Shelley nonetheless had a sound grasp of the concepts and implications of some of the most important scientific work of her day. In her novel, she distinguishes between that scientific research which attempts to describe accurately the functionings of the physical universe and that which attempts to *control* or *change* the universe through human intervention. Implicitly she celebrates the former, which she associates most closely with the work of Erasmus Darwin, while she calls attention to the dangers inherent in the latter, found in the work of Davy and Galvani.

Victor Frankenstein chooses to work within the newly established field of chemical physiology. He must thus become familiar with recent experiments in the disparate fields of biology, chemistry, mechanics, physics, and medicine. The need to span the entire range of science is stressed by Victor's chemistry professor, M. Waldman, who observes that 'a man would make but a very sorry chemist, if he attended to that department of human knowledge alone' and therefore advises Victor 'to apply to every branch of natural philosophy, including mathematics' (p. 43).

After his misguided and self-taught education in the theories of the medieval and renaissance alchemists, Cornelis Agrippa, Paracelsus, and Albertus Magnus, Victor Frankenstein at the age of fifteen was suddenly forced to acknowledge the ignorance of these pseudo-scientists when, during a storm in the Jura, lightning struck a nearby tree:

> As I stood at the door, on a sudden I beheld a stream of fire issue from an old and beautiful oak, which stood about twenty yards from our house; and so soon as the dazzling light vanished, the oak had

> disappeared, and nothing remained but a blasted stump. When we visited it the next morning, we found the tree shattered in a singular manner. It was not splintered by the shock, but entirely reduced to thin ribbands of wood. I never beheld any thing so utterly destroyed.
>
> The catastrophe of this tree excited my extreme astonishment; and I eagerly inquired of my father the nature and origin of thunder and lightning. He replied, 'Electricity'; describing at the same time the various effects of that power. He constructed a small electrical machine, and exhibited a few experiments; he made also a kite, with a wire and string, which drew down that fluid from the clouds.
>
> This last stroke completed the overthrow of Cornelius Agrippa, Albertus Magnus, and Paracelsus, who had so long reigned the lords of my imagination.
>
> (p. 35)

In the first edition of *Frankenstein*, Victor is introduced to the recent discoveries of Benjamin Franklin by his father, but in her later edition, Mary Shelley remembered that she had described the Frankenstein family as not interested in science.[2] In 1831, she therefore attributed Victor Frankenstein's initiation into legitimate science to an unnamed 'man of great research in natural philosophy' who happened to join them and who then 'entered on the explanation of a theory which he had formed on the subject of electricity and galvanism' which Victor found at once 'new and astonishing' (pp. 238–9).

At the University of Ingolstadt, Victor enrols in courses in chemistry and natural philosophy, inspired by the charismatic M. Waldman. Both Victor's and Professor Waldman's concept of the nature and utility of chemistry is based upon Humphry Davy's famous introductory lecture to a course in chemistry given at the newly founded Royal Institution on 21 January 1802.[3] Immediately published as *A Discourse, Introductory to a Course of Lectures on Chemistry* in 1802, this pamphlet is probably the work that Mary Shelley read on Monday, 28 October 1816, just before working on her story of Frankenstein. Her Journal entry for that day notes: 'Read the Introduction to Sir H. Davy's "Chemistry"; write'.[4] Waldman's enthusiasm for and description of the benefits to be derived from the study of chemistry seem to be based on Davy's remarks, as does Victor Frankenstein's belief that chemistry might discover the secret of life itself.

Davy probably also supplied Mary Shelley's description of the first parts of Professor Waldman's introductory lecture on chemistry – the opening 'recapitulation of the history of chemistry and the various improvements made by different men of learning', followed by 'a cursory view of the present state of the sciences', an explanation of several key terms and a few preparatory experiments – which comes not so much from Davy's *Discourse* as from Davy's later textbook, *Elements of Chemical Philosophy* (London, 1812), which Percy Shelley ordered from Thomas Hookham on 29 July 1812.[5] This may be the book listed in Mary's *Journal* on 29, 30 October, 2 and 4 November 1816, when Mary notes that she 'read Davy's "Chemistry" with Shelley' and then alone. A glance at the table of contents of this book would have given Mary Shelley the outline she attributes to Waldman: a brief history, followed by a discussion of several specific elements and compounds, with descriptions of experiments performed. The contents probably also provided her with the description of the lectures on natural philosophy that Victor Frankenstein attended in Geneva while still living at home:

> Some accident prevented my attending these lectures until the course was nearly finished. The lecture being therefore one of the last was entirely incomprehensible to me. The professor discoursed with the greatest fluency of potassium and boron, of sulphates and oxyds, terms to which I could affix no idea.
>
> (p. 36)

Davy's *Discourse*, written to attract and keep a large audience, provided Mary Shelley with both the content and the rhetoric of Waldman's final panegyric on modern chemistry, the panegyric that directly inspired Victor Frankenstein's subsequent research. Waldman concludes

> the ancient teachers of this science ... promised impossibilities, and performed nothing. The modern masters promise very little; they know that metals cannot be transmuted, and that the elixir of life is a chimera. But these philosophers, whose hands seem only made to dabble in dirt, and their eyes to pore over the microscope or crucible, have indeed performed miracles. They penetrate into the recesses of nature, and shew how she works in her hiding places. They ascend into the heavens; they have discovered how the blood circulates, and the nature of the air we breathe. They have acquired new and almost unlimited powers; they can command the thunders of heaven, mimic the earthquake, and even mock the invisible world with its own shadows.
>
> (p. 42)

Davy, in his celebration of the powers of chemistry, asserted that 'the phenomena of combustion, of the solution of different substances in water, of the agencies of fire; the production of rain, hail, and snow, and the conversion of dead matter into living matter by vegetable organs, all belong to chemistry.'[6] Arguing that chemistry is the basis of many other sciences, including mechanics, natural history, minerology, astronomy, medicine, physiology, pharmacy, botany, and zoology, Davy insists

> how dependent, in fact, upon chemical processes are the nourishment and growth of organised beings; their various alterations of form, their constant production of new substances; and, finally, their death and decomposition, in which nature seems to take unto herself those elements and constituent principles which, for a while, she had lent to a superior agent as the organs and instruments of the spirit of life!
> (p. 8)

After detailing the necessity of chemical knowledge to all the operations of common life, including agriculture, metal-working, bleaching, dyeing, leather-tanning, and glass and porcelain-making, Davy paints an idealistic portrait of the contemporary chemist, who is informed by a science that

> has given to him an acquaintance with the different relations of the parts of the external world; and more than that, it has bestowed upon him powers which may be almost called creative; which have enabled him to modify and change the beings surrounding him, and by his experiments to interrogate nature with power, not simply as a scholar, passive and seeking only to understand her operations, but rather as a master, active with his own instruments.
> (p. 16)

Here Davy introduces the very distinction Mary Shelley wishes to draw between the scholar-scientist who seeks only to understand the operations of nature and the master-scientist who actively interferes with nature. But where Davy obviously prefers the master-scientist Mary Shelley sees his instrumental activities as profoundly dangerous.

Davy sketches a visionary picture of the master-scientist of the future, who will discover the still unknown general laws of chemistry:

> For who would not be ambitious of becoming acquainted with the most profound secrets of nature; of ascertaining her hidden operations; and of exhibiting to men that system of knowledge which relates so intimately to their own physical and moral constitution?
> (p. 17)

These are Waldman's chemists, who 'penetrate into the recesses of nature and show how she works in her hiding places.' The result of such activity, Davy confidently predicts, will be a more harmonious, cooperative, and healthy society. True, he cautions, 'We do not look to distant ages, or amuse ourselves with brilliant, though delusive dreams, concerning the infinite improveability of man, the annihilation of labour, disease, and even death' (p. 22). But even as Davy apparently disavows the very dreams that would inspire Victor Frankenstein, Davy claims for his own project something very similar: 'we reason by analogy from simple facts. We consider only a state of human progression arising out of its present condition. We look for a time that we may reasonably expect, for a bright day of which we already behold the dawn' (p. 22). Having boldly stated the social benefits to be derived from the pursuit of chemistry, Davy concludes his *Discourse* by insisting on the personal gratifications to be gained: 'it may destroy diseases of the imagination, owing to too deep a sensibility; and it may attach the affections to objects, permanent, important, and intimately related to the interests of the human species', even as it militates against the 'influence of terms connected only with feeling' and encourages instead a rational contemplation of the universal order of things (p. 26).

In fairness to Davy, he had a great deal of scepticism about the very field that Victor Frankenstein chooses to enter, the new field of chemical physiology. Commenting on just the kind of enterprise Frankenstein pursues, the search for the principle of life itself, Davy warns

> if the connexion of chemistry with physiology has given rise to some visionary and seductive theories; yet even this circumstance has been useful to the public mind in exciting it by doubt, and in leading it to new investigations. A reproach, to a certain degree just, has been thrown upon those doctrines known by the name of the chemical physiology; for in the applications of them speculative philosophers have been guided rather by the analogies of words than of facts. Instead of slowly endeavouring to lift up the veil concealing the wonderful phenomena of living nature; full of ardent imaginations, they have vainly and presumptuously attempted to tear it asunder.
>
> (p. 9)

Mary Shelley clearly heeded Davy's words, for she presents Victor Frankenstein as the embodiment of hubris, of that Satanic or

Faustian presumption which blasphemously attempts to tear asunder the sacred mysteries of nature.

But in contrast to Davy, Mary Shelley doubted whether chemistry itself – in so far as it involved a 'mastery' of nature – produced only good. She substituted for Davy's complacent image of the happy scientist living in harmony with both his community and himself the frightening image of the alienated scientist working in feverish isolation, cut off both physically and emotionally from his family, friends, and society. Victor Frankenstein's scientific researches not only bring him no physical or emotional pleasure but they also leave him, as Laura Crouch has observed, disgusted with the entire scientific enterprise.[7] Detached from a respect for nature and from a strong sense of moral responsibility for the products of one's research, purely objective thought and scientific experimentation can and do produce monsters. Mary Shelley might have found trenchant support for her view in Humphry Davy's praise for one of chemistry's most notable achievements: 'in leading to the discovery of gunpowder, [chemistry] has changed the institutions of society, and rendered war more independent of brutal strength, less personal, and less barbarous.'[8]

In contrast to Davy, Erasmus Darwin provided Mary Shelley with a powerful example of what she considered to be 'good' science, a careful observation and celebration of the operations of all-creating nature with no attempt radically to change either the way nature works or the institutions of society. Percy Shelley acknowledged the impact of Darwin's work on his wife's novel when he began the Preface to the 1818 edition of *Frankenstein* with the assertion that 'the event on which this fiction is founded has been supposed, by Dr Darwin, and some of the physiological writers of Germany, as not of impossible occurrence' (p. 1). To what suppositions, theories and experiments, by Erasmus Darwin and others, did Percy Shelley allude? Mary Shelley, in her Preface to the 1831 edition, referred to an admittedly apocryphal account of one of Dr Darwin's experiments. During one of Byron's and Shelley's many long conversations to which she was 'a devout but nearly silent listener,' Mary Shelley recalled

> various philosophical doctrines were discussed, and among others the nature of the principle of life, and whether there was any probability of its ever being discovered and communicated. They talked of the

> experiments of Dr Darwin (I speak not of what the doctor really did or said that he did, but, as more to my purpose, of what was then spoken of as having been done by him), who preserved a piece of vermicelli in a glass case till by some extraordinary means it began to move with voluntary motion.
>
> (p. 227)

Even though Mary Shelley acknowledges that the animated piece of vermicelli is probably a fiction, Erasmus Darwin's theories have significant bearing on her purpose in *Frankenstein*.

Erasmus Darwin was most famous for his work on evolution and the growth of plants, and it is this work that Mary Shelley affirmed. Victor Frankenstein is portrayed as a direct opponent of Darwin's teachings, as an anti-evolutionist and a parodic proponent of an erroneous 'Creation Theory'. The basic tenets of Erasmus Darwin's theories appear in his major works, *The Botanic Garden* (1789, 1791), *Zoonomia; or the Laws of Organic Life* (1793), *Phytologia* (1800), and *The Temple of Nature* (1803).[9]

Eighteenth-century scientists generally conceived of the universe as a perfect, static world created by divine fiat at a single moment in time. This universe, metaphorically represented as a Great Chain of Being, manifested myriad and minute gradations between species, but these relationships were regarded as fixed and permanent, incapable of change. As Linnaeus, the great eighteenth-century classifier of all known plant-life, insisted in his *Systema Naturae* (1735), 'Nullae species novae' – no new species can come into existence in a divinely ordered, perfect world. But by the end of the eighteenth century, under pressure from Herschel's new discoveries in astronomy, Cuvier's palaeontological researches, William Smith's studies of fossil stratification, Sprengel's work on botanical cross-breeding and fertilisation, and observations made with an increasingly powerful microscope, together with a more diffuse Leibnizian 'natural theology' that emphasised the study of nature's varied interactions with human populations, the orthodox Linnaean concept of an immutable physical universe had begun to weaken.[10]

Erasmus Darwin was inspired by the researches of Comte du Buffon, the 'father of evolution',[11] who in his huge *Histoire naturelle* (44 volumes, 1749–1804) had described myriads of flora and fauna and interspersed among them comments on the progressive 'degeneration' of life forms from earlier and more uniform species, often caused by environmental or climatic changes. Although he adhered to the concept of the *scala naturae* and the immutability of species, Buffon was the first to discuss seriously such central evolutionary problems as the origin of the earth, the extinction of species, the theory of 'common descent', and in particular the reproductive isolation between two incipient species.[12] Significantly, it was to Buffon that Victor Frankenstein turned after his early disillusionment with the alchemists, and Buffon whom he 'still read ... with delight' (p. 36).[13] But it was Erasmus Darwin who for English readers first synthesised and popularised the concept of the evolution of species through natural selection over millions of years.

By 1803, Darwin had accepted, on the basis of shell and fossil remains in the highest geological strata, that the earth must once have been covered by water and hence that all life began in the sea. As Darwin concisely summed up this theory of evolution in *The Temple of Nature*:

> Cold gills aquatic form respiring lungs,
> And sounds aerial flow from slimy tongues.
>
> (*The Temple of Nature*, I, 11. 333–4)

Meditating on the suggestion that mankind descended from 'one family of monkeys on the banks of the Mediterranean' that learned to use and strengthen the thumb muscle and 'by this improved use of the sense of touch ... acquired clear ideas, and gradually became men,' Darwin speculated

> perhaps all the productions of nature are in their progress to greater perfection! an idea countenanced by modern discoveries and deductions concerning the progressive formation of the solid parts of the terraqueous globe, and consonant to the dignity of the Creator of all things.
>
> (*The Temple of Nature*, p. 54)

Darwin further suggested that such evolutionary improvement is the direct result of sexual selection:

> A great want of one part of the animal world has consisted in the desire of the exclusive possession of the females; and these have acquired weapons to bombard each other for this purpose, as the very thick, shield-like, horny skin on the shoulder of the boar is a defence only against animals of his own species, who strike obliquely upwards, nor are his tushes for other purposes, except to defend himself, as he is not naturally a carnivorous animal. So the horns of the stag are not sharp to offend his adversary, but are branched for the purpose of parrying or receiving the thrusts of horns similar to

> his own, and have therefore been formed for the purpose of combating other stags for the exclusive possession of the females; who are observed, like the ladies in the times of chivalry, to attend the car of the victor.
>
> (*Zoonomia*, 1794, I:503)

Erasmus Darwin anticipated the modern discovery of mutations, noting in his discussion of monstrous births that monstrosities, or mutations, may be inherited: 'Many of these enormities of shape are propagated, and continued as a variety at least, if not as a new species of animal. I have seen a breed of cats with an additional claw on every foot' (*Zoonomia*, 1794, I:501).

In relation to *Frankenstein*, Erasmus Darwin's most significant evolutionary concept was that of the hierarchy of reproduction. Again and again, in *Zoonomia*, in *The Botanic Garden*, in *Phytologia*, and in *The Temple of Nature*, Darwin insisted that sexual reproduction is at a higher evolutionary level than hermaphroditic or solitary paternal propagation. As Darwin commented in his Note on 'Reproduction' for *The Temple of Nature*:

> The miscroscopic productions of spontaneous vitality, and the next most inferior kinds of vegetables and animals, propagate by solitary generation only; as the buds and bulbs raised immediately from seeds, the lycoperdon tuber, with probably many other fungi, and the polypus, volvox, and taenia. Those of the next order propagate both by solitary and sexual reproduction, as those buds and bulbs which produce flowers as well as other buds or bulbs; and the aphis and probably many other insects. Whence it appears, that many of those vegetables and animals, which are produced by solitary generation, gradually become more perfect, and at length produce a sexual progeny.
>
> A third order of organic nature consists of hermaphrodite vegetables and animals, as in those flowers which have anthers and stigmas in the same corol; and in many insects, as leeches, snails, and worms; and perhaps all those reptiles which have no bones ...
>
> And, lastly, the most perfect orders of animals are propagated by sexual intercourse only.
>
> (pp. 36–7)

This concept of the superiority of sexual reproduction over paternal propagation was so important to Darwin that it forced him to revise radically his concept of reproduction in his third, 'corrected' edition of *Zoonomia* (1801). In 1794, Darwin had argued, following Aristotle, that male plants produce the seed or embryon, while female plants provide only nourishment to this seed, and by analogy, had contended 'that the mother does not contribute to the formation of the living ens in normal generation, but is necessary only for supplying its nutriment and oxigenation' (*Zoonomia*, 1794, I:487). He then attributed all monstrous births to the female, saying that deformities result from either excessive or insufficient nourishment in the egg or uterus (p. 497). But by 1801, Darwin's observations of both animal and vegetable hybrids had convinced him that both male and female seeds contribute to the innate characteristics of the species:

> We suppose that redundant fibrils with formative appetencies are produced by, or detached from, various parts of the male animal, and circulating in his blood, are secreted by adapted glands, and constitute the seminal fluid, and that redundant molecules with formative aptitudes or propensities are produced by, or detached from, various parts of the female, and circulating in her blood, are secreted by adapted glands, and form a reservoir in the ovary; and finally that when these formative fibrils, and formative molecules, become mixed together in the uterus, that they coalesce or embrace each other, and form different parts of the new embryon, as in the cicatricula of the impregnated egg.
>
> (*Zoonomia*, 1801, II:296–7)

Interestingly, while Darwin no longer attributed monstrous births to uterine deficiencies or excesses, he continued to hold the *male imagination* at the moment of conception responsible for determining both the sex of the child and its outstanding traits:

> I conclude, that the act of generation cannot exist without being accompanied with ideas, and that a man must have at this time either a general idea of his own male form, or of the forms of his male organs; or of an idea of the female form, or of her organs, and that this marks the sex, and the peculiar resemblances of the child to either parent.
>
> (*Zoonomia*, 1794, I:524; 1801, II:270)

The impact of the female imagination on the seed in utero is less intense, argued Darwin, because its impact lasts for a longer period of time and is therefore more diffuse. It follows that Darwin, in 1801, attributed the bulk of monstrous births to the *male* imagination, a point of obvious relevance to *Frankenstein*.

Erasmus Darwin's work on what he called 'the economy of vegetation' has equally significant implications for *Frankenstein*.

Darwin's comments in *Phytologia* on plant nutrition, photosynthesis, and the use of fertilisers and manures for the first time put gardening and agriculture on a sound scientific basis.[14] Again and again in this lengthy work, Darwin emphasised the necessity to recycle all organic matter. His discussion of manures runs to over twenty-five thousand words and is by far the largest section in this book on plant agriculture. The best manures, Darwin reports, are

> organic matters, which ... will by their slow solution in or near the surface of the earth supply the nutritive sap-juice to vegetables. Hence all kinds of animal and vegetable substances, which will undergo a digestive process, or spontaneous solution, as the flesh, fat, skin, and bones of animals; with their secretions of bile, saliva, mucus; and their excretions of urine and ordure; and also the fruit, meal, oil, leaves, wood of vegetables, when properly decomposed on or beneath the soil, supply the most nutritive food to plants.
>
> (*Phytologia*, p. 254)

He urges every gardener and farmer to save all organic matter for manure, 'even the parings of his nails and the clippings of his hair' (*Phytologia*, p. 241), and further urges the heretical notion that the soil nourished by the decomposition of human bodies ought to be available for growing plants. Mourning the waste of rich soil in churchyards and cemeteries, he argues that

> proper burial grounds should be consecrated out of towns, and divided into two compartments, the earth from one of which, saturated with animal decomposition, should be taken away once in ten or twenty years, for the purposes of agriculture; and sand or clay, or less fertile soil, brought into its place.
>
> (*Phytologia*, p. 243)

Mary Shelley was introduced to Darwin's thought by her father and again by her husband, who had been heavily influenced by Darwin's evolutionary theories while writing *Queen Mab*. Percy Shelley first read *The Botanic Garden* in July 1811, as he reported to Thomas Hogg, and in December 1812 he ordered Darwin's *Zoonomia* and *The Temple of Nature* from the booksellers Hookham and Rickman.[15] The extensive impact of Darwin's theories of evolution and agriculture and his poetic language on Percy Shelley's Notes to *Queen Mab*, 'The Cloud', 'The Sensitive Plant', and *Prometheus Unbound* has been well-documented.[16] It is clear that Darwin's work remained vivid in Percy Shelley's mind throughout the period in which Mary Shelley was writing *Frankenstein*, as his prefatory comment to the novel testifies.

Reading *Frankenstein* in the context of Darwin's writings, we can see that Mary Shelley directly pitted Victor Frankenstein, that modern Prometheus, against those gradual evolutionary processes of nature so well described by Darwin. Rather than letting organic life-forms evolve slowly over thousands of years according to natural processes of sexual selection, Victor Frankenstein wants to originate a new life-form quickly, by chemical means. In his Faustian thirst for knowledge and power, he dreams:

> Life and death appeared to me ideal bounds, which I should first break through, and pour a torrent of light into our dark world. A new species would bless me as its creator and source; many happy and excellent natures would owe their being to me.
>
> (p. 49)

Significantly, in his attempt to create a new species, Victor Frankenstein substitutes solitary paternal propagation for sexual reproduction. He thus reverses the evolutionary ladder described by Darwin. And he engages in a concept of science that Mary Shelley deplores, the notion that science should manipulate and control rather than describe, understand, and revere nature.

Moreover, his male imagination at the moment of conception is fevered and unhealthy; as he tells Walton:

> Every night I was oppressed by a slow fever, and I became nervous to a most painful degree; ... my voice became broken, my trembling hands almost refused to accomplish their task; I became as timid as a love-sick girl, and alternate tremor and passionate ardour took the place of wholesome sensation and regulated ambition.
>
> (p. 51)

Under such mental circumstances, according to Darwin, the resultant creation could only be a monster. Frankenstein has further increased the monstrousness of his creation by making a form that is both larger and more simple than a normal human being. As he acknowledges to Walton:

> As the minuteness of the parts formed a great hindrance to my speed, I resolved, contrary to my first intention, to make the being of a

> gigantic stature; that is to say, about eight feet in height, and proportionably large.
>
> (p. 49)

Darwin had observed that nature moves 'from simpler things to more compound' (*Phytologia*, 118). In defying nature's law, Victor Frankenstein has created not a more perfect species but a degenerate one.

In his attempt to override evolutionary development and to create a new species *sui generis*, Victor Frankenstein becomes a parodic perpetrator of the orthodox creationist theory. On the one hand, he denies the unique power of God to create organic life. At the same time he confirms the capacity of a single creator to originate a new species. By playing God, Victor Frankenstein has simultaneously upheld the creationist theory and parodied it by creating only a monster. In both ways, Victor Frankenstein has blasphemed against the natural order of things. He has moved down rather than up the evolutionary ladder – he has constructed his creature not only out of dead human organs collected from charnel houses and dissecting rooms, but also out of animal organs and tissue removed from 'the slaughter-house' (p. 50). And he has denied the natural mode of human reproduction through sexual procreation.

Victor Frankenstein has perverted evolutionary progress in yet another way. Despite Darwin's insistence that all dead organic matter – including decomposing human flesh and bones found in cemeteries – ought to be saved for compost-heaps and manure, Victor Frankenstein has removed human flesh and bones from graveyards. And he has done so not in order to generate life organically through what Darwin described as 'spontaneous animal vitality in microscopic cells'[17] but to create a new life-form through chemical engineering. Frankenstein has thus disrupted the natural life-cycle. His attempt to speed up the transformation of decomposing organic material into new life-forms by artificial means has violated the rhythms of nature.

Mary Shelley's novel implicitly invokes Darwin's theory of gradual evolutionary progress to suggest both the error and the evils of Victor Frankenstein's bad science. The genuine improvement of the species can result only from the conjunction of male and female sexuality. In trying to have a baby without a woman, Victor Frankenstein has failed to give his child the mothering and nurturance it requires, the very nourishment that Darwin explicitly equated with the female sex. Victor Frankenstein's failure to embrace his smiling creature with parental love, his horrified rejection of his own creation, spells out the narrative consequences of solitary paternal propagation. But even if Frankenstein had been able to provide his child with a mother's care, he could not have prevented his creature's ostracism and misery. At best he would have produced another Elephant Man, a benevolent but still much maligned freak.

It is therefore a triple failure of imagination that curses Victor Frankenstein. First, by not imaginatively identifying with his creation, Frankenstein fails to give his child the parental support he owes to it. He thereby condemns his creature to become what others behold, a monster. Secondly, by imagining that the male can produce a higher form of evolutionary species by lateral propagation than by sexual procreation, Frankenstein defines his own imagination as profoundly anti-evolutionary and thus anti-progressive. Third, in assuming that he can create a perfect species by chemical means, Frankenstein defies a central tenet of Romantic poetic ideology: that the creative imagination must work spontaneously, unconsciously, and above all organically, creating forms that are themselves organic heterocosms.

Moreover, in trying to create a human being as God created Adam, out of earth and water, all at once, Victor Frankenstein robs nature of something more than fertiliser. 'On a dreary night in November, ... with an anxiety that almost amounted to agony', Victor Frankenstein infused 'a spark of being into the lifeless thing that lay' at his feet (p. 52). At that moment Victor Frankenstein became the modern Prometheus, stealing fire from the gods to give to mankind and thus overthrowing the established, sacred order of both earth and heaven. At that moment he transgressed against nature.

To understand the full implications of Frankenstein's transgression, we must recognise that Victor Frankenstein's stolen 'spark of life' is not merely fire; it is also that recently discovered caloric fluid called electricity. Victor's interest in legitimate science was first aroused by the sight of lightning destroying an old oak tree; it was then that he learned of the existence of electricity and replicated Benjamin Franklin's experiment with kite and key to draw down 'that fluid from the clouds' (p. 35). In the late eighteenth century, there was widespread interest in the implications of Franklin's and Father Beccaria's discoveries of the existence of atmospheric mechanical electricity generated through such machines as the Leyden jar. Many scientists explored the possibility, derived from Newton's concept of the ether as an elastic medium capable of transmitting the pulsations of light, heat, gravitation, magnetism, and electricity, that the atmosphere was filled with a thin fluid that was positively and negatively charged and that could be identified as a single animating principle appearing under multiple guises (as light, heat, magnetism, etc.). Erasmus Darwin speculated that the perpetual necessity of the human organism for breathing suggests that 'the spirit of animation itself is thus acquired from the atmosphere, which if it be supposed to be finer or more subtle than the electric matter, could not long be retained in our bodies and must therefore require perpetual renovation' (*Botanic Garden*, Canto I, Note to line 401). And Humphry Davy, founder of the field of electrochemistry, first gave authoritative voice to a theory of matter as electrically charged atoms. In his *Elements of Chemical Philosophy*, Davy argued:

> Whether matter consists of indivisible corpuscles, or physical points endowed with attraction and repulsion, still the same conclusions may be formed concerning the powers by which they act, and the quantities in which they combine; and the powers seem capable of being measured by their electrical relations, and the quantities on which they act of being expressed by numbers.
>
> (p. 57)

He further concluded that

> it is evident that the particles of matter must have space between them; and ... it is a probable inference that [each body's] own particles are possessed of motion; but ... the motion, if it exists, must be a vibratory or undulatory motion, or a motion of the particles round their axes, or a motion of particles round each other.
>
> (p. 95)

Reading Darwin and Davy encouraged Percy Shelley in scientific speculations that he had embarked upon much earlier, as a school boy at Dr Greenlaw's Syon House Academy in 1802. Inspired by the famous lectures of Dr Adam Walker, which he heard again at Eton, Shelley began ten years of experiments with Leyden jars, microscopes, magnifying glasses, and chemical mixtures. His more memorable experiments left holes in his clothes and carpets, attempted to cure his sister Elizabeth's chilblains with a galvanic battery, and electrified a family tomcat. Shelley early learned to think of electricity and the processes of chemical attraction and repulsion as modes of a single polarised force. Adam Walker even identified electricity as the spark of life itself. At the conclusion of his discussion of electricity in his *A System of Familiar Philosophy*, Walker enthused

> Its power of exciting muscular motion in apparently dead animals, as well as of increasing the growth, invigorating the stamina, and reviving diseased vegetation, prove its relationship or affinity to the *living principle*. Though, Proteus-like, it eludes our grasp; plays with our curiosity; tempts enquiry by fallacious appearances and attacks our weakness under so many perplexing subtitles; yet it is impossible not to believe it the soul of the material world, and the paragon of elements![18]

Percy Shelley's basic scientific concepts had long been familiar to Mary Shelley, ever since the early days of their relationship when he ritually celebrated his birthday by launching fire balloons.[19] That Percy Shelley endorsed Adam Walker's identification of life with electricity is everywhere apparent in his poetry. The imagery of *Prometheus Unbound* explicitly associates electricity with love, light, and life itself, as in the final act of the poem where the Spirit of the Earth, earlier imaged as a Cupid-figure linked to his mother Asia/Venus, becomes a radiant orb – or 'ten thousand orbs involving and involved' – of pure energy. And on the forehead of the spirit sleeping within this 'sphere within sphere' is a 'star' (or negative electrode) that shoots 'swords of azure fire' (the blue flame of electrical discharges) or

> Vast beams like spokes of some invisible wheel
> Which whirl as the orb whirls, swifter than thought,
> Filling the abyss with sun-like lightnings,
> And perpendicular now, and now transverse,
> Pierce the dark soil, and as they pierce and pass,
> Make bare the secrets of the earth's deep heart.
> (*Prometheus Unbound*, IV, 241, 243, 270, 271, 274–9)

When Victor Frankenstein steals the spark of being, then, he is literally stealing Jupiter's lightning bolt, as Benjamin Franklin had proved. But in Percy Shelley's terms, he is stealing the very life of nature, the source of both love and electricity.

To appreciate fully the science that lies behind Victor Frankenstein's endeavours, however, we must remember that in the 1831 edition of *Frankenstein*, Mary Shelley explicitly associated electricity with galvanism. Victor Frankenstein is there disabused of his belief in the alchemists by a 'man of great research in natural philosophy' who introduces him to 'a theory which he had formed on the subject of electricity and galvanism' (p. 238); and in her Preface, Mary Shelley linked the attempt to give life to dead matter with galvanism. After referring to Dr Darwin's vermicelli experiment, she writes:

> Not thus, after all, would life be given. Perhaps a corpse would be re-animated; galvanism had given token of such things: perhaps the component parts of a creature might be manufactured, brought together, and endued with vital warmth.
>
> (p. 227)

In 1791 the Bolognese physiologist Luigi Galvani published his *De Viribus Electricitatis in Motui Musculari (or Commentary on the Effects of Electricity on Muscular Motion)*[20] in which he came to the conclusion that animal tissue contained a heretofore neglected innate vital force, which he called 'animal electricity' but which was subsequently widely known as 'galvanism'. This force activated both nerves and muscles when they were connected by an arc of metal wires connected to a pile of copper and zinc plates. Galvani believed that his new vital force was a form of electricity different from both the 'natural' form of electricity produced by lightning or by the torpedo fish and electric eel and the 'artificial' form produced by friction (i.e. static electricity). Galvani argued that the brain is the most important source of the production of this 'electric fluid' and that the nerves acted as conductors of this fluid to other nerves and muscles, the tissues of which act much like the outer and inner surfaces of the widely used Leyden jar. Thus the flow of animal electric fluid provided a stimulus which produced contractions or convulsions in the irritable muscle fibres.

Galvani's theories made the British headlines in December 1802, when in the presence of their Royal Highnesses the Prince of Wales, the Duke of York, the Duke of Clarence, and the Duke of Cumberland, Galvani's nephew, disciple and ardent defender, Professor Giovanni Aldini of Bologna University, applied a Voltaic pile connected by metallic wires to the ear and nostrils of a recently killed ox-head. At that moment, 'the eyes were seen to open, the ears to shake, the tongue to be agitated, and the nostrils to swell, in the same manner as those of the living animal, when irritated and desirous of combating another of the same species'.[21] But Professor

Aldini's most notorious demonstration of galvanic electricity took place on 17 January 1803. On that day he applied galvanic electricity to the corpse of the murderer Thomas Forster. The body of the recently hanged criminal was collected from Newgate where it had lain in the prison yard at a temperature of 30 degrees Fahrenheit for one hour by the President of the College of Surgeons, Mr Keate, and brought immediately to Mr Wilson's Anatomical Theatre where the following experiments were performed. When wires attached to a pile composed of 120 plates of zinc and 120 plates of copper were connected to the ear and mouth of the dead criminal, Aldini later reported, 'the jaw began to quiver, the adjoining muscles were horribly contorted, and the left eye actually opened.'[22] When the wires were applied to the dissected thumb muscles they 'induced a forcible effort to clench the hand'; when applied to the ear and rectum, they 'excited in the muscles contractions much stronger ... The action even of those muscles furthest distant from the points of contact with the arc was so much increased as almost to give an appearance of re-animation.' And when volatile alkali was smeared on the nostrils and mouth before the Galvanic stimulus was applied, 'the convulsions appeared to be much increased ... and extended from the muscles of the head, face, and neck, as far as the deltoid. The effect in this case surpassed our most sanguine expectations,' Aldini exulted, and remarkably concluded that 'vitality might, perhaps, have been restored, if many circumstances had not rendered it impossible.'[23] Here is the scientific prototype of Victor Frankenstein, restoring life to dead bodies.

In further experiments conducted by Aldini in 1804, the bodies of human corpses became violently agitated and one even raised itself as if about to walk; arms alternately rose and fell; and one forearm was made to hold a weight of several pounds, while the fists clenched and beat violently the table upon which the body lay. Natural respiration was also artificially re-established and, through pressure exerted against the ribs, a lighted candle placed before the mouth was several times extinguished.[24]

Aldini's experiments on the severed heads of oxen, frogs' legs, dogs' bodies, and human corpses were replicated widely throughout Europe in the early 1800s. His colleagues at bologna, Drs Vassali-Eandi, Rossi, and Giulio, reported to the Academy of Turin on 15 August 1802, that they had been able to excite contractions even in the involuntary organs of the heart and digestive system,[25] while applications of galvanic electricity to vegetables, animals, and humans were conducted in Germany by F. H. A. Humboldt, Edmund Schmück, C. J. C. Grapengiesser, and Johann Caspar Creve.[26] Their experiments were reported in 1806 by J. A. Heidmann in his *Theorie der Galvanischen Elektrizität*, while the theoretical implications of galvanism were expounded by Lorenz Oken in his influential *Lehrbuch der Naturephilosophie* (Leipzig, 1809–10). Oken argued that polarity is the first and only force in the world; that galvanism or electrical polarity is therefore the principle of life; and that organic life is galvanism in a state of homogeneous mass.[27]

Events so notorious and so widely reported in the popular press must have been discussed in both the Shelley and the Godwin households at the time and would have been recalled, however inaccurately, by Shelley and Byron in their conversations about the possibility of reanimating a corpse. Indeed, the popular interest in galvanic electricity reached such a pitch in Germany that a Prussian edict was passed in 1804 forbidding the use of decapitated criminals' heads for galvanic experiments. It is probably to these events, as well as to the experiments of Humboldt, Grapengiesser, and Creve and the expositions of Heidmann and Oken that Percy Shelley referred in his Preface to *Frankenstein* when he insisted that 'the event on which this fiction is founded has been supposed, by Dr Darwin and some of the physiological writers of Germany, as not of impossible occurrence' (p. 6). Even though Erasmus Darwin never fully endorsed the revolutionary theory of Galvani and Volta that electricity is the cause of muscular motion, he was convinced that electricity stimulated plant growth.[28]

Mary Shelley's familiarity with these galvanic experiments came not only from Shelley and Byron, but also from Dr William Polidori. As a medical student with a degree from the University of Edinburgh, Polidori had been exposed to the latest galvanic theories and experiments by the famous Edinburgh physician, Dr Charles Henry Wilkinson, whose review of the literature, *Elements of Galvanism in Theory and Practice*, was published in 1804. Dr Wilkinson continued research on galvanism and developed his own galvanic treatments for intermittent fevers, amaurosis, and quinsy, with which he reported several successes.[29]

Mary Shelley based Victor Frankenstein's attempt to create a new species from dead organic matter through the use of chemistry and electricity on the most advanced scientific research of the early nineteenth century. Her vision of the isolated scientist discovering the secret of life is no mere fantasy but a plausible prediction of what science might accomplish. As such, *Frankenstein* has rightly been hailed as the first legitimate example of that genre we call science fiction. Brian Aldiss has tentatively defined science fiction as 'the search for a definition of man and his status in the universe which will stand in our advanced but confused state of knowledge (science), and is characteristically cast in the Gothic or post-Gothic mould.' And Eric Rabkin and Robert Scholes have identified the conventional elements of science fiction as 'speculation and social criticism, hardware and exotic adventure'.[30] We might expand these criteria to say that science fiction is a genre that (1) is grounded on valid scientific research; (2) gives a persuasive prediction of what science might be able to accomplish in the foreseeable future; and (3) offers a humanistic critique of either specific technological inventions or the very nature of scientific thinking.

Frankenstein is notable both for its grasp of the nature of the seventeenth-century scientific revolution and for its perspicacious analysis of the dangers inherent in that enterprise. Mary Shelley provides us with the first portrait of what the popular media has since caricatured as the 'mad scientist', a figure that finds its modern apotheosis in Stanley Kubrick's Dr Strangelove (1964). But Mary Shelley's portrait of Victor Frankenstein is both more subtle and more persuasive than subsequent media versions.

Mary Shelley recognised that Frankenstein's passion for his scientific research is a displacement of normal emotions and healthy human relationships. Obsessed by his vision of the limitless power to be gained from his newly discovered capacity to bestow animation, Victor Frankenstein devotes all his time and 'ardour' to his experimental research, the creating of a human being. He becomes oblivious to the world around him, to his family and friends, even to his own health. As he admits, 'my cheek had grown pale with study, and my person become emaciated with confinement' (p. 49) as 'a resistless, and almost frantic impulse, urged me forward; I seemed to have lost all soul or sensation but for this one pursuit' (p. 50). In his compulsive desire to complete his experiment, he ignores the beauty of nature and stops corresponding with his father and Elizabeth. 'I could not tear my thoughts from my employment, loathsome in itself; but which had taken hold of my imagination. I wished, as it were, to procrastinate my feelings of affection, until the great object of my affection was completed' (manuscript version of 50:29–33). Frankenstein has clearly substituted his scientific research for normal emotional interactions. His only 'object of affection' has become the experiment on the laboratory table before him.

In his ability to substitute work for love, a dream of personal omnipotence for a dream of familial interdependence, Victor Frankenstein possesses a personality that has recently been characterised by Evelyn Fox Keller as typical of the modern scientist. Keller argues from her psychological survey of physicists working at Harvard University that the professional scientific demand for 'objectivity' often masks a prior psychological alienation from the mother, an alienation that can lead scientists to feel uncomfortable with their emotions and sexuality. The scientists she studied, when compared to the norm, typically felt more estranged from their mothers, were more emotionally repressed, had a relatively low sex-drive, and tended to feel more comfortable with objects than with people.[31] Their professional detachment often precluded a concern with ethics and politics in their research. They preferred to leave the problems resulting from the social application of their discoveries to others. Frankenstein's failure to take personal responsibility for the outcome of his experiment thus anticipates the practice of many modern scientists.

Mary Shelley developed the character of Victor Frankenstein as a calculated inversion of the eighteenth-century 'man of feeling'. Influenced by Shaftesbury's philosophical argument that sympathy is the basis of human morality and by the fictional treatments of this idea – Henry Mackenzie's *The Man of Feeling*, Godwin's *Fleetwood, or The New Man of Feeling*, Laurence Sterne's *A Sentimental Journey* and Rousseau's *La Nouvelle Héloïse* which she heard Percy Shelley read aloud that summer of 1816 – Mary Shelley embodied in Victor Frankenstein the very opposite of the sentimental hero. Her isolated protagonist has given both 'heart and soul' to his work, callously indifferent to the anxiety his silence might cause his father and his fiancée. As such he has truly 'lost all soul' (p. 50). He has cut himself off from all moral feeling, from the capacity either to perceive or to enact goodness, as Shaftesbury defined it.

That Mary Shelley endorsed the ideal of the man of feeling as a moral exemplar is revealed not only in her association of the alienated Victor Frankenstein with Faust and Satan but also in her cameo portrait of the Russian boat-master whom Walton employs. This character functions in the novel as a moral touchstone of disinterested sympathy from which to measure the fall of both Frankenstein and Walton. The master 'is a person of an excellent disposition, and is remarkable in the ship for his gentleness, and the mildness of his discipline' (p. 14). He is entirely altruistic. When the girl he had obtained permission to marry told him that she loved another man, he not only gave her up but bestowed his small fortune on his impoverished rival and then tried to persuade her father to consent to the love-match. When her father refused, thinking himself honour-bound to the sea-master, the master left Russia and refused to return until the girl had married her lover. But despite the master's noble character, Walton finds the master's sympathetic involvement in the communal life of the ship narrow and boring.

Walton is aware of his own emotional limitations. Throughout the novel, he desperately seeks a friend, some man who would 'participate my joy, ... sympathise with me, ... approve or amend my plans ... [and have] affection enough for me to endeavour to regulate my mind' (p. 13–14). Walton's desire is modelled directly on Godwin's Fleetwood, who also desperately sought a friend:

> I saw that I was alone, and I desired to have a friend, ... a friend ... whose kindness shall produce a conviction in my mind, that I do not stand alone in the world ... a friend, who is to me as another self, who joys in all my joys, and grieves in all my sorrows, not with a joy or grief that looks like compliment, not with a sympathy that changes into smiles when I am no longer present, though my head continues bent to the earth with anguish ... Friendship, in the sense in which I felt the want of it, has been truly said to be a sentiment that can grasp but one individual in its embrace.[32]

But Godwin's novel clearly demonstrates that Fleetwood's sentimental desire for a 'brother of my heart' masks a selfish need to possess the beloved entirely. His jealousy leads to a paranoic suspiciousness that destroys the only genuine friendship Fleetwood ever finds, that with his wife Mary Macneil. In contrast, Mary Macneil articulates an ideal of true friendship, a concept that Godwin had learned from Mary Wollstonecraft:

> I am not idle and thoughtless enough, to promise to sink my being and individuality in yours. I shall have distinct propensities and preferences ... In me you will have a wife, and not a passive machine. But, whenever a question occurs of reflection, of experience, of judgement, or of prudential consideration, I shall always listen to your wisdom with undissembled deference. In every thing indifferent, or that can be made so, I shall obey you with pleasure. And in

> return I am sure you will consider me as a being to be won with kindness, and not dictated to with the laconic phrase of authority.[33]

From the perspective provided by Godwin's *Fleetwood*, we can see that Walton's concept of friendship, which some have hailed as the positive moral value in the novel,[34] is badly flawed. Walton seeks an alter-ego, a mirror of his self who will reflect back his own joys and sorrows, adding only the wisdom that an older Walton would in time have discovered for himself. Rather than a relationship of genuine altruism and self-sacrifice, or a partnership of independent yet mutually supportive persons, Walton's concept of friendship is in fact another form of egoism. He is therefore given the friendship of his genuine alter-ego, Victor Frankenstein, a 'friendship' that, being none, is found only to be lost. As Walton laments, 'I have longed for a friend; I have sought one who would sympathise with and love me. Behold, on these desert seas I have found such a one; but, I fear, I have gained him only to know his value, and lose him' (p. 209).

Both Walton and Frankenstein devote their emotional energy not to empathic feelings or domestic affections but to egoistic dreams of conquering the boundaries of nature or of death. Not only have they diverted their libidinal desires away from normal erotic objects, but in the process they have engaged in a particular mode of thinking which we might call 'scientific'. Frankenstein and Walton are both the products of the scientific revolution of the seventeenth century. They have been taught to see nature 'objectively', as something separate from themselves, as passive and even dead matter – as the 'object of my affection' – that can and should be penetrated, analysed, and controlled. They thus accord nature no living soul or 'personhood' requiring recognition or respect.

Wordsworth had articulated the danger inherent in thinking of nature as something distinct from human consciousness. A reader of Wordsworth, Mary Shelley understood nature in his terms, as a sacred all-creating mother, a living organism or ecological community with which human beings interact in mutual dependence. To defy this bond, as both Frankenstein and Walton do, is to break one's ties with the source of life and health. Hence Frankenstein literally becomes sick in the process of carrying out his experiment: 'every night I was oppressed by a slow fever, and I became nervous to a most painful degree' (p. 51); and at its completion, he collapses in 'a nervous fever' that confines him to his sickbed for several months.

But Mary Shelley's critique of objective, rationalistic thought goes beyond Wordsworth's organicist notion that 'we murder to dissect'. Perhaps because she was a woman, she perceived that inherent in most scientific thought was a potent gender identification. Professor Waldman taught Frankenstein that scientists 'penetrate into the recesses of nature, and shew how *she* works in *her* hiding places' (p. 42, my emphasis). In Waldman's trope, nature is a passive female who can be penetrated in order to satisfy male desire. Waldman's metaphor is derived directly from the writings of the leading British scientists of the seventeenth and eighteenth centuries. Francis Bacon had heralded the seventeenth-centry scientific revolution as a calculated attempt to enslave female nature. Bacon's metaphor of a passive, possessable female nature strikingly altered the traditional image of nature as Dame Kind, an 'all-creating' and bounteous Mother Earth who singlehandedly bore and nourished her children. But it was Bacon's metaphor that structured most of the new scientific writing in England in the eighteenth century. Isaac Barrow, Newton's teacher, declared that the aim of the new philosophy was to 'search Nature out of her Concealments, and unfold her dark Mysteries',[35] while Robert Boyle noted contemptuously that 'some men care only to know Nature, others desire to command her'.[36] Henry Oldenburg, a future Secretary of the Royal Society, invoked Bacon to support his assertion that the 'true sons of learning' are those men who do not remain satisfied with the well-known truths but rather 'penetrate from Nature's antechamber to her inner closet'.[37] As Brian Easlea concludes, many seventeenth-century natural philosophers and their successors viewed the scientific quest as a virile masculine penetration into a passive female nature, a penetration that would, in Bacon's words, not merely exert a 'gentle guidance over nature's course' but rather 'conquer and subdue her' and even 'shake her to her foundations'.[38] This vision of nature was visually encoded in Ernest Barrias' large, bare-breasted female statue that in 1902 was placed at the entrance of the grand staircase of the Faculté de Médecine of the Université de Paris, bearing the inscription: 'LA NATURE SE DEVOILANT DEVANT LA SCIENCE'.

Caroline Merchant, Evelyn Fox Keller, and Brian Easlea have drawn our attention to the negative consequences of this identification of nature as the passive female.[39] Construing nature as the passive Other has led, as Merchant shows, to the increasing destruction of the environment and the disruption of the delicate ecological balance between humankind and nature. Moreover, as Keller has suggested in her studies of how the social construction of gender has affected the making of science, the professional scientific demand for 'objectivity' and detachment often masks an aggressive desire to dominate the female sex object. The result can be a dangerous division between what C. P. Snow called the 'two cultures', between the power-seeking practices of science and the concerns of humanists with moral responsibility, emotional communion, and spiritual values. The scientist who analyses, manipulates, and attempts to control nature unconsciously engages in a form of oppressive sexual politics. Construing nature as the female Other, he attempts to make nature serve his own ends, to gratify his own desires for power, wealth, and reputation.

Frankenstein's scientific project is clearly an attempt to gain power. Inspired by Waldman's description of scientists who 'acquired new and almost unlimited powers' (p. 42), Frankenstein has sought both the power of a father over his children, and, more omnipotently, of God over creation. More subtly, yet more pervasively, Frankenstein has sought power over the female. He has 'pursued nature to her hiding places' (p. 49) in an attempt not only to penetrate nature and show how her hidden womb works but actually to steal or appropriate that womb. To usurp the power of reproduction is to usurp the power of production as such. Marx identified childbirth as the primary example of pure, or unalienated, labour. Victor Frankenstein's enterprise can be viewed from a Marxist perspective as an attempt to exploit nature or labour in the service of a ruling class. Frankenstein wishes to harness the modes of reproduction in order to become the acknowledged, revered, and gratefully obeyed father of a new species. His project is thus identical with that of bourgeois capitalism: to exploit nature's resources for both commercial profit and political control.[40]

Among these resources are animal and human bodies. Collecting bones and flesh from charnel-houses, dissecting rooms, and slaughter-houses, Frankenstein sees these human and animal organs as nothing more than the tools of his trade, no different from his other scientific instruments. In this sense he is identical with the factory owner who gathers men, his disembodied 'hands' as Dickens's Bounderby would say, to manipulate his machines. We can therefore see Frankenstein's creature,[41] as Franco Moretti has suggested, as the proletariat, 'a *collective* and *artificial* creature',[41] dehumanised by the mechanised modes of technological production controlled by the industrial scientist and, in modern times, by the computer. Elizabeth Gaskell first identified Frankenstein's monster with the nineteenth-century British working-class in *Mary Barton* (1848):

> The actions of the educated seem to me typified in those of Frankenstein, that monster of many human qualities, ungifted with a soul, a knowledge of the difference between good and evil.
>
> The people rise up to life; they irritate us, they terrify us, and we become their enemies. Then, in the sorrowful moment of our triumphant power, their eyes gaze on us with a mute reproach. Why have we made them what they are; a powerful monster, yet without the inner means for peace and happiness?
>
> (ch. 15)

But this misshapen and alienated worker, Frankenstein's monster, has the power to destroy his maker, to seize the technology of production (the creature carries the creation in his pocket) and force it to serve his own ends.

In the second edition of the novel, Mary Shelley further identifies Frankenstein's capitalist project with the project of colonial imperialism. Clerval here announces his intention to join the East India Company:

> He came to the university with the design of making himself complete master of the oriental languages, as thus he should open a field for the plan of life he had marked out for himself. Resolved to pursue no inglorious career, he turned his eyes toward the East, as affording scope for his spirit of enterprise.
>
> (pp. 243–4)

Frankenstein's enthusiastic affirmation of Clerval's plan signals Mary Shelley's recognition of the expanding and increasingly dangerous degree of cultural and scientific control over the resources of nature, whether dead matter or living races. Her awareness of the similarity between Frankenstein's scientific enterprise and Clerval's imperialist project may have been triggered by the Parliamentary Debates on the slave trade in 1824. The foreign secretary and leader of the House of Commons, George Canning, in a speech opposing the freeing of the Negro slaves in the West Indies, explicitly identified the slaves with Frankenstein's monster:

> To turn [the Negro] loose in the manhood of his physical strength, in the maturity of his physical passions, but in the infancy of his uninstructed reason, would be to raise up a creature resembling the splendid fiction of a recent romance; the hero of which constructs a human form, with all the corporeal capabilities of man, and with the thews and sinews of a giant; but being unable to impart to the work of his hands a perception of right and wrong, he finds too late that he has only created a more than mortal power of doing mischief, and himself recoils from the monster which he has made.[42]

Writing during the early years of Britain's industrial revolution and the age of Empire, Mary Shelley was aware of the damaging consequences of a scientific, objective, alienated view of both nature and human labour. Uninhibited scientific and technological develpement, without a sense of moral responsibility for either the processes or products of these new modes of production, could easily, as in Frankenstein's case, produce monsters. A creature denied both parental love and peers; a working class denied access to meaningful work but condemned instead, in Ruskin's words, to make the same glass bead over and over; a colonised and degraded race: all are potential monsters, dehumanised by their uncaring employers and unable to feel the bonds of citizenship with the capitalist society in which they live. Moreover, these workers can become more powerful than their makers. As Frankenstein's creature asserts, 'You are my creator, but I am your master; – obey!' (p. 165), a prophecy whose fulfilment might take the form of bloody revolutions in which the oppressed overthrow their masters.

Even more important is Mary Shelley's implicit warning against the possible dangers inherent in the technological developments of modern science. Although we have not yet discovered Frankenstein's procedure for reanimating corpses, recent research in biochemistry – the discovery of DNA, the technique of gene-splicing, and the development of extra-uterine fertilisation – has brought us to the point where human beings are able to manipulate life-forms in ways previously reserved only to nature and chance. The replacement of natural childbirth by the mechanical eugenic control systems and baby-breeders envisioned in Aldous Huxley's *Brave New World* or Marge Piercy's *Woman on the Edge of Time* is now only a matter of time and social will. Worse by far, of course, is the contemporary proliferation of nuclear weapons systems resulting from the Los Alamos Project and the political decision to drop atomic bombs on Hiroshima and Nagasaki in 1945. As Jonathan Schell has so powerfully reminded us in *The Fate of the Earth*, as such docudramas as 'The Day After' (1983) and 'Threads' (1984) have starkly portrayed, a morally irresponsible scientific development has released a monster that can destroy human civilisation itself. As Frankenstein's monster proclaims, 'Remember that I have power; ... I can make you so wretched that the light of day will be hateful to you' (p. 165). Mary Shelley's tale of horror is no fantastical ghost story, but rather a profound insight into the probable consequences of 'objective' – gendered – or morally insensitive scientific and technological research.

From Anne K. Mellor, *Mary Shelley: Her Life, Her Fiction, Her Monsters* (London, 1988), pp. 89–114.

NOTES

[Anne Mellor's feminist literary criticism uncovers the gendered metaphors that are embedded in the scientific texts cited by Mary Shelley as influences on her novel. The argument centres on the way the female author resists the patriarchal imperatives of scientific discourse by presenting Victor Frankenstein in a critical light as one who disastrously partakes of its underlying masculine attempts to control, master and appropriate the power of feminine nature. The scientific transgression of natural laws is linked to a feminist critique by Shelley of the male Romantic imagination which, in its egocentricity, excludes all relationships and bonds with anything or anyone other than its own idealisations. In contrast, Mellor argues, the novel advocates a more evolutionary, sympathetic and understanding model of scientific practice. The book from which this chapter is taken addresses issues of politics, creativity, gender and culture and the novel in similarly feminist terms. Ed.]

1. Benjamin Farrington, trans., '"Temporis Partus Masculus": An Untranslated Writing of Francis Bacon,' *Centaurus*, I (1951), 197. For a full discussion of Bacon's use of gender metaphors, see Evelyn Fox Keller, *Reflections on Gender and Science* (New Haven and London, 1985), ch. 2. All references to *Frankenstein* will be to the 1818 edition: ed. James Rieger (New York, 1974; repr. Chicago, 1982).
2. A marginal note on the Thomas copy of the 1818 Frankenstein beside this passage, probably in Mary Shelley's own hand, comments 'you said your family was not scientific [sic]' (reported by James Rieger [ed.], *Frankenstein*, p. 35 n. 8).
3. On the importance of this introductory lecture to Humphry Davy's career, see Sir Harold Hartley, *Humphry Davy* (London, 1966), p. 41. Roger Sharrock has traced Davy's debt to William Wordsworth's 'Preface to *The Lyrical Ballads* of 1800' in 'The Chemist and the Poet:

Sir Humphry Davy and the Preface to the *Lyrical Ballads', Notes and Records of the Royal Society*, 17 (1962), 57.

4. *Mary Shelley's Journal*, ed. Frederick L. Jones (Norman, Oklahoma, 1947), p. 67; Laura Crouch has persuasively argued that the 'Discourse' is the book listed by Mary Shelley in her Journal under Books Read in 1816 as 'Introduction to Davy's Chemistry' ('Davy's *A Discourse, Introductory to a Course of Lectures on Chemistry*: A Possible Scientific Source of *Frankenstein,' Keats–Shelley Journal*, 27 [1978], 35–44). Mary Shelley would have known of Humphry Davy's work since childhood; she may even have been introduced to him when Davy dined with Godwin on 16 February 1801. See Samuel Holmes Vasbinder, 'Scientific Attitudes in Mary Shelley's *Frankenstein*: Newtonian Monism as a Base for the Novel', *DAI*, 37 (1976), 2842A (Kent State University).
5. *The Letters of Percy Shelley*, ed. Frederick L. Jones (Oxford, 1964), I:319.
6. Sir Humphry Davy, *A Discourse, Introductory to a Course of Lectures on Chemistry* (London, 1802), pp. 5–6. All further references to this edition are cited in the text.
7. Laura Crouch, 'Davy's *A Discourse*', p. 43.
8. Sir Humphry Davy, *Elements of Chemical Philosophy* (London, 1812), p. 58.
9. Erasmus Darwin, *The Botanic Garden* (London, Part I: 'The Economy of Vegetation,' 1791; Part II: 'The Loves of the Plants,' 1789); *Zoonomia: or The Laws of Organic Life* (London, 1794; third 'Corrected' edition, 1801); *Phytologia: or the Philosophy of Agriculture and Gardening* (London, 1800); *The Temple of Nature* (London, 1803). All further references to these editions are cited in the text.
10. See Loren Eiseley, *Darwin's Century: Evolution and the Men Who Discovered It* (Garden City, NJ, 1958), chs 1 and 2; and Ernst Mayr, *The Growth of Biological Thought: Diversity, Evolution, and Inheritance* (Cambridge, 1982), pp. 301–41, for excellent summaries of pre-evolutionary and early evolutionary theories.
11. Mayr, *Growth of Biological Thought*, p. 335.
12. Mayr, *Growth of Biological Thought*, pp. 329–37.
13. Percy Shelley also read Buffon attentively. In his journal letter to Peacock of 23 July 1816, Shelley alludes to the first volume of Buffon's work, *La Théorie de la terre*, in the course of describing the glaciers of Mont Blanc: 'I will not pursue Buffons sublime but gloomy theory, that this earth which we inhabit will at some future period be changed into a mass of frost' (*Letters of Percy Shelley*, ed. Frederick L. Jones, I:499).

14. Desmond King-Hele, *Erasmus Darwin* (London, 1963), p. 3.

15. *Letters of Percy Shelley*, ed. Frederick L. Jones, I:129, 342, 345.

16. For Erasmus Darwin's influence on Percy Shelley's thought and poetry, see Carl Grabo, *A Newton among Poets – Shelley's Use of Science in 'Prometheus Unbound'* (Chapel Hill, 1930), pp. 22–74; Desmond King-Hele, *Erasmus Darwin*, pp. 144–51, and *Shelley – His Thought and Work* (London, 1960), pp. 162–4; Kenneth Neill Cameron, *The Young Shelley – Genesis of a Radical* (London, 1951), pp. 121, 240; and Robert M. Maniquis, 'The Puzzling *Mimosa*: Sensitivity and Plant Symbols in Romanticism', *Studies in Romanticism*, 8 (1969), 129–55.

17. Erasmus Darwin discusses this process in *The Temple of Nature*, Additional Note 1: 'Spontaneous Vitality of Miscroscopic Animals', pp. 1–11.

18. Adam Walker, *A System of Familiar Philosophy* (London, 1799), p. 391.

19. Richard Holmes, *Shelley – The Pursuit* (New York, 1975), pp. 150, 344.

20. Luigi Galvani, *De Viribus Electricitatis in Motui Musculari. Commentarius* (Bologna, 1791); *Commentary on the Effects of Electricity on Muscular Motion*, trans. M. G. Foley, with notes and Introduction by I. Bernard Cohen (Norwalk, Conn., 1953).

21. Giovanni Aldini, *An Account of the Late Improvements in Galvanism, with a series of Curious and Interesting Experiments performed before the Commissioners of the French National Institute and repeated lately in the Anatomical Theatres of London; to which is added, An Appendix, containing the author's Experiments on the Body of a Malefactor executed at New Gate* (London, 1803), p. 54. This book is an English translation of the original French text, *Essay Théorique et Expérimentale sur le Galvanisme* published in Paris in 1802 and translated into German by F. H. Martens and published at Leipzig in 1804.

22. Aldini, *Galvanism*, p. 193.

23. Aldini, *Galvanism*, pp. 195, 194, 194.

24. These results are reported by Paul Fleury Mottelay, in his *Bibliographical History of Electricity and Magnetism* (London, 1922), which gives a complete set of references to Aldini's experiments, pp. 305–7.

25. Reported by Dr Giulio in Aldini, *Galvanism*, pp. 204–8.

26. See F. H. A. Humbold, *Sur Galvanisme*, trans. J. F. N. Jadelot (Paris, 1799); Edmund Joseph Schmück, 'On the action of galvanic electricity on the *mimosa pudica*,' cited in Mottelay, *Bibliographical History of Electricity*, p. 332; C.J.C. Grapengieser, *Versuche den Galvanismus*

(Berlin, 1801, 1802); and Johann Caspar Creve, *Beiträge zu Galvanis versuchen* (Frankfurt and Leipzig, 1793).

27. See Paul Mottelay, *Bibliographical History of Electricity*, pp. 402–4.

28. Erasmus Darwin, *The Botanic Garden*, Part I, p. 463.

29. Charles Henry Wilkinson, *Elements of Galvanism in Theory and Practice*, 2 vols (London, 1804), pp. 269–70. Wilkinson's treatise is heavily dependent upon the earlier dissertations on the subject of galvanism prepared by Johann C. L. Reinhold for his medical degree at Magdeburg in 1797 and 1798.

30. Brian W. Aldiss, *Billion Year Spree – The History of Science Fiction* (London, 1973), p. 8. Cf. Robert Scholes and Eric S. Rabkin, *Science Fiction: History, Science, Vision* (New York, 1977), p. 38. Aldiss, Scholes and Rabkin concur that *Frankenstein* is the first legitimate example of science fiction. For an analysis of the way *Frankenstein* has been misread by male science-fiction writers, see Judith A. Spector, 'Science Fiction and the Sex War: A Womb of One's Own', *Literature and Psychology*, 31 (1981), 21–32.

31. Evelyn Fox Keller, 'Gender and Science', *Psychoanalysis and Contemporary Thought*, I (1978), 409–33; see also her *Reflections on Gender and Science*, ch. 4.

32. William Godwin, *Fleetwood or, the New Man of Feeling*, 3 vols, (London, 1805; repr. New York and London, 1979), II: 143–5.

33. William Godwin, *Fleetwood*, II: 278–9.

34. See, for example, Robert Kiely, *The Romantic Novel in England* (Cambridge, 1972), p. 166.

35. Isaac Barrow, *The Usefulness of Mathematical Learning Explained and Demonstrated* (London, 1734; repr. 1970), pp. xxix–xxx.

36. Robert Boyle, *The Works of Robert Boyle*, ed. Thomas Birch, 6 vols (London, 1772), I:310.

37. Henry Oldenburg, *The Correspondence of Henry Oldenburg*, ed. A. R. Hall and M. B. Hall (Madison, 1965), I:113.

38. Francis Bacon, *The Works of Francis Bacon*, ed. J. Spedding, R. L. Ellis, and D. N. Heath (new edn, 1879–90; Facsimile, Stuttgart-Bad Cannstatt, 1962, 7 vols), II:42, 373. For a discussion of the sexual metaphors utilised in much seventeenth- and eighteenth-century English scientific writing, see Brian Easlea, *Science and Sexual Oppression – Patriarchy's Confrontation with Woman and Nature* (London, 1981), p. 86; chs 3, 4, 5.

39. Caroline Merchant, *The Death of Nature: Women, Ecology and the Scientific Revolution* (San Francisco, 1980); see also Evelyn Fox Keller,

Reflections on Gender and Science, chs 4–9; and Brian Easlea, *Science and Sexual Oppression*.

40. As Caroline Merchant concludes, 'The removal of animistic, organic assumptions about the cosmos constituted the death of nature – the most far-reaching effect of the Scientific Revolution. Because nature was now viewed as a system of dead, inert particles moved by external, rather than inherent forces, the mechanical framework itself could legitimate the manipulation of nature. Moreover, as a conceptual framework, the mechanical order had associated with it a framework of values based on power, fully compatible with the directions taken by commercial capitalism' (*The Death of Nature*, p. 193).
    For a useful study of the way *Frankenstein* condemns bourgeois patriarchy and the concept of male motherhood, see Burton Hatlen, 'Milton, Mary Shelley and Patriarchy', in *Rhetoric, Literature and Interpretation*, ed. Harry R. Garvin (Lewisburg, Pa, 1983), pp. 19–47.

41. Franco Moretti, *Signs Taken for Wonders – Essays in the Sociology of Literary Form*, trans. S. Fischer, D. Forgacs, and D. Miller (London, 1983), p. 85.

42. George Canning, 'Ameliorization of the Condition of the Slave Population in the West Indies (House of Lords)', [Hansard's] *Parliamentary Debates*, n. s. 10 (16 March 1824), cols. 1046–1198 [1103].

6

Bearing Demons: Frankenstein's Circumvention of the Maternal

MARGARET HOMANS

Married to one romantic poet and living near another, Mary Shelley at the time she was writing *Frankenstein* experienced with great intensity the self-contradictory demand that daughters embody both the mother whose death makes language possible by making it necessary and the figurative substitutes for that mother who constitute the prototype of the signifying chain. At the same time, as a mother herself, she experienced with great intensity a proto-Victorian ideology of motherhood, as Mary Poovey has shown.[1] This experience leads Shelley both to figure her writing as mothering and to bear or transmit the words of her husband.[2] Thus Shelley not only practises the daughter's obligatory and voluntary identification with the literal, as do Dorothy Woodsworth and Charlotte and Emily Brontë, but she also shares with George Eliot and Elizabeth Gaskell (and again with Charlotte Brontë) their concern with writing as literalisation, as a form of mothering. It is to Shelley's handling of these contradictory demands, and to her criticism of their effect on women's writing, that my reading of *Frankenstein* will turn.

Frankenstein portrays the situation of women obliged to play the role of the literal in a culture that devalues it. In this sense, the novel is simultaneously about the death and obviation of the mother and about the son's quest for a substitute object of desire. The novel criticises the self-contradictory male requirement that that substitute at once embody and not embody (because all embodiment is a reminder of the mother's powerful and forbidden body) the object of desire. The horror of the demon that Frankenstein creates is that it is the literalisation of its creator's desire for an object, a desire that never really seeks its own fulfilment.

Many readers of *Frankenstein* have noted both that the demon's creation amounts to an elaborate circumvention of normal heterosexual procreation – Frankenstein does by himself with great difficulty what a heterosexual couple can do quite easily – and that each actual mother dies very rapidly upon being introduced as a character in the novel.[3] Frankenstein's own history is full of the deaths of mothers. His mother was discovered, as a poverty-stricken orphan, by Frankenstein's father. Frankenstein's adoptive sister and later fiancée, Elizabeth, was likewise discovered as an orphan, in poverty, by Frankenstein's parents.[4] Elizabeth catches scarlet fever, and her adoptive mother, nursing her, catches it herself and dies of it. On her deathbed, the mother hopes for the marriage of Elizabeth and Frankenstein and tells Elizabeth, 'You must supply my place to my younger children' (ch. 3). Like Shelley herself, Elizabeth is the death of her mother and becomes a substitute for her. Justine, a young girl taken in by the Frankenstein family as a beloved servant, is said to cause the death of her mother; and Justine herself, acting as foster mother to Frankenstein's little brother, William, is executed for his murder. There are many mothers in the Frankenstein circle, and all die notable deaths.

The significance of the apparently necessary destruction of the mother first emerges in Frankenstein's account of his preparations for creating the demon, and it is confirmed soon after the demon comes to life. Of his early passion for science, Frankenstein says, 'I was ... deeply smitten with the thirst for knowledge' (ch. 2). Shelley confirms the Oedipal suggestion here when she writes that it is despite his father's prohibition that the young boy devours the archaic books on natural philosophy that first raise his ambitions to discover the secret of life. His mother dies just as Frankenstein is preparing to go to the University of Ingolstadt, and if his postponed trip there is thus motivated by her death, what he finds at the university becomes a substitute for her: modern scientists, he is told, 'penetrate into the recesses of nature and show how she works in her hiding-places' (ch. 3). Frankenstein's double, Walton, the polar explorer who rescues him and records his story, likewise searches for what sound like sexual secrets, also in violation of a paternal prohibition. Seeking to 'satiate [his] ardent curiosity', Walton hopes to find the 'wondrous power which attracts the needle' (letter 1). Frankenstein, having become 'capable of bestowing animation upon lifeless matter', feels that to arrive 'at once at the summit of my desires was the most gratifying consummation of my toils'. And his work to create the demon adds to this sense of an Oedipal violation of Mother Nature: dabbling 'among the unhallowed damps of the grave', he 'disturbed, with profane fingers, the tremendous secrets of the human frame' (ch. 4). This violation is necrophiliac. The mother he rapes is dead; his researches into her secrets, to usurp her powers, require that she be dead.[5]

Frankenstein describes his violation of nature in other ways that recall what William Wordsworth's poetry reveals when read in conjunction with Dorothy Wordsworth's journals. Of the period during which he is working on the demon, Frankenstein writes,

> The summer months passed while I was thus engaged, heart and soul, in one pursuit. It was a most beautiful season; never did the fields bestow a more plentiful harvest or the vines yield a more luxuriant vintage, but my eyes were insensible to the charms of nature .... Winter, spring and summer passed away during my labours; but I did not watch the blossom or the expanding leaves – sights which before always yielded me supreme delight – so deeply was I engrossed in my occupation.
>
> (ch. 4)

Ignoring the bounteous offering nature makes of itself and substituting for it his own construction of life, what we, following Thomas Weiskel, might call his own reading of nature, Frankenstein here resembles William Wordsworth, reluctantly and ambivalently allowing himself to read nature, to impose on nature apocalyptic patterns of meaning that destroy it. Dorothy Wordsworth herself makes an appearance in the text of *Frankenstein*, if indirectly, and her presence encodes a shared women's critique of the romantic reading of nature. Much later in the novel, Frankenstein compares his friend Clerval to the former self William Wordsworth depicts in 'Tintern Abbey', a self that he has outgrown but that his sister retains. Shelley quotes (with one major alteration) the lines beginning, 'The sounding cataract / Haunted him like a passion' and ending with the assertion that the colours and forms of natural objects (rock, mountain, etc.) were

> a feeling, and a love,
> That had no need of a remoter charm,
> By thought supplied, or any interest
> Unborrow'd from the eye.[6]

If Clerval is like Dorothy, then Frankenstein is like William, regrettably destroying nature by imposing his reading on it.

When, assembled from the corpse of nature, the demon has been brought to life and Frankenstein has recognised – oddly only now that is alive – how hideous it is, Frankenstein falls into an exhausted sleep and dreams the following dream:

> I thought I saw Elizabeth, in the bloom of health, walking in the streets of Ingolstadt. Delighted and surprised, I embraced her, but as I imprinted the first kiss on her lips, they became livid with the hue of death; her features appeared to change, and I thought that I held the corpse of my dead mother in my arms; a shroud enveloped her form, and I saw the grave-worms crawling in the folds of the flannel. I started from my sleep with horror.
>
> (ch. 5)

He wakes to see the demon looking at him, hideous, but clearly loving. The dream suggests that to bring the demon to life is equivalent to killing Elizabeth, and that Elizabeth dead is equivalent to his mother dead. Elizabeth may have been the death of the mother, but now that she has replaced her, she too is vulnerable to whatever destroys mothers.[7] And, indeed, the dream is prophetic: the demon will much later kill Elizabeth, just as the demon's creation has required both the death of Frankenstein's own mother and the death and violation of Mother Nature. To bring a composite corpse to life is to circumvent the normal channels of procreation; the demon's 'birth' violates the normal relations of family, especially the normal sexual relation of husband and wife. Victor has gone to great lengths to produce a child without Elizabeth's assistance, and in the dream's language, to circumvent her, to make her unnecessary, is to kill her, and to kill mothers altogether.

Frankenstein's creation, then, depends on and then perpetuates the death of the mother and of motherhood. The demon's final, and greatest, crime is in fact its murder of Elizabeth, which is, however, only the logical extension of its existence as the reification of

Frankenstein's desire to escape the mother. The demon is, to borrow a phrase from Shelley's *Alastor*, 'the spirit of' Frankenstein's 'solitude'. Its greatest complaint to Frankenstein is of its own solitude, its isolation from humanity, and it promises that if Frankenstein will make it a mate, 'one as hideous as myself.... I shall become a thing of whose existence everyone will be ignorant' (ch. 17). That is, no longer solitary, the demon will virtually cease to exist, for its existence is synonymous with its solitude. But, on the grounds that 'a race of devils would be propagated upon the earth', Frankenstein destroys the female demon he is in the process of creating, thus destroying yet another potential mother, and the demon promises, 'I shall be with you on your wedding-night' (ch. 20). If the demon is the form taken by Frankenstein's flight from the mother, then it is impossible that the demon should itself find an embodied substitute for the mother, and it will prevent Frankenstein from finding one too.

The demon's promise to be present at the wedding night suggests that there is something monstrous about Frankenstein's sexuality. A solipsist's sexuality is monstrous because his desire is for his own envisionings rather than for somebody else, some other body. The demon appears where Frankenstein's wife should be, and its murder of her suggests not so much revenge as jealousy. The demon's murder of that last remaining potential mother makes explicit the sequel to the obviation of the mother, the male quest for substitutes for the mother, the quest that is never intended to be fulfilled. Elizabeth suggests in a letter to Frankenstein that his reluctance to marry may stem from his love for someone else, someone met, perhaps, in his travels or during his long stay in Ingolstadt. 'Do you not love another?' she asks (ch. 22). This is in fact the case, for the demon, the creation of Frankenstein's imagination, resembles in many ways the romantic object of desire, the beloved invented to replace, in a less threatening form, the powerful mother who must be killed.[8] This imagined being would be an image of the self, because it is for the sake of the ego that the mother is rejected in the first place. Created right after the death of the mother to be, as Victor says, 'a being like myself' (ch. 4), the demon may be Adam, created in God's image. Indeed, this is what the demon thinks when it tells Frankenstein, 'I ought to be thy Adam, but I am rather the fallen angel' (ch. 10). But it is also possible, as Gilbert and Gubar suggest, that the demon is Eve, created from Adam's imagination.[9]

When the demon takes shelter in the French cottager's shed, it looks, repeating Milton's Eve's first act upon coming to life, into the mirror of a 'clear pool' and is terrified at its own reflection: 'I started back' (ch. 12). Here is the relevant passage from Milton, from Eve's narration in book 4 of her memory of the first moments of her creation.[10] Hearing the 'murmuring sound / Of waters issu'd from a Cave and spread / Into a liquid Plain', Eve looks

> into the clear
> Smooth Lake, that to me seem'd another Sky.
> As I bent down to look, just opposite,
> A Shape within the wat'ry gleam appear'd
> Bending to look on me, I started back,
> It started back, but pleas'd I soon return'd ...
> (4.ll.453–63)

But the disembodied voice instructs her, 'What there thou seest fair Creature is thyself' (l.468), and tells her to follow and learn to prefer him 'whose image thou art' (ll.471–2). Christine Froula argues that the fiction of Eve's creation by a paternal God out of the flesh of Adam values the maternal and appropriates it for the aggrandisement of masculine creativity.[11] Frankenstein revises this paradigm for artistic creation: he does not so much appropriate the maternal as bypass it, to demonstrate the unnecessariness of natural motherhood and, indeed, of women. Froula points out that in this 'scene of canonical instruction', Eve is required to turn away from herself to embrace her new identity, not as a self, but as the image of someone else.[12] Created to the specifications of Adam's desire, we later learn – 'Thy likeness, thy fit help, thy other self, / Thy wish, exactly to thy heart's desire' (8.ll.450–1) – Eve is, like Frankenstein's demon, the product of imaginative desire. Milton appropriates the maternal by excluding any actual mother from the scene of creation. Eve is the form that Adam's desire takes once actual motherhood has been eliminated; and in much the same way, the demon is the form taken by Frankenstein's desire once his mother and Elizabeth as mother have been circumvented. These new creations in the image of the self are substitutes for the powerful creating mother and place creation under the control of the son.

That the demon is, like Eve, the creation of a son's imaginative desire is confirmed by another allusion both closer to Shelley and closer in the text to Elizabeth's question, 'Do you not love another?' Mary Poovey has argued that the novel criticises romantic egotism, specifically, Percy Shelley's violation of the social conventions that bind humans together in families and societies. As the object of desire of an imaginative overreacher very like Percy Shelley himself, the demon substitutes for the fruitful interchange of family life the fruitlessness of self love, for what Frankenstein loves is an image of himself. The novel was written when Percy Shelley had completed, of all his major works besides *Queen Mab*, only *Alastor*, the archetypal poem of the doomed romantic quest, and it is to this poem that Mary Shelley alludes.[13] Just before Frankenstein receives Elizabeth's letter, just after being acquitted of the murder of his friend Clerval, Frankenstein tells us, 'I saw around me nothing but a dense and frightful darkness, penetrated by no light but the glimmer of two eyes that glared upon me' (ch. 21). This is a direct allusion to a passage in *Alastor* in which the hero, who has quested in vain after an ideal female image of his own creation, sees

> two eyes,
> Two starry eyes, hung in the gloom of thought,
> And seemed with their serene and azure smiles
> To beckon him.
>
> (ll.489–92)

In *Alastor*, these eyes belong to the phantom maiden, the 'fleeting shade' whom the hero pursues to his death, a beloved who is constructed out of the poet's own visionary narcissism. The girl he dreams and pursues has a voice 'like the voice of his own soul / Heard in the calm of thought' (ll.153–4), and like him, she is 'Herself a poet' (l.161). In the novel, the starry eyes become glimmering, glaring eyes, alternately the eyes of the dead Clerval and the 'watery, clouded eyes of the monster, as I first saw them in my chamber at Ingolstadt' (ch. 21). This conflation of the eyes of the poet's beloved with the eyes of the demon suggests, even more surely than the allusion to Eve, that the demon is the form, not only of Frankenstein's solipsism, of his need to obviate the mother, but also of the narcissism that constitutes the safety of the ego for whose sake the mother is denied. The monster is still the object of Frankenstein's desire when Elizabeth writes to him, just as its creation was the object of his initial quest.[14] It is this monster, the monster of narcissism, that intervenes on the wedding night, substituting Frankenstein's desire for his own imagining for the consummation of his marriage, just as the visionary maiden in *Alastor* takes the place both of the dead Mother Nature of the poet's prologue and of the real maiden the hero meets, attracts, and rejects in the course of his quest.

That the demon is a revision of Eve, of emanations, and of the object of romantic desire, is confirmed by its female attributes. Its very bodiliness, its identification with matter, associates it with traditional concepts of femaleness. Further, the impossibility of Frankenstein giving it a female demon, an object of its own desire, aligns the demon with women, who are forbidden to have their own desires. But if the demon is really a feminine object of desire, why is it a he? I would suggest that this constitutes part of Shelley's exposure of the male romantic economy that would substitute for real and therefore powerful female others a being imagined on the model of the male poet's own self. By making the demon masculine, Shelley suggests that romantic desire seeks to do away, not only with the mother, but also with all females so as to live finally in a world of mirrors that reflect a comforting illusion of the male self's independent wholeness. It is worth noting that just as Frankenstein's desire is for a male demon, Walton too yearns, not for a bride, but for 'the company of a man who could sympathise with me, whose eyes would reply to mine' (letter 2).[15]

It may seem peculiar to describe the demon as the object of Frankenstein's romantic desire, since he spends most of the novel suffering from the demon's crimes. Yet in addition to the allusions to Eve and the 'fleeting shade' in *Alastor* that suggest this, it is clear that while Frankenstein is in the process of creating the demon, he loves it and desires it; the knowledge that makes possible its creation is the 'consummation' of his 'toils'. It is only when the demon becomes animated that Frankenstein abruptly discovers his loathing for his creation. Even though the demon looks at its creator with what appears to be love, Frankenstein's response to it is unequivocal loathing. Why had he never noticed before the hideousness of its shape and features? No adequate account is given, nor could be, for as we shall see, this is what most mystifies and horrifies Shelley about her own situation. Frankenstein confesses, 'I had desired it with an ardour that far exceeded moderation; but now that I had finished, the beauty of the dream vanished, and breathless horror and disgust filled my heart' (ch. 5). The romantic quest is always doomed, for it secretly resists its own fulfilment: although the hero of *Alastor* quests for his dream maiden and dies of not finding her, his encounter with the Indian maid makes it clear that embodiment is itself an obstacle to desire, or more precisely, its termination.

Frankenstein's desire for his creation lasts only so long as that creation remains uncreated, the substitution for the too-powerful mother of a figure issuing from his imagination and therefore under his control.

We might say that the predicament of Frankenstein, as of the hero of *Alastor*, is that of the son in Lacan's revision of the Freudian Oedipal crisis. In flight from the body of the mother forbidden by the father, a maternal body that he sees as dead in his urgency to escape it and to enter a paternal order constituted of its distance from the mother, the son seeks figurations that will at once make restitution for the mother and confirm her death and absence by substituting for her figures that are under his control. Fundamentally, the son cannot wish for these figurative substitutes to be embodied, for any *body* is too reminiscent of the mother and is no longer under the son's control, as the demon's excessive strength demonstrates; the value of these figurations is that they remain figurations. In just this way, romantic desire does not desire to be fulfilled, and yet, because it seems both to itself, and to others to want to be embodied, the romantic quester as son is often confronted with a body he seems to want but does not.[16] Thus Frankenstein thinks he wants to create the demon, but when he has succeeded, he discovers that what he really enjoyed was the process leading up to the creation, the seemingly endless chain of signifiers that constitute his true, if unrecognised, desire.

Looking at *Alastor* through *Frankenstein*'s reading of it, then, we see that the novel is the story of a hypothetical case: what if the hero of *Alastor* actually got what he thinks he wants? What if desire were embodied, contrary to the poet's deepest wishes? That Shelley writes such a case suggests that this was her own predicament. In real life, Percy Shelley pursued her as the poet and hero of *Alastor* pursue ghosts and as Frankenstein pursues the secrets of the grave. That he courted the adolescent Mary Godwin at the grave of her mother, whose writing he admired, already suggests that the daughter was for him a figure for the safely dead mother, a younger and less powerfully creative version of her. Yet when he got this substitute, he began to tire of her, as he makes quite explicit in *Epipsychidion*, where he is not embarrassed to describe his life in terms of an interminable quest for an imaginary woman. Mary starts out in that poem as one 'who seemed / As like the glorious shape which I had dreamed' (ll. 277–8) but soon becomes 'that Moon' with 'pale and waning lips' (l. 309). The poet does not seem to notice that each time an embodiment of the ideal turns out to be unsatisfactory, it is not because she is the wrong woman, but because the very fact of the embodiment inevitably spoils the vision. Emily, the final term in the poem's sequence of women, remains ideal only because she has not yet been possessed, and indeed at the end of the poem, the poet disintegrates and disembodies her, perhaps to save himself from yet one more disappointment. Shelley was for herself never anything but embodied, but for Percy Shelley it seems to have been a grave disappointment to discover her substantiality, and therefore her inadequacy for fulfilling his visionary requirements. *Frankenstein* is the story of what it feels like to be the undesired embodiment of romantic imaginative desire. The demon, rejected merely for being a body, suffers in something of the way that Shelley must have felt herself to suffer under the conflicting demands of romantic desire: on the one hand, that she must embody the goal of Percy's quest, and on the other, his rejection of that embodiment.

Later in the novel, when the demon describes to Frankenstein its discovery and reading of the 'journal of the four months that preceded my creation', the discrepancy between Percy's conflicting demands is brought to the fore. The demon notes that the journal records 'the whole detail of that series of disgusting circumstances' that resulted in 'my accursed origins', and that 'the minutest description of my odious and loathsome person is given, in language which painted your own horrors and rendered mine indelible' (ch. 15). This summary suggests that while Frankenstein was writing the journal during the period leading up to the demon's vivification, he was fully aware of his creature's hideousness. Yet Frankenstein, in his own account of the same period, specifically says that it was only when 'I had finished, the beauty of the dream vanished, and breathless horror and disgust filled my heart' (ch. 5). If Frankenstein is right about his feelings here, why should his journal be full of 'language which painted [his] horrors'? Or, if the account in the journal is correct, if Frankenstein was aware from the start of his creature's 'odious and loathsome person', why does he tell Walton that the demons appeared hideous to him only upon its awakening? If the text of this journal is, like *Alastor*, the record of a romantic quest for an object of desire, then the novel is presenting us with two conflicting readings of the poem – Frankenstein's or Percy's and the demon's or Shelley's – confirming our sense that Shelley reading *Alastor* finds in it the story of Percy's failure to find in her the object of his desire, or the story of his desire not to find the object of his desire, not to find that she is the object.

A famous anecdote about the Shelleys from a few days after the beginning of the ghost story contest in which *Frankenstein* originated lends support to this impression of Shelley's experience. Byron was reciting some lines from Coleridge's *Christabel* about Geraldine, who is, like the demon, a composite body, half young and beautiful, half (in the version Byron recited) 'hideous, deformed, and pale of hue'. Percy, 'suddenly shrieking and putting his hands to his head, ran out of the room with a candle'. Brought to his senses, he told Byron and Polidori that 'he was looking at Mrs Shelley' while Byron was repeating Coleridge's lines, 'and suddenly thought of a woman he had heard of who had eyes instead of nipples'.[17] If disembodied eyes are, in *Alastor*, what are so alluring to the hero about his beloved, eyes in place of nipples may have been Percy's hallucination of the horror of having those ideal eyes re-embodied in the form of his real lover. This is an embodiment that furthermore calls attention to its failure to be sufficiently different from the mother, whose nipples are for the baby so important a feature. An actual woman, who is herself a mother, does not fit the ideal of disembodied femininity, and the vision of combining real and ideal is a monster. Mary's sense of herself viewed as a collection of incongruent body parts – breasts terminating in eyes – might have found expression in the demon, whose undesirable corporeality is expressed as its being composed likewise of ill-fitting parts. *Paradise Lost*, *Alastor*, and other texts in this tradition compel women readers to wish to embody, as Eve does, imaginary ideals, to be glad of this role in masculine life; and yet at the same time, they warn women readers that they will suffer for such embodiment.

It requires only a transposing of terms to suggest the relevance of this reading of *Frankenstein* to the myth of language in its form as the romantic quest. The demon is about the ambivalent response of a woman reader to some of our culture's most compelling statements of woman's place in the myth. That the mother must vanish and be replaced by never quite embodied figures for her is equivalent to the vanishing of the referent (along with that time with the mother when the referent had not vanished) to be replaced by language as figuration that never quite touches its objects. Women's role is to be that silent or lost referent, the literal whose absence makes figuration possible. To be also the figurative substitute for that lost referent is, Shelley shows, impossible, for women are constantly reminded that they are the mother's (loathed, loved) body, and in any case, 'being' is incompatible with being a figure. The literal provokes horror in the male poet, or scientist, even while he demands that women literalise his vision.

That Shelley knew she was writing a criticism, not only of women's self-contradictory role in androcentric ontology, but also of the gendered myth of language that is part of that ontology, is suggested by the appearance of a series of images of writing at the very end of the novel. Once again, the demon is the object of Frankenstein's quest, pursued now in hate rather than in love. Frankenstein is preternaturally motivated in his quest by an energy of desire that recalls his passion when first creating the demon, and that his present quest depends on the killing of animals recalls his first quest's dependence on dead bodies. Frankenstein believes that 'a spirit of good' follows and directs his steps: 'Sometimes, when nature, overcome by hunger, sank under the exhaustion, a repast was prepared for me in the desert that restored and inspirited me .... I will not doubt that it was set there by the spirits that I had invoked to aid me' (ch. 24). He says this, however, directly after pointing out that the demon sometimes helped him. Fearing 'that if I lost all trace of him I should despair and die, [he] left some mark to guide me', and Frankenstein also notes that the demon would frequently leave 'marks in writing on the barks of the trees or cut in stone that guided me and instigated my fury'. One of these messages includes the information, 'You will find near this place, if you follow not too tardily, a dead hare; eat and be refreshed'. Frankenstein, it would seem, deliberately misinterprets the demon's guidance and provisions for him as belonging instead to a spirit of good: his interpretation of the demon's marks and words is so figurative as to be opposite to what they really say. The demon, all body, writes appropriately on the body of nature messages that refer, if to objects at a distance, at least at not a very great distance ('you will find near this place ...'). Frankenstein, however, reads as figuratively as possible, putting as great a distance as possible between what he actually reads and what he interprets. His reading furthermore puts a distance between himself and the object of his quest, which he still cannot desire to attain; figurative reading would extend indefinitely the pleasure of the quest itself by forever putting off the moment of capture. Just at the moment when Frankenstein thinks he is about to reach the demon, the demon is transformed from a 'mark', as if a mark on a page, into a 'form', and Frankenstein seeks to reverse this transformation. One of Frankenstein's sled dogs has died of exhaustion, delaying him, 'suddenly my eye caught a dark speck upon the dusky plain'; he utters 'a wild cry of ecstasy' upon 'distinguish[ing) a sledge and the distorted proportions of a well-known form within' (ch. 24). Frankenstein's response, however, is to take an hour's rest: his real aim, which he does not admit, is to keep the demon at the distance where he remains a 'dark speck', a mark on the white page of the snow, his signification forever deferred.[18]

At the same time that *Frankenstein* is about a woman writer's response to the ambiguous imperative her culture imposes upon her, it is also possible that the novel concerns a woman writer's anxieties about bearing children, about generating bodies that would have the power to displace or kill the parent. Ellen Moers first opened up a feminist line of inquiry into the novel by suggesting that it is a 'birth myth', that the horror of the demon is Shelley's horror, not only at her own depressing experience of childbirth, but also at her knowledge of the disastrous consequences of giving birth (or of pregnancy itself) for many women in her vicinity.[19] The list is by now familiar to Shelley's readers. First, Mary Wollstonecraft died eleven days after she gave birth to Mary; then, during the time of the writing of the novel, Fanny Imlay, Mary's half-sister, drowned herself in October 1816 when she learned that she was her mother's illegitimate child by Gilbert Imlay; Harriet Shelley was pregnant by another man when she drowned herself in the Serpentine in December 1816; and Claire Clairmont, the daughter of the second Mrs Godwin, was, scandalously, pregnant by Byron, much to the embarrassment of the Shelleys, with whom she lived.[20] Illegitimate pregnancy, that is, a pregnancy over which the woman has particularly little control, brings either death to the mother in childbirth (Wollstonecraft) or shame, making visible what ought to have remained out of sight, the scene of conception (Claire), a shame that can itself result in the death of both mother (Harriet Shelley) and child (Fanny).

At the time of the conception of the novel, Mary Godwin had herself borne two illegitimate children: the first, an unnamed girl, died four days later, in March 1815; the second was five months old. In December 1816, when Harriet Shelley died and Shelley had finished chapter 4 of the novel, she was pregnant again. With but a single parent, the demon in her novel is the world's most monstrously illegitimate child, and this illegitimate child causes the death of that parent as well as of the principle of motherhood, as we have seen. Read in connection with the history of disastrous illegitimacies, the novel's logic would seem to be this: to give birth to an illegitimate child is monstrous, for it is the inexorable life of these babies, especially those of Mary Wollstonecraft and of Harriet Shelley, that destroys the life of the mother. Subsequently, as Marc Rubenstein argues, the guilty daughter pays for the destruction of her own mother in a fantasy of being destroyed by her own child.[21]

Once a conception has taken objective form, it has the power to destroy its own source, to transform the mother herself into the literal. In the Brontës' novels, childbirth is structurally equivalent to (and indeed also often situated in) the coming true of dreams, which has, like childbirth, an ironic relation to the original conception. Shelley's 1831 introduction to her novel makes a comparable equation of giving birth, the realisation of a dream, and writing. As many readers have pointed out, this introduction to her revised version of the novel identifies the novel itself with the demon, and both with a child.[22] She tells of being asked every morning if she had thought of a story, as if a story, like a baby, were necessarily to be conceived in the privacy of the night. And at the close of the introduction she writes, 'I bid my hideous progeny go forth and prosper', and she refers to the novel in the next sentence as 'the offspring of happy days'. The genesis of the novel, furthermore, is in a dream that she transcribes, a dream moreover that is about the coming true of a dream. One night, she says, after listening to conversation about the reanimation of corpses, 'Night waned upon this talk .... When I placed my head on my pillow I did not sleep, nor could I be said to think. My imagination, unbidden, possessed and guided me.' Then follows her account of the famous dream of 'the pale student of unhallowed arts kneeling beside the thing he had put together', the 'hideous phantasm of a man' stirring 'with an uneasy, half-vital motion', and the 'artist' sleeping and waking to behold 'the horrid thing ... looking on him with yellow, watery, but speculative eyes'. Waking in horror from her dream, she at first tries 'to think of something else', but then realises that she has the answer to her need for a ghost story: '"What terrified me will terrify others; and I need only describe the spectre which had haunted my midnight pillow." ... I began that day with the words, "It was on a dreary night of November", making only a transcript of the grim terrors of my waking dream.' Making a transcript of a dream – that is, turning an idea into the 'machinery of a story' – a dream that is about the transformation of a 'phantasm' into a real body, is equivalent here to conceiving a child. She makes it very clear that her dream takes the place of a sexual act ('Night waned ... When I placed my head on my pillow ... I saw the pale student'), just as the book idea she can announce the next day substitutes for a baby. The terrifying power of the possibility that her dream might be true encodes the terrifying power of conception and childbirth. In Deutsch's language, 'she who has created this new life must obey its power; its rule is expected, yet invisible, implacable.'[23]

Despite Ellen Moer's delineation of the resemblance of the demon to the apprehensions a mother might have about a baby, it is the introduction that supplies the most explicit evidence for identifying demon and book with a child. Mary Poovey has demonstrated that this introduction has a significantly different ideological cast from the original version of the novel (or even from the revised novel). Written in 1831, fourteen years after the novel itself and following the death of Percy Shelley (as well as the deaths of both the children who were alive or expected in 1816–17), the introduction takes pains to distance itself from the novel, and it aims to bring the writing of the novel further within the fold of the conventional domestic life Shelley retrospectively substitutes for the radically disruptive life she in fact led.[24] Referring obliquely to her elopement with Percy and its effect on her adolescent habit of inventing stories, for example, she writes, 'After this my life became busier, and reality stood in place of fiction.' Echoed later by Robert Southey's remark to Charlotte Brontë that 'literature cannot be the business of a woman's life', Shelley's busyness refers largely to her responsibilities as a mother and wife. When she describes her endeavour to write a ghost story she repeats this term for family responsibility: 'I busied myself to *think of a story*.' This echo suggests that her busyness with story writing is somehow congruent with, not in conflict with, her 'busier' life as a wife and mother. It makes the novel, 'so very hideous an idea', seem somehow part of the busy life of a matron. It is this effort to domesticate her hideous idea, that may be at the bottom of her characterising it as a 'hideous progeny'. If the novel read in this light seems, like *Jane Eyre* and *Wuthering Heights*, to be full of a horror of childbirth, that may only be the result of the impossibility of changing the basic story of the 1817 novel, the result of assembling mismatched parts.

Thus the novel may be about the horror associated with motherhood, yet this reading seems unduly influenced by the superimpositions of the introduction, and furthermore it ignores the novel's most prominent feature, that the demon is not a child born of woman but the creation of a man.[25] Most succinctly put, the novel is about the collision between androcentric and gynocentric theories of creation, a collision that results in the denigration of maternal childbearing through its circumvention by male creation. The novel presents Mary Shelley's response to the expectation, manifested in such poems as *Alastor* or *Paradise Lost*, that women embody and yet not embody male fantasies. At the same time, it expresses a woman's knowledge of the irrefutable independence of the body, both her own and those of the children that she produces, from projective male fantasy. While a masculine being – God, Adam, Percy Shelley, Frankenstein – may imagine that his creation of an imaginary being may remain under the control of his desires. Mary Shelley knows otherwise, both through her experience as mistress and wife of Percy and through her experience of childbirth. Shelley's particular history shows irrefutably that children, even pregnancies, do not remain under the control of those who conceive them.

Keats writes that 'the Imagination may be compared to Adam's dream – he awoke and found it truth'.[26] In *Paradise Lost*, narrating his recollection of Eve's creation, Adam describes how he fell into a special sleep – 'Mine eyes he clos'd, but op'n left the Cell / Of Fancy my internal sight' (8.ll.460–1) – then watched, 'though sleeping', as God formed a creature

> Manlike, but different sex, so lovely fair,
> That what seem'd fair in all the World, seem'd now
> Mean, or in her summ'd up.
>
> (8. ll. 471–3)

This is 'Adam's dream'. But what of 'he awoke and found it truth'? Adam wakes, 'To find her, or for ever to deplore / Her loss' (ll.479–80), and then, 'behold[s] her, not far off, / Such as I saw her in my dream' (ll. 481–2), yet what Keats represses is that the matching of reality to dream is not so neat as these lines suggest.[27] Eve comes to Adam, not of her own accord, but 'Led by her Heav'nly Maker' (l. 485), and as soon as he catches sight of her, Adam sees Eve turn away from him, an action he ascribes to modesty (and thus endeavours to assimilate to his dream of her) but that Eve, in book 4, has already said stemmed from her preference for her image in the water. Though designed by God for Adam 'exactly to thy heart's desire' (8. l. 451), Eve once created has a mind and will of her own, and this independence is so horrifying to the male imagination that the Fall is ascribed to it.

It is neither the visionary male imagination alone that Mary Shelley protests, then, nor childbirth itself, but the circumvention of the maternal creation of the new beings by the narcissistic creations of male desire. While Keats can gloss over the discrepancy between Adam's dream and its fulfilment, Shelley cannot. As Frankenstein is on the verge of completing the female demon, it is for her resemblance to Eve that he destroys her. Just as Adam says of Eve, 'seeing me, she turn'd' (8. l. 507), Frankenstein fears the female demon's turning from the demon toward a more attractive image: 'She also might turn with disgust from him to the superior beauty of man' (ch. 20). Also like Eve, who disobeys a prohibition agreed upon between Adam and God before her creation, she 'might refuse to comply with a compact made before her creation', the demon's promise to leave Europe. Frankenstein typifies the way in which the biological creation of necessarily imperfect yet independent beings has always been made to seem, within an androcentric economy, monstrous and alarming. Although Mary Wollstonecraft would in any case have died of puerperal fever after Mary's birth, her earlier pregnancy with Fanny and the pregnancies of Harriet Shelley, Claire Clairmont, and Mary Godwin would have done no harm had they not been labelled 'illegitimate' by a society that places a premium on the ownership by a man of his wife's body and children. The novel criticises, not childbirth itself, but the male horror of independent embodiment. This permits us to speculate that the horror of childbirth in *Jane Eyre* and *Wuthering Heights* stems from the Brontës' identification with an androcentric perspective. To a certain extent, as a writer in a culture that defines writing as a male activity and as opposite to motherhood, Shelley too must share the masculine perspective, with its horror of embodiment and its perennial re-enacting of Adam's affront at Eve's turning away. For whatever reason, however, perhaps because of her direct experience of the mother's position, Shelley is able to discern the androcentrism in her culture's view of the relation of childbearing to writing, and thus she enables us to interpret her own painful exposure of it.

At the site of the collision between motherhood and romantic projection another form of literalisation appears as well. While it is important how Shelley reads texts such as *Alastor* and *Paradise Lost*, it is also important to consider, perhaps more simply, that her novel reads them. Like the Brontës' novels, whose gothic embodiments of subjective states, realisation of dreams, and literalised figures all literalise romantic projection, Shelley's novel literalises romantic imagination, but with a different effect and to a different end. Shelley criticises these texts by enacting them, and because enactment or embodiment is both the desire and the fear of such texts, the mode of her criticism matters. Just as the heroes of these poems seem to seek, but do not seek, embodiments of their visionary desires, these poetic texts seem to seek embodiment in 'the machinery of a story'. For in the ideology of postromantic culture, it is part of a woman's duty to transcribe and give form to men's words, just as it is her duty to give form to their desire, or birth to their seed, no matter how ambivalently men may view the results of such projects. In the same passage in the introduction to the novel in which Shelley makes the analogy between the book and a child, between the conception of a story and the conception of a baby, and between these things and the coming true of a dream, she also identifies all these projects with the transcription of important men's words. Drawing on the ideology of maternity as the process of passing on a male idea, Shelley describes her book-child as the literalisation of two poets' words:

> Many and long were the conversations between Lord Byron and Shelley to which I was a devout but nearly silent listener. During one of these, various philosophical doctrines were discussed, and among others the nature of the principle of life, and whether there was any probability of its ever being discovered and communicated .... Perhaps a corpse would be reanimated; galvanism had given token of such things: perhaps the component parts of a creature might be manufactured, brought together, and endued with vital warmth.

Directly following this passage appears her account of going to bed and vividly dreaming of the 'student of unhallowed arts' and the 'hideous phantasm', the dream of which she says she made 'only a transcript' in transferring it into the central scene of her novel, the dream that equates the conception of a book with the conception of a child.

Commentators on the novel have in the past taken Shelley at her word here, believing, if not in her story of transcribing a dream, then certainly in her fiction of transcribing men's words.[28] Mario Praz, for example, writes 'All Mrs Shelley did was to provide a passive reflection of some of the wild fantasies which, as it were, hung in the air about her.'[29] Harold Bloom suggests that 'what makes *Frankenstein* an important book' despite its 'clumsiness' is 'that it contains one of the most vivid versions we have of the Romantic mythology of the self, one that resembles Blake's *Book of Urizen*, Shelley's *Prometheus Unbound*, and Byron's *Manfred*, among other works'.[30] It is part of the subtlety of her strategy to disguise her criticism of such works as a passive transcription, to appear to be a docile wife and 'devout listener' to the conversations of important men. Indeed, central to her critical method is the practice of acting out docilely what these men tell her they want from her, to show them the consequences of their desires. She removes herself beyond reproach for 'putting [her]self forward', by formulating her critique as a devout transcription, a 'passive reflection', a 'version' that 'resembles'. She inserts this authorial role into her novel in the form of a fictive M.S., Walton's sister, Margaret Saville, to whom his letters containing Frankenstein's story are sent and who silently records and transmits them to the reader.

Now that we have assembled the parts of Shelley's introductory account of the novel's genesis, we can see that she equates childbearing with the bearing of men's words. Writing a transcript of a dream that was in turn merely the transcript of a conversation is also giving birth to a hideous progeny conceived in the night. The conversation between Byron and Shelley probably represents Shelley's and Byron's poetry, the words, for example, of *Alastor* that she literalises in her novel. That the notion of motherhood as the passive transcription of men's words is at work here is underscored by the allusion this idea makes to the Christ story. 'Perhaps a corpse would be reanimated' refers initially, not to science's power, but to that occasion, a myth but surely still a powerful one even in this den of atheists, when a corpse was reanimated, which is in turn an allusion to the virgin birth. Like the creations of Adam and Eve, which excluded the maternal, Christ's birth bypassed the normal channels of procreation. It is this figure, whose birth is also the literalisation of a masculine God's Word, who serves as the distant prototype for the reanimation of corpses. And within the fiction, the demon too is the literalisation of a word, an idea, Frankenstein's theory given physical form. As Joyce Carol Oates remarks, the demon 'is a monster-son born of Man exclusively, a parody of the Word or Idea made Flesh'.[31] The book-baby literalises Shelley's and Byron's words, the words of their conversation as figures for Shelley's words in *Alastor*, just as the demon–baby literalises Frankenstein's inseminating words. Christ literalises God's Word through the medium of a woman, Mary, who passively transmits Word into flesh without being touched by it. Literalisations again take place through the medium of a more recent Mary, who passively transcribes (or who seems to), who adds nothing but the 'the platitude of prose' and 'the machinery of a story' to the words of her more illustrious male companions who for their own writing prefer 'the music of the most melodious verse'. It is precisely the adding of this 'machinery', which would seem only to facilitate the transmission of the ideas and figures of poetry into the more approachable form of a story, that subverts and reverses what it appears so passively to serve.

The demon literalises the male romantic poet's desire for a figurative object of desire, but it also literalises the literalisation of male literature. While telling Frankenstein the story of its wanderings and of its education by the unknowing cottagers, the demon reports having discovered in the woods 'a leathern portmanteau containing ... some books. I eagerly sized the prize and returned with it to my hovel' (ch. 15). The discovery of these books – *Paradise Lost*, Plutarch's *Lives*, and *The Sorrows of Werther* – is followed in the narrative, but preceded in represented time, by the demon's discover of another book, Frankenstein's 'journal of the four months that preceded [the demon's] creation'.[32] Both *Frankenstein*, the book as baby, and the demon as baby literalise these books, especially *Paradise Lost* – the demon is Satan, Adam, and Eve, while Frankenstein himself is Adam, Satan, and God – as well as a number of other prior texts, among them, as we have seen, *Alastor*, but also the book of Genesis, Coleridge's 'Rime of the Ancient Mariner', Aeschylus's *Prometheus Bound*, Wordsworth's 'Tintern Abbey', William Godwin's *Caleb Williams*, and many others. At the same time and in the same way, the demon is the realisation of Frankenstein's words in the journal of his work on the demon, a journal that is in some ways equivalent to (or a literalisation of) *Alastor*, since both record a romantic quest for what was 'desired ... with an odour that far exceeded moderation'. The demon, wandering about the woods of Germany carrying these books, the book of his own physical origin and the texts that contribute to his literary origin, embodies the very notion of literalisation with which everything about him seems to be identified. To carry a book is exactly what Mary Shelley does in bearing the words of the male authors, in giving birth to a hideous progeny that is at once book and demon. Carrying the books of his own origin, the demon emblematises the literalisation of literature that Shelley, through him, practises.

I have pointed out earlier that Mary Shelley would not see childbirth itself as inherently threatening apart from the interference in it by a masculine economy. Likewise, writing or inventing stories is not inherently monstrous – witness her retrospective account in the introduction of how, before life became 'busier', she used to 'commune with the creatures of my fancy' and compose unwritten stories out of doors: 'It was beneath the trees of the grounds belonging to our house, or on the bleak sides of the woodless mountains near, that my true compositions, the airy flights of my imagination, were born and fostered.' Like both Cathys in *Wuthering Heights* in their childhood, indeed, probably like the young Brontës themselves, Mary Shelley's imagination prior to the fall into the Law of The Father – in her case, elopement, pregnancy, and marriage – is at one with nature and also does not require to be written down. The metaphor of composition as childbirth – 'my true compositions ... were born and fostered' – appears here as something not only harmless but celebratory. It is only when both childbirth and a woman's invention of stories are subordinated to the Law of the Father that they become monstrous; it is only when such overpowering and masculinist texts as Genesis, *Paradise Lost*, and *Alastor* appropriate this Mary's body, her female power of embodiment, as vehicle for the transmission of their words, that monsters are born. When God appropriates maternal procreation in Genesis or *Paradise Lost*, a beautiful object is created; but through the reflex of Mary Shelley's critique, male circumvention of the maternal creates a monster. Her monster constitutes a criticism of such appropriation and circumvention, yet it is a criticism written in her own blood, carved in the very body of her own victimisation, just as the demon carves words about death in the trees and rocks of the Arctic. She is powerless to stop her own appropriation and can only demonstrate the pain that appropriation causes in the woman reader and writer.

From Margaret Homans, *Bearing the Word: Language and Female Experience in Nineteenth-century Women's Writing* (Chicago, 1986), pp. 100–19.

NOTES

[The book from this essay is exerpted focuses on the work of several nineteenth-century women writers and addresses the absence of the maternal figure as both a literal source of creativity and a metaphorical site of creative substitution in women's writing, thus reversing and resisting the impositions of male meanings and metaphors. In its focus on women's writing, desire and language, Margaret Homans' essay adapts Lacanian psychoanalysis and de Manian deconstruction in order to address in feminist terms the effects of and resistance to patriarchal language. Psychoanalysis is used to disclose the narcissistic patterns of male desire which, excluding or appropriating the role and power of the mother, attempts to make literal or objectify in language its own idealised versions of masculinity. In Frankenstein's appropriation of the secret of life from feminine nature and in Walton's attempt to conquer virgin soil femininity is associated with natural objects and negative states like death. Male desire never supplants the creative power and difference of female sexuality, however, because it fails to realise or make literal its own narcissistic imaginings. Using Paul de Man's deconstructive version of language as simultaneously literal and metaphorical in form and function, Homans demonstrates how the metaphors that are applied to women can never be fully literalised or objectified: there are differences in the representation of women that remain both irreducible and unstable, allowing other meanings and metaphors to take positive significance in women's writing. Ed.]

1. Mary Poovey, *The Proper Lady and the Woman Writer* (Chicago, 1984), pp. 114–42. Hereafter I will refer to Mary Shelley as Shelley (except where her unmarried name is necessary for clarity) and to her husband as Percy.
2. Sandra Gilbert and Susan Gubar's reading of the novel focuses on its 'apparently docile submission to male myths' and identifies it specifically as 'a fictionalised rendition of the meaning of *Paradise Lost* to women' (*The Madwoman in the Attic* (New Haven, 1979), pp. 219, 221). Although my interest in Shelley as a reader of prior, masculine texts, as well as some of my specific points about the novel's reading of Milton, overlaps with theirs, I am putting these concerns to uses different from theirs.
3. For example, Robert Kiely writes that Frankenstein 'seeks to combine the role of both parents in one, to eliminate the need for the woman in the creative act, to make sex unnecessary' (*The Romantic Novel in England* [*Cambridge*, 1972], p. 164). Marc Rubenstein remarks on 'the series of motherless family romances which form the substance of Frankenstein's past' ('"My Accursed Origin": The Search for the Mother in *Frankenstein*,' *Studies in Romanticism*, 15[1976], 177). The general argument of his psychoanalytic reading of the novel is that the

novel represents Shelley's quest for her own dead mother. U. C. Knoepflmacher, in the course of arguing that the novel portrays a daughter's rage at her parents, mentions 'the novel's attack on a male's usurpation of the role of mother' ('Thoughts on the Aggression of Daughters', in *The Endurance of Frankenstein: Essays on Mary Shelley's Novel*, ed. George Levine and U. C. Knoepflmacher [Berkeley, 1979], p. 105). Mary Jacobus writes that 'the exclusion of woman from creation symbolically "kills" the mother' ('Is There a Woman in This Text?' *New Literary History*, 14 [1982], 131). Barbara Johnson suggests that the novel focuses on 'eliminations of the mother' as well as on 'the fear of somehow effecting the death of one's own parents' ('My Monster/My Self', *Diacritics*, 12 [1982], 2–10). Christine Froula's argument about the maternal in Milton, although it focuses on the author's appropriation of the maternal for masculine creativity (as differentiated from its circumvention or elimination) helped to stimulate my thinking. See Christine Froula, 'When Eve Reads Milton: Undoing the Canonical Economy', *Critical Inquiry*, 10 (1983), 321–47.

4. I am following, in this reading, the 1831 revised text of the novel; in the 1818 version, Elizabeth is Frankenstein's cousin. All quotations from the novel will be from the Signet edition (Mary Shelley, *Frankenstein, Or the Modern Prometheus* [New York, 1965]), which prints the text of 1831. Future references will be cited in the text by chapter number or by letter number for the letters that precede the chapter sequence. See also James Reiger's edition of the 1818 version, with revisions of 1823 and 1831 (Chicago, 1982).

5. Rubenstein notes the sexual nature of Walton's quest, as well as the maternal associations of those aspects of nature on which Frankenstein carries out his research ('My Accursed Origin', 174–5, 177). Kiely notes the necrophilia of the passage from *Alastor*'s invocation to Mother Nature, and suggests its similarity to Frankenstein's 'penetrating the recesses of nature' (*The Romantic Novel*, pp. 162–3).

6. Quoted p. 149: Frankenstein quotes lines 76–83 of the poem, altering the original 'haunted *me* like a passion' to fit a third person.

7. In the context of arguing that the novel critiques the bourgeois family, Kate Ellis shows that Frankenstein's mother passes on to Elizabeth her 'view of the female role as one of constant, self-sacrificing devotion to others', and she suggests that 'Elizabeth's early death, like her adopted mother's, was a logical outgrowth of the female ideal she sought to embody' ('Monsters in the Garden: Mary Shelley and the Bourgeois Family', in *The Endurance of Frankenstein*, p. 131). My argument would explain why what created this 'female ideal' also determined the interchangeability of mother and daughter.

8. Harold Bloom suggests the resemblance between the demon and Blake's emanations or Shelley's epipsyche, in his afterword to the

Signet edition of the novel, p. 215. The essay is reprinted in *Ringers in the Tower* (Chicago, 1971), pp. 119–29. Peter Brooks makes a similar point when he writes, 'fulfilment with Elizabeth would mark Frankenstein's achievement of a full signified in his life, accession to plenitude of being – which would leave no place in creation for his daemonic projection, the Monster' ('Godlike Science/Unhallowed Arts: Language and Monstrosity in *Frankenstein*', *New Literary History*, 9 [1978], 599). Ellis also suggests, though for different reasons, that the demon is a representative for Elizabeth ('Monsters in the Garden', 136). Jacobus writes that Frankenstein 'exchang[es] a woman for a monster', and she discusses Frankenstein's preference for imagined over actual beings ('Is There a Woman in This Text?', 131).

9. Gilbert and Gubar suggest first that 'the part of Eve *is* all the parts' and then discuss at length the demon's resemblance to Eve (*The Madwoman*, pp. 230, 235–44. However, in describing this resemblance, they focus primarily on the patriarchal rejection of women's bodies as deformed and monstrous, as well as on Eve's motherlessness, but not, as I do here, on Eve as Adam's imaginative projection. Joyce Carol Oates also suggests the demon's resemblance to Eve, also using the scene I am about to discuss, in 'Frankenstein's Fallen Angel', *Critical Inquiry*, 10 (1984), 547.

10. Quotations from *Paradise Lost* are from *Complete Poems and Major Prose of John Milton*, ed. Merritt Hughes (Indianapolis, 1957), and are cited in the text by book and line numbers. Other critics have noted Shelley's allusion to this Miltonic scene; see for example, Brooks, 'Godlike Science', 595.

11. Froula writes, 'Through the dream of the rib Adam both enacts a parody of birth and gains possession of the womb by claiming credit for woman herself.' Milton, she goes on to argue, re-enacts Adam's solution to his 'womb envy' by analogously repressing female power in his account of the origin of his poem: 'The male Logos called upon to articulate the cosmos against an abyss of female silence overcomes the anxieties generated by the tension between visible maternity and invisible paternity by appropriating female power to itself in a parody of parthenogenesis' ('When Eve Reads Milton', 332, 338; and see passim 326–40).

12. Ibid., pp. 326–8.

13. All quotations from Shelley's verse are from the Reiman and Powers edition of his works.

14. Gilbert and Gubar also discuss narcissistic love in the novel, although with reference only to the potentially incestuous relation between Frankenstein and Elizabeth, not with reference to the demon (*The Madwoman*, p. 229). My reading would suggest that Frankenstein's

relation to Elizabeth is far less narcissistic than his relation to the demon; in his descriptions of Elizabeth, he focuses on her difference from him, which is what I believe makes her like the mother and therefore threatening.

15. Jaya Mehta pointed out to me the significance of this aspect of Walton, in a seminar paper at Yale in 1984.

16. Kiely discusses 'the sheer concreteness' of the demon, though his concern is with the mismatching between ideal and real in the novel (*The Romantic Novel*, p. 161).

17. *The Diary of Dr. John William Polidori*, ed. W. M. Rossetti (London, 1911), pp. 128–9, entry for 18 June 1816. Cited also by Rubenstein, who reads it as a story about 'maternal reproach' and connects it with Frankenstein's dream of his dead mother ('My accursed Origin', 184–5). I am grateful to Marina Leslie for her discussion of this episode in a seminar paper at Yale in 1984.

18. Peter Brooks's essay on *Frankenstein* also connects the plot of desire with the plot of language in the novel, but to a somewhat different effect. Brooks argues that the demon's acquisition of the 'godlike science' of language places him within the symbolic order. Trapped at first, like any baby, within the specular order of the imaginary, the demon is first judged only by its looks; it is only when it masters the art of rhetoric that the monster gains sympathy. But, Brooks continues, despite the promise that the symbolic seems to hold, the monster's failure to find an object of love removes its life from the signifying 'chain' of human interconnectedness and makes of it instead a 'miserable series', in which one signifier refers always to another with 'no point of arrest'. Thus Brooks sees the monster as a dark and exaggerated version of all life within the symbolic, where desire is never satisfied and where there is no transcendental signified. Although I agree with much of what Brooks writes, I would argue that in its materiality and its failure to acquire an object of desire, the demon enters the symbolic primarily as the (dreaded) referent, not as signifier. The negative picture of the demon's materiality is a product of its female place in the symbolic, and not of any lingering in the realm of the imaginary (which Brooks, with other readers of Lacan, views as tragic). I would also argue that the novel presents, not a vision of the condition of human signification, but a targeted criticism of those in whose interests the symbolic order constitutes itself in the ways that it does.

19. Ellen Moers, *Literary Women* (New York, 1977), p. 140.

20. Ibid., pp. 145–7.

21. This is the general tendency of Rubenstein's argument, carrying the material Moers presents into a psychoanalytic frame.

22. See Rubenstein, 'My Accursed Origin', 168, 178–1; Poovey, *The Proper Lady*, pp. 138–42.

23. Deutsch, *Motherhood*, p. 215.

24. One of the central tenets of Poovey's argument concerns Shelley's endeavour in her 1831 revisions to make the novel more conservative, more in keeping with a proto-Victorian ideology of the family (see *The Proper Lady*, pp. 133–42). Poovey argues, however, that both versions of the novel oppose romantic egotism's assault on the family.

25. Gilbert and Gubar assert as part of their argument that everyone in the novel is Eve that 'Frankenstein has a baby' and that as a consequence he becomes female (*The Madwoman*, p. 232). I would argue, to the contrary, that Frankenstein's production of a new life is pointedly masculine, that it matters to the book that he is a man circumventing childbirth, not a woman giving birth.

26. Letter of 22 November 1817 to Benjamin Bailey, in *Letters of John Keats*, ed. Robert Gittings (London, 1970), p. 37.

27. I am indebted to Suzanne Raitt for her discussion of this point in a seminar at Yale in 1984.

28. Rubenstein also argues that Shelley deliberately created the impression that she merely recorded Percy and Byron's conversation as part of a project to make her creativity seem as passive and maternal as possible. He discusses at length the analogy she sets up between conceiving a child and conceiving a book, and he specifically suggests that the men's words in conversation are like men's role in procreation, which was, in the early nineteenth century, thought to involve the man actively and the woman only passively: 'She is trying to draw for us a picture of her imagination as a passive womb, inseminated by those titans of romantic poetry' ('My Accursed Origin', 181). I would agree with everything Rubenstein says, although I am using this idea for a somewhat different purpose: he is using it to show how the novel is about Shelley's effort to make restitution for her dead mother.

29. Mario Praz, *The Romantic Agony*, trans. Angus Davidson (London, 1933), p. 114. Cited by Moers and also by Rubenstein in support of his argument discussed in note 28 above.

30. Harold Bloom, 'Afterword', *Frankenstein*, p. 215. It is worth noting that *Frankenstein* preceded *Prometheus Unbound* and was of course written in ignorance of the *Book of Urizen*.

31. Oates, 'Frankenstein's Fallen Angel', 552.

32. Gilbert and Gubar, who focus much of their argument on Shelley's reading of *Paradise Lost*, connect that reading to the demon's reading of the poem, as well as connecting Shelley's listening to her husband and Byron with the demon's listening to the DeLaceys.

7

Narratives of Seduction and the Seductions of Narrative: The Frame Structure of *Frankenstein*

BETH NEWMAN

The unnamed narrator of Conrad's *Heart of Darkness* offers a well-known cautionary metaphor for reading narratives – particularly frame narratives, fictions like *Frankenstein*, *Wuthering Heights* and *The Turn of the Screw* (as well as *Heart of Darkness* itself) that contain a story within a story. The narrator tells us that for Marlow the meaning of a story 'was not inside like a kernel but outside, enveloping the tale which brought it out only as a glow brings out a haze ...'[1] Conrad does not define precisely what 'inside' and 'outside' are, which leaves considerable leeway for the reader. But he does extend the metaphor, restating it by figuring it in the formal structure of the text. He offers us Marlow's story not by itself, but embedded in another – enclosed in a frame that completes it and is completed by it, 'as a glow brings out a haze'.[2] By tracing the narrator's conversion in the frame from a complacent faith in the superiority of the West to Marlow's anti-imperialism, *Heart of Darkness* makes meaning something that happens on the margins, along the edges of a narrative, as much as something that we discover within it. We cannot hope to extract a single 'kernel' of meaning from Marlow's story, nor from those of Frankenstein, Nelly Dean, or James's governess, but must attend instead to the relations between the stories in the centre and those in the frame, and listen to the dialogue between the voices that speak them.

If we consider Marlow's story by itself, it directs insistently back to the frame that completes it. First, its imagery repeats and complicates the metaphor of absent (or hazy and spectral) centre suggested by the frame narrator. The jungle in which Marlow's quest takes place, like the objects it contains (a bottomless bucket, the broken-down steamer that Marlow commands), is riddled with holes, trenches randomly dug and abandoned in the name of 'progress'. At the dramatic centre of the story is Kurtz, himself an enigma, whom we come to know more by what is revealed about him in his absence than through anything he says or does when he finally appears in his own person. Even in the few scenes where he is present in the narrative, he is just barely there: physically he has dwindled to a mere spectre, a skeleton barely capable of casting a shadow; spiritually he is 'hollow at the core'. Yet he retains some of his power: '"Kurtz discoursed. A voice! A voice! It rang deep to the very last. It survived his strength to hide in the magnificent folds of eloquence the barren darkness of his heart."'[2] Kurtz's voice again directs us back to the frame, where Marlow too is reduced to a voice: 'It had become so pitch dark', the nameless narrator recalls, 'that we listeners could hardly see one another. For a long time already [Marlow], sitting apart, had been no more to us than a voice.'[3] These descriptions of Kurtz and Marlow are unsettling because they suggest voice without body, language without a source, discourse uttered without a human subject. In so describing his characters, Conrad raises some of the issues latent in narrative framing, a device that tends at once to emphasise and to annul the individuality of the various tellers it presents. Furthermore, by drawing our attention to the voices of Kurtz and Marlow, he calls our attention as well to another issue involved in narrative framing, the issue of textual voice.

Heart of Darkness, then, is a paradigmatic example of the frame narrative, a conventional narrative structure that had lain in disuse for some time before Conrad disinterred it and breathed new life into it. Because Conrad's famous novella comes close to making explicit many of the issues that framing involves, it serves usefully to frame an inquiry into the structure of *Frankenstein*, the novel that concerns me here. The image that *Heart of Darkness* presents of a disembodied voice telling a story serves almost as a metaphor for what *Frankenstein*, *Wuthering Heights*, *The Turn of the Screw*, and many other frame narratives suggest about storytelling: that a story can be cut off from its origin in a particular speaker and tell itself in other speakers, who to some extent are shaped by it instead of shaping it. Such a conception of the narrative act contradicts one of the central tenets of most approaches to narrative theory, the idea that no story exists apart from a shaping human intelligence, and that every story bears the mark of this shaping intelligence.[4] The paradox of frame narratives like *Frankenstein* and *Wuthering Heights* is that they present first person narrators whose singular and even bizarre stories suggest highly individualised tellers, but they ask us to believe that the stories they contain are repeated virtually word for word by other, quite different tellers; and in the process they efface a particular set of markers in the text that would permit us to distinguish the individual tellers, those tonal markers and indices of character inscribed in the narration itself, markers often loosely called 'voice'.

In my reading of *Frankenstein* I will argue that within what one might call the framework of the text, story and character turn out to be separable, even opposing elements, which do not fuse in the creation of narrative discourse. That is, *Frankenstein* does not offer us multiple narrators in order to provide multiple points of view, each of which expresses the unique psychology of the character who tells a given story. Nevertheless this is the approach generally taken by critics who set out to explain the complex narrative structure of *Wuthering Heights*, an approach which leads in turn to the questions of unreliability that surface repeatedly in the criticism. The problem with reading either *Frankenstein* or *Wuthering Heights* along these lines is that both of these novels, being firmly rooted in a Gothic tradition, represent character differently than do later works of nineteenth-century realism. Both Shelley and Brontë represent human personality in terms of abstractions, in terms of general qualities or states of mind that are often rendered symbolically and obliquely, rather than through the kind of careful and explicit analysis of individual psychology that realistic novels offer. Consequently they are less concerned with the motivations in individual psychology for the telling of a given story than with general tendencies in the nature of narrative itself. Even James, who is equally interested in both these aspects of fiction, is more coy than usual about the reliability of the governess in *Turn of the Screw*, so that it is finally impossible to determine whether the ghosts are real or a figment of an overheated, neurotic imagination. So while

James's fictional oeuvre represents the perfection of points of view as a fictional device, and his prefaces create the poetic that accounts for its effects, *Turn of the Screw* nevertheless bears instructive similarities to *Frankenstein* and *Wuthering Heights*. While Shelley and Brontë do not specifically ask us to be suspicious of the reliability of their narrators, they do cast suspicion on the stories they tell, though in another way, one common as well to *Turn of the Screw*. In all three works storytelling itself is suspect: narrative has become, in these novels, a form of seduction. It serves both as a way of seducing a listener, and as a means of displacing and sublimating desire that cannot be satisfied directly. As spoken narratives that get written down only by another teller, the stories in these fictions, from Shelley to Conrad and James, cast suspicion as well on the medium through which their tellers pursue their aims of seduction – the speaking voice.[5]

Frankenstein, the reader will recall, contains an elaborate series of frames. Working from the outside in we start with an epistolary narrative, the letters of a Captain Walton to his sister Mrs Saville, who remains safely at home in England while he seeks fame, glory and the North Pole. His letters announce the discovery and rescue of a stranger – Frankenstein – who tells his bizarre story to Walton, who then includes it in his letters home. Frankenstein's story contains yet another, the confessions of the monstrous creature he has created and abandoned; and the Monster includes within his own narrative the story of the De Laceys, the family of exiles he tries pathetically and unsuccessfully to adopt as his own. As we pass from teller to teller, peeling back one story to discover another as though peeling an onion, we progress not only through time but also toward some goal that seems the more powerful and important for being so palpably *within*; it is as though we were moving toward the kernel that Marlow's tales refuse us. Put another way, this series of narratives creates the same kinds of expectations as those set in motion by what Roland Barthes has called the 'hermeneutic code',[6] but instead of being encoded in words alone – in the 'lexia' – the presence of some enigma is signalled by the layering of stories, by the system of frames.

Though we receive this Chinese box of stories-within-stories in the form of writing, the packet of letters that Walton sends his sister, most of what we read is Walton's transcription of two oral narratives. In this respect *Frankenstein*, with its roots in the novels and romances of the previous century, takes a hackneyed convention and turns it nearly inside out. Instead of an editor producing a (supposedly) found manuscript, an already written document, Walton turns oral narratives into writing. Unlike the narratives he transcribes, Walton's letters to his sister are addressed to someone absent from the narrative situation, someone removed in time and place. This is only another way of saying that they are written, not spoken, but it reveals something important about how the outermost layer of narration differs from the others: Mrs Saville, safe at home in England, is cut off from the chain of narratives and the dangers they pose. But what are their dangers, and what do they have to do with the opposition of speech and writing? As we shall see, the dangers are in the seductiveness of narrative, particularly narratives that are literally given voice.

When Frankenstein first boards Walton's ship, the cold, hunger and exhaustion he has suffered in his search for the Monster have deprived him of speech, but as he regains this faculty he begins to insinuate himself very quickly into Walton's heart. In a letter to his sister Walton praises Frankenstein's gentleness and wisdom, but what impresses him most is something else: 'When he speaks, although his words are culled with the choicest art, yet they flow with rapidity and unparalleled eloquence' (p. 27).[7] Frankenstein's fluency as a speaker makes him almost divine in Walton's eyes (p. 10), and Walton is not alone in being moved by Frankenstein's powers of oratory: 'Even the sailors feel the power of his eloquence; when he speaks, they no longer despair: he rouses their energies, and while they hear his voice they believe these vast mountains of ice are mole-hills which will vanish before the resolutions of man' (p. 213). But Walton suggests that Frankenstein's eloquence – his fluency with words and his ability to manipulate language – is only part of what makes him persuasive; its effects upon his men last only 'while they hear his voice'. There is something spellbinding in that alone; as long as Frankenstein speaks, Walton and his crew cannot choose but hear.[8] Its effects are even more profound upon Walton, who imagines that he can hear Frankenstein's 'full-toned voice swell[ing] in my ears' long after it has ceased, and that his sister, when she reads his transcription of Frankenstein's story, will not be moved as much as he, 'who hear[s] it from his own lips' (p. 31). Like the Ancient Mariner's glittering eye, Frankenstein's voice compels attention – but it does so without seeming to compel, wooing its listeners to receptivity through its richness and resonance.

Frankenstein raises the issue of the human voice in order to complicate it, and to call our attention to the differences between reading a story and hearing one spoken aloud. It insists on a difference between the voice of Frankenstein and that of the Monster, which 'though harsh, had nothing terrible in it' (p. 132), but that difference is inaccessible to us as we read. We are more apt to be struck by the similarities in the way the Monster and Frankenstein express themselves, since they both use the same kind of heightened language, and since both speak with an eloquence more expressive of a shared Romantic ethos than of differences in character. In fact, Walton's voice, the other significant voice in the text, is scarcely different. The novel fails to provide significant differences in tone, diction and sentence structure that alone can serve, in a written text, to represent individual human voices, and so blurs the distinction that it asks us to make between the voices of its characters.

Such differences in tone, diction and sentence structure have to do with another kind of voice than that with which we began; instead of voice in the physiological sense we are here concerned with voice in a textual sense. So conceived, voice is no longer the sensible medium of expression that lingers in Walton's ears but something more abstract. As a quasi-technical term often used to refer to properties of writing, voice is a metaphor that invokes precisely what is absent in the discourse to which it applies: the sounds produced by the organs of speech. Frame narratives, by giving the words of one speaker over to another, often force us to confront voice in this textual sense. Through an extended ventriloquism, a word-for-word repetition of another speaker's discourse, *Frankenstein* further blurs the distinctions between the voices of its narrators. That is, by transferring a given narrative from teller to teller, it complicates the question that most theories of narrative – particularly those that stress point of view – begin by asking: who is speaking?

Frankenstein, by juxtaposing three tendentious narratives, seems to encourage a point-of-view approach. It presents confessional first-person narrators whose stories sound the note of self-justification so loudly that they immediately invite suspicion, the kind of suspicion that point-of-view criticism teaches us to entertain. Each story is then transferred to a new teller who repeats it as an event in his own tale, which now serves as a frame. Putting such stories in someone else's mouth might seem to be a way of distancing the reader from a narrator so that we can see through the story he tells; framing might seem to provide a perspective that heightens the distance. That is, it might seem that the purpose of a narrative technique that transfers a story from teller to teller is to direct the reader to questions of point of view, and more specifically to questions of reliability. But each teller in the chain of narrative embeddings accepts the story he hears without question, and repeats it unchanged. As a result, we are given no new perspective; we are instead offered a series of stories that corroborate one another, in a sameness of voice that blurs the distinctions between tellers instead of heightening them. The frame structure of *Frankenstein* thus suggests that 'point of view' is not the point at all. In fact, the logic of *Frankenstein* violates the main premise of point-of-view criticism by suggesting that its narratives are not expressions of individual human psyches. In other words, a story is emphatically separable from the character who first tells it; once a narrative has been uttered, it exists as a verbal structure with its own integrity, and can, like myth, think itself in the minds of men (and women). Being infinitely repeatable in new contexts, it has achieved autonomy; it now functions as a text, having been severed from its own origins, divested of its originating voice. The mark of this severance is the frame itself.[9]

The mutual independence of story and character becomes visible and problematic in *Frankenstein* in an episode that seems otherwise marginal, even digressive. This is the story of Justine, the young woman who (like Elizabeth Lavenza, Frankenstein's sister-bride) was adopted into the Frankenstein household while still a child. In terms of plot, Justine is merely functional, introduced only to be quickly killed off. We hear of her for the first time in a letter Frankenstein receives from Elizabeth after he has created the Monster and long after he has finished describing his family life. Elizabeth spends four paragraphs reminding Frankenstein who Justine is. To a lengthy summary of Justine's life story Elizabeth appends a significant *non sequitur* about 'darling William', the baby of the Frankenstein clan, and closes her letter with a spate of gossipy details, a whole can of red herrings served up to distract us from the fishy digression the narrative has just taken. The importance to the plot of this apparent digression eventually becomes clear: Mary Shelley is setting up the first of the monster's murders – the murder of William – for which Justine will soon be found guilty. But as we read this, the narrative machinery itself begins to creak and groan; we sense that it is making itself ready for an event that hasn't yet been prepared. This hitch in the works is doubly marked, not only by the way the narrative changes direction here, but also by Elizabeth's being forced, briefly, into the unidiomatic (if theoretically possible) voice of second-person narration: '"Justine, you may remember, was a great favourite of yours"' she writes (p. 65).[10] Curiously, just as the coherence of *Frankenstein* threatens to dissolve into a peculiar narrative ineptness it is preparing us for Justine's trial, an episode about narratives that fail to cohere. Moreover, by dispersing the story of Justine's innocence across multiple voices, the novel enacts the division of voice and character that is suggested by its frames.

In a sense, narrative itself is implicated in Justine's troubles. In the first place, the evidence that links Justine to the murder is circumstantial, which means that it assumes a narrative form: a series of apparently related events is distributed into a pattern of cause and effect, and so into a single, coherent plot; this plot, being narratable, is plausible, and being plausible begins to seem true. Thus the discovery upon Justine of a miniature stolen from the murdered William tells a story that ends in Justine's guilt. Further, what finally condemns Justine is precisely her inability to counter that story with a coherent narrative of her own. From the first, the only account she can give of herself is 'confused and unintelligible' (p. 82). When she is called to the witness stand in her own defence, she refuses to plead her case with studied eloquence, with careful rhetoric: '"I do not pretend that my protestations should acquit me; I rest my innocence on a plain and simple explanation of the facts which have been adduced against me"' (p. 82). But is precisely because she cannot explain these facts – that is, because they remain from her point of view, unnarratable – that she is found guilty.

Justine is not content simply to admit her fatal inability to compose a coherent narrative. She incriminates herself further by rejecting the very arguments which might have exonerated her:

> 'I know ... how heavily and fatally this one circumstance [of the miniature] weighs against me, but I have no power of explaining it; and when I have expressed my utter ignorance, I am only left to conjecture concerning the probabilities by which it might have been placed in my pocket. But here I am also checked. I believe that I have no enemy on earth, and none surely would have been so wicked as to destroy me wantonly. Did the murderer place it there? I know of no opportunity afforded him for so doing; or, if I had, why should he have stolen the jewel, to part with it again so soon?'
>
> (pp. 83–4)

Realising that she can offer no alternative to the story that seems to have shaped itself around her, Justine makes the only appeal that remains to her. She appeals in the name of character. As she begins her plea in self-defence she says, 'I hope the character I have always borne will incline my judges to a favourable interpretation, where any circumstance appears doubtful or suspicious' (p. 83). Against the force of a story that seems to assemble itself from diverse pieces of evidence and to tell against her, she offers the argument of character, the hope that however incoherent her own explanation, she will be judged a reliable narrator. But the story proves far more eloquent and persuasive to its hearers than does the innocent victim, Justine, who has no story to tell.

In appealing to character, Justine is anticipating the way many twentieth-century critics will read novels like *Frankenstein* – and more problematically, like *Wuthering Heights*, with its supposedly 'unreliable' or 'incompetent' narrators. At the same time, the judge and the courtroom mob use against Justine the reverse of her own argument, showing that the knife cuts both ways. We'll judge your character on the basis of your narrative, they say, using the kind of logic that, in its extreme form, can turn Nelly Dean into a villain.[11] But the court is as wrong about Justine's character as Justine is inept as a narrator. The episode of Justine's trial thus implicitly challenges the habit of reading all narratives primarily as expressions of character, and figures the separability of character and narrative by opposing them to one another. Justine really is innocent, though her testimony fails to explain effects in terms of causes, and so is it itself guilty of breaking the most basic law of narrative. Her character bears no relation to the incriminating evidence of her own testimony, to the story she inadvertently tells about herself.

If character is not implicated in *Frankenstein*'s narratives, gender is; for like Elizabeth, who narrates unidiomatically (though not quite ungrammatically), Justine is a woman. Gender may determine another of Justine's problems as a narrator as well: she speaks 'in an audible although variable voice' (p. 83). Lacking the recognisable consistency of the Monster's voice which 'though harsh, had nothing terrible in it' (p. 132) and the authority of Frankenstein's resonant, 'full-toned voice' (p. 31), Justine's 'variable voice' adds to the pall of unreliability cast by her incoherent narrative. In fact, her 'variable voice' exacerbates the incoherence of her story, for coherence depends on the very self-consistency that her voice, like the story it tries to tell, lacks. But Justine's story really does cohere –

though only in being completed by other voices. Begun in Elizabeth's letter, continued in the letter from Frankenstein's father and in Frankenstein's account of the trial, it is concluded only much later, by the Monster's voice.

The Monster is the one circumstance of which judge, jury and Justine are alike ignorant, the missing cause that would make Justine's story hold together. As we eventually discover, it is of course he who strangles William in a fit of rage and orchestrates Justine's condemnation by planting the miniature, which he took from William, upon her. His narrative expertise, which later exercises its effects on Frankenstein, reveals itself here in another way: he tells a persuasive story (this time, a fictional one) not discursively but in figures, using William's corpse, the stolen miniature and the body of Justine. The story that seemed to assemble itself of its own accord and to end in Justine's guilt thus turns out to have a narrator after all.

Why does the monster tell this story? Before he puts the miniature in the pocket of Justine's dress, he finds that the picture of Frankenstein's mother arouses his desire, a desire that he transfers to the living woman he discovers sleeping on some straw at his feet. Bending over Justine, he whispers '"Awake, fairest, thy lover is near"' (p. 143). This scene has been described as a perverse fantasy of rape, but the Monster's language expresses tenderness rather than violence, and a desire to use not force, but more subtle forms of persuasion. He envisions not a rape but a seduction, at least until he perceives that this attempt to seduce must fail. He then plants the picture upon Justine, knowing precisely the story it will tell: '"the murder I have committed because I am for ever robbed of all that she could give me, she shall atone"' (p. 144). As a substitute for a seduction that can never succeed and a sexual union that can never take place, he engineers the fiction of Justine's guilt – and so offers himself the consolation of revenge. But this time he does not seek revenge by engaging in violence directly, as he has a few moments before in strangling William. Rather, this act of revenge takes the form of a narrative which, like the abortive seduction it displaces, serves to discharge pent-up, frustrated desire. Again like the seduction, the narrative takes as its object the body of a woman, Justine.

The story the Monster tells about Justine is thus an act of sublimation, the rewriting of a grotesque would-be love story as a murder mystery. It forges a link between acts of narration and acts of seduction, which are related here not through equivalence, but through displacement and transformation.[12] In a somewhat different manner, the frame structure will reiterate this link between narration and seduction. The Monster's story about Justine is not the only place in *Frankenstein* where a scene of seduction is revised into something new, or an act of storytelling displaces – or even becomes – an attempt to seduce. We can detect a scene of seduction transformed at the centre of the novel's many frames, in the Monster's account of his ill-fated desire to befriend the De Laceys. In this case the story under revision comes from another novel: it rewrites the scene that sets up Ambrosio's seduction in M. G. Lewis's *The Monk*.[13]

The parallels are subtle but significant. At the beginning of the scene, Ambrosio, the monk of the title, considers the perils of his role as the confessor of 'the fairest and noblest dames of Madrid': 'I must accustom my eyes to objects of temptation, and expose myself to the seduction of luxury and desire'.[14] Ambrosio must make himself, in other words, as good as blind to the charms of physical beauty, just as De Lacey is blind to the horrors of physical monstrosity. But he fails: a beautiful woman has already begun to work her arts of seduction upon him by disguising herself as a young man, the novice Rosario, who becomes Ambrosio's most devoted follower. As the scene unfolds, Rosario plaintively tells Ambrosio the story of his sorrows, just as De Lacey briefly becomes the Monster's confidant in *Frankenstein*. Their stories are strikingly similar. '"I have no relation or friend upon earth,"' the Monster tells De Lacey (p. 133); Rosario's complaint is much the same: 'I have no friend! The whole wide world cannot furnish an heart that is willing to participate in the sorrows of mine"' (p. 80). Both the Monster and Rosario seek to manipulate their confidants by playing on their sympathies, and to that end both tell stories about themselves that dissemble the truth by displacing it onto other characters. Rosario offers a story about his sister Matilda and the Monster tells De Lacey about 'a French family' who educated him. Finally, both Rosario and the Monster reveal the true identities of the characters in their tales:

> 'Do not fly me!' she cried. 'Leave me not abandoned to the impulse of despair! ... I acknowledge my sister's story to be my own! I am Matilda; you are her beloved.'
>
> (p. 81)

> '[S]ave and protect me! You and your family are the friends whom I seek. Do not desert me in the hour of trial!'
>
> (p. 135)

Thus the Monster tries to win De Lacey by a ruse very similar to Matilda's (that is, Rosario's), and like Matilda, ends by throwing himself at the mercy of his listener. But Mary Shelley doesn't simply adapt this scene to her own purposes; she offers a revision that is meaningful for what it suggests about the anxieties of gender. Matilda in *The Monk* is not telling the whole truth at her moment of truth; she turns out later to be the Devil, or least one of his emissaries. If Matilda's/Rosario's confession ('I am a woman') becomes, later on in *The Monk*, 'I am a Devil', it is revised in *Frankenstein* to something different: 'I am a Monster.'[15] Perhaps this is why the Monster's discursive narratives, like those of Elizabeth and Justine, ultimately fail. In the final analysis, one that considers the role of gender in *Frankenstein*, the Monster's stories become tales told by a woman in a novel by a woman who feared that such tales – like her own – would be understood as signifying nothing.

The Monster's failure to win De Lacey, followed by the failure of his pathetic attempt to win Justine, brings him to tell his story once again, more fully and less obliquely, to Frankenstein. This retelling is the entire confessional narrative embedded in Frankenstein's own, which introduces it and serves as its frame. Though it too will fail, the Monster's story affects Frankenstein forcibly, as it must, for it is a story with a purpose. Its *end* (that is, its purpose) is also one of the most conventional *endings* (that is, closures) of literary plots: a sexual union. The Monster concludes his story with the following demand:

> 'We may not part until you have promised to comply with my requisition. I am alone, and miserable; man will not associate with me; but one as deformed and horrible as myself would not deny herself to me ... This being you must create.'
>
> (p. 144)

Once more an act of narration in *Frankenstein* takes the form of a displaced seduction. Though Frankenstein is himself the object of the Monster's rhetoric, its aim is still the satisfaction of desire, a sexual consummation. But this time, the link between narrative and seduction defines a relation between distinct parts of the novel – that is, between one of its extended acts of storytelling and the narrative situation that serves as its frame.

From a rhetorical standpoint, the Monster's story is exceedingly well shaped. William Labov's studies of so-called 'natural narratives' suggest that for a story to be successful, it must forestall the most withering critique of all: the response, 'So what?'[16]

Storytellers, then, continually employ various strategies for warding off the 'so what'; that is, successful narrators manage things so that their stories have 'point'. Because we think of texts as bounded objects, framed and delimited, we have learned to seek the point of a narrative within the story itself. But the Monster's story (like the one Marlow tells in *Heart of Darkness*) makes meaning – narrowly construed, the point – something that happens on the outside. The point of his narrative leads outside the story itself, to its (fictive) audience, breaking through the self-enclosed structure of a story with a beginning, middle and end. At the moment of its conclusion it reaches outside itself with its demand, producing not a structure with closure but an opening into further discourse, implicating its own listener, violating its own frame.

The ending of the Monster's narrative calls our attention to something else, to a particular linguistic utterance on which all of *Frankenstein* turns. As a rhetorical act, his story has an immediate purpose: to bind Frankenstein to a promise. The danger of the Monster's eloquence, the danger that Frankenstein warns Walton against, is precisely its ability to bind his listener to a promise, and so to make the effects of his eloquence outlast the duration of its own utterance, the time during which it is given voice. Yet this is equally what Frankenstein tries to do at the end of his long confession, and equally the purpose behind the telling of his own story. In the same speech in which he warns Walton of the Monster's eloquence, Frankenstein, soaring to new rhetorical heights of his own, attempts to elicit a promise from his interlocutor:

> Oh! When will my guiding spirit, in conducting me to the demon, allow me the rest I so much desire; or must I die, and he yet live? If I do, swear to me, Walton, that he shall not escape, that you will seek him, and satisfy my vengeance in his death.
>
> (p. 208)

Frankenstein promised Walton a didactic story, a tale from which he might 'deduce an apt moral' (p. 30) about the perils of seeking glory in death-defying acts of bravery and ambition. Ambivalent himself about the moral he would have Walton draw, he reveals that his real point, his true narrative purpose, is neither to instruct nor to delight, but to exact a promise. Frankenstein's 'hideous narration' thus repeats the gesture of the monstrous narrative it frames: in his attempt to bind Walton to some future action, he generates a chain of contracts, a chain of narratives whose 'points' lie outside of the stories themselves. And yet each of these narratives is embedded in another, is framed. The syntactic placement of these narratives (one inside the other) moves the reader inward, setting up a pulsion toward a centre, creating a spatial image for narrative as something closed, finite, contained by its own borders – a middle set off from the rest of language by a beginning and an end. And yet the rhetorical strategy of the narrative chain moves continually outward, implicating through each narration someone outside the tale. Contradictory though this may seem, there is really nothing surprising about it; we are confronting a fresh instance of framing's double logic, the tendency of the frame simultaneously to establish boundaries and to announce, even to invite, their violation.[17]

More surprising is the persistence of the *promise* in each of the novel's laminations. If Frankenstein's confession tells the story of his promise to the Monster, Walton's letters tell the story of his promise to his crew. This story begins with the rumblings of mutiny, so fearful are his sailors of the mountains of ice that surround the ship and threaten to crush it. His men approach him to make 'a requisition which, in justice, I could not refuse' (p. 214):

> They insisted ... that I should engage with a solemn promise, that if the vessel should be freed I would instantly direct my course southward.
>
> (p. 214)

Walton consents. Unlike Frankenstein, he keeps his promise, perhaps having drawing an 'apt moral' from Frankenstein's story after all. Nevertheless, Walton disregards the oath with which Frankenstein attempted to bind him. Given the opportunity, he does not destroy the Monster.

Promises kept and promises broken – this pattern repeats itself elsewhere, at the very beginning of the novel and at the heart of the Monster's narrative.[18] It gives point to a story Walton tells his sister, a digression which, taken by itself, leaves us with a Labovian 'So what?' The central character of this digression is Walton's master-at-arms, who never appears in the novel *in propria persona*. After acquiring a respectable fortune in prize money from his conquests at sea, he had fallen in love with 'a young Russian lady of moderate fortune', and now had enough money and property to win the consent of the woman's father. But he soon discovered that the woman loved someone else, though her father would not consent to their marriage because the man was too poor. In an extravagantly self-denying gesture, Walton's master-at-arms presented his prize money and his farm to his rival and pressed the woman's father to consent to the new match. The father, feeling bound in honour, refused to break his promise until the master-at-arms forced his hand by leaving the country. Walton's immediate reason for telling this story is to demonstrate how sorely he needs a friend, for though his ship's master is a model of kindliness and even a 'noble fellow', he is no companion for someone who admires eloquence and loves a good story as much as Walton does. The problem, as Walton puts it, is that he is 'as silent as a Turk' (p. 21).[19]

This Orientalist simile, which embeds within it some of the 'incidental imperialist sentiment' expressed elsewhere in the text, directs us to the real point of this story which, again, lies partly outside of its own bounds.[20] At the geometrical centre of *Frankenstein*, in the Monster's story-within-Frankenstein's story-within-Walton's story, the story of the De Laceys once more tells about a promise of a daughter's hand. But whereas the father of the Russian lady keeps his promise, this time the promise is treacherously broken. The villain is Safie's father, who is responsible for the De Laceys' poverty and exile, and who compounds this injury by offering his daughter to Felix in marriage only to renege. The story of the master-at-arms now becomes meaningful as a story in which a promise is scrupulously, almost stubbornly kept. Thus a story on the outside of *Frankenstein*, a brief digression in the outermost of the novel's many narrative frames, illuminates the story at the centre of these frames. And the story in the centre sheds some light on the strange simile with which Walton dismisses the master-at-arms, for Safie's father, though not particularly silent, is (in the novel's parlance) a 'Turk'.

One problem with this pattern of promises is that Frankenstein's promise – which in a sense grounds all the other promises, making them meaningful by analogy to itself – is really a promise *manqué*. For Frankenstein never actually utters the words 'I promise', though the Monster's conditions are that he '"promise ... to comply with my requisition"' (p. 144). Indeed, it is the Monster who makes all of the promises on that misty afternoon atop Montanvert: '"I swear to you, by the earth which I inhabit, and by you that made me, that with the companion you bestow, I will quit the neighbourhood of man ..."' The monster's narrative, with its concluding 'proposition'

(p. 147), begins to take a familiar shape. He speaks forcibly and persuasively; he makes extravagant promises, binding himself to another for all eternity; he swears 'by the fire of love that burns in [his] heart' (p. 148), and he wins consent from someone who yields gradually and reluctantly. The whole narrative has the structure of an elaborate seduction.

We don't ordinarily think of the promise as basic to seduction. The essence of seduction might seem rather to be in its etymology: 'to lead astray'. But Robert Meister, a student of seductions literary and otherwise, denies this altogether. He observes that

> In order to arrive at a satisfactory definition of seduction, it is essential to dismiss the notion that seduction is equivalent to leading astray; its possibilities are so *promising* that it cannot be defined in one equation.[21]

One is reluctant to speculate about these promising possibilities, but Shoshana Felman, whose much more interesting book about seduction celebrates and exploits such verbal coincidences, might observe that promising is rather one of the conditions of the possibility of seduction. Exploring the seductions of various Don Juans and of J. L. Austin's speech-act theory, Felman argues that '[t]he rhetoric of seduction may be summarised by the performative utterance *par excellence:* "I promise"'. Unlike Meister, she does hazard 'one equation' with which to define seduction: 'to seduce is to produce felicitous language' (p. 28).

In its general, non-technical sense, *felicitous* might aptly (felicitously?) describe the Monster's discourse, for his oratorical flair, his studied use of the many tropes at the rhetorician's disposal,[23] he has 'a special ability for suitable manner or expression' – which is how the dictionary defines *felicitous*. But the word has a technical meaning as well. It has been used by Austin to describe certain performative speech acts, that is, utterances such as 'I promise', which neither inform nor describe but instead constitute an action in their own utterance. These cannot be logically true or false, but Austin argues that they can either succeed or misfire. For example, the utterance that declares two people married can either be legal and binding, if it is uttered by the right person under the right circumstances, or else it can have no force at all – for example, during a rehearsal or in a play.[24] Only in the first case is the utterance 'felicitous'.

To seduce, then, is to produce language that hits the mark, that succeeds in its aim. But by this definition, the Monster's narrative, for all its resemblance to the seductions of Don Juan, fails miserably. Whereas Don Juan's speech acts never fail to end in sex acts, the Monster's language in this respect is stubbornly infelicitous, his efforts to seduce inevitably misfiring. For Frankenstein ultimately breaks his promise, denying the Monster the mate he desires, even though he had agreed upon the mate as 'the justice due both to him and my fellow creatures' (p. 148). In the last analysis narration itself – the Monster's medium of seduction – fails, as it had earlier failed Justine, though not for the same reasons.

The price of failure is high. The results are violence and death, which *Frankenstein* seems to suggest, lie somewhere beyond narration, as though narrative were a means of staving them off. Had the Monster succeeded in his narrative task, had his persuasiveness outlasted his giving it voice, he would not have visited upon Frankenstein the chain of deaths that culminates finally in Frankenstein's own.[25] At the same time, death is the very stuff of narrative in *Frankenstein*, the set of events that compose the plot. In a sense, death generates narrative as surely as it is the origin of the Monster himself, who was assembled from bits and pieces taken from charnel houses. For Frankenstein's desire to create new life – the precondition of the whole series of monstrous events that form his 'hideous narration' – is largely a response to the death of his mother, which he calls 'the first misfortune of my life' (p. 42). It is his desire to reverse the most basic plot of all, the ending of life in death, that engenders his scientific discoveries and the horror story they bring about: 'I thought, that if I could bestow animation upon lifeless matter, I might in process of time ... renew life where death had apparently devoted the body to corruption' (p. 54). *Frankenstein* suggests a morphology of narrative texts that makes death the beginning instead of the end.

Death is only one conventional solution to narrative's need for closure and a sense of an ending. Though nineteenth-century realism will often strenuously deny it or admit it only with a resigned and world-weary irony, there is still at least the narrative possibility of living happily ever after, the ending offered by countless folk tales and suggested by comedy and romance. Domestic tranquillity serves as a fit ending to literary plots because it represents repose and stability, even stasis; it is what gets disrupted so that narrative can be produced. In many respects, narrative and domesticity are opposed to one another, each coming into being only at the expense of the other. (It remains for nineteenth-century realism, particularly Jane Austen's novels of manners, to show how they might co-exist.) Such an opposition is an organising principle of romance, whose episodic plots spin out, with untiring narrative vigour, story after story of heightened experience that takes place far from the hearth.[26]

In the many stories within *Frankenstein*, marital/sexual contentment and the repose of domesticity are promised repeatedly, and repeatedly disrupted. To the broken promises we have already seen we may add other images of domestic paradises lost: not only the marriage of Frankenstein and Elizabeth, violently ended by Elizabeth's murder on their wedding night, but also the destruction of the Frankenstein family, which begins with the mother's death and ends only when there is no one left. But the novel's most poignant vision of domestic tranquillity is not the short, happy picture of family life with which it begins; nor does it occur, as in *Wuthering Heights*, at the end of the novel as its consummation. Rather, it occupies the centre of the novel, in the story of the De Laceys, whose benevolence and kindness toward one another in adversity provide the Monster with his sentimental education. Significantly, theirs is the most radically disrupted story of the many embedded narratives *Frankenstein* contains. Just as the De Laceys are beginning, in their humble way, to prosper (Felix and Safie having been reunited, and material conditions being less austere), the Monster invades. The novel offers no suggestion of how their story ends; they simply flee, abandoning their cottage forever. *Frankenstein* makes domestic tranquillity an unattainable ideal, a state that can never, in the world it represents, be achieved. Its impossibility is symbolised by the De Laceys, the Monster's only 'family', who live in perpetual exile not only from their native land but finally from the novel as well.[27]

Not only is domestic tranquillity disrupted at the centre of the novel, but it is also excluded at the margins, in the frame. Walton directs the entire package of letters, including his transcription of Frankenstein's narrative, home to 'dear England' and his sister, Mrs Saville. With her 'husband, and lovely children' (p. 213), the absent Mrs Saville provides a final image of domesticity, but it lies wholly without the novel, outside of its many frames, beyond all of its narratives and hopelessly unconnected to any of them.

But since the framing of Frankenstein's and the Monster's stories serves to implicate something exterior to themselves, why is Mrs Saville not likewise implicated by the act of reading Walton's narrative; why is she not seduced by it? She is kept safely outside the scheme of the novel precisely because she is *reading*, because what she confronts is the written word. The novel's logic suggests that Walton, by offering her a transcription of the stories he hears, exposes her merely to a simulacrum, a representation of a monstrous story in a different medium. Deprived of the speaking voice, severed from its origins, the story can no longer exercise its seductive hold, its ability to exact promises. Thus transformed, the monstrous narrative is domesticated; Mrs Saville can read the story without any danger to herself. It may, as Walton fears, make her blood 'congeal with horror' (p. 209), but it poses her no real threat. Like Medusa's head in Perseus's mirror, what she reads is only an image of monstrosity; it therefore loses its power and its danger.

The frames thus mark the exclusion of Mrs Saville – and the reader as well – from the horror of the narratives they contain, and signal an immunity from the seductiveness of the voices that first utter them. At the same time, each frame that we pass through as we read makes the matter at the centre seem more highly charged, more significant, more invested with power. We read Gothic novels like *Frankenstein* precisely because we want our blood to 'congeal with horror', and the frames, by promising something powerfully horrifying at their centre, heighten the effect; hence the affinity of frame structures for the Gothic. Just as frames in general serve at once to delimit and extend, so do the frames around Gothic and supernatural fictions signify at once something highly charged, even dangerous, and the barriers that protect us from it.

As though to protect his version of Romanticism from what might have seemed to him a monstrous perversion of it. Percy Bysshe Shelley appended to *Frankenstein* a frame of his own, a peculiarly defensive statement of supposedly authorial intention. The 'chief concern' of the novelist, he asserted, 'has been limited to ... the exhibition of the amiableness of domestic affection, and the excellence of universal virtue'.[28] With these words, Shelley usurped the voice, domesticated (in every sense) a powerful story, and greatly reduced its meaning, offering that meaning to use almost as a hard, smooth kernel, deftly extracted from the whole. He then went further, denying on behalf of Mary Shelley any implications 'prejudicing any philosophical doctrine of whatever kind'. First representing *Frankenstein* as a story that exhibits precisely what it repeatedly disrupts and defers, he finally dismisses Mary Shelley's mythmaking altogether by assuring us that, after all, it signifies nothing. Perhaps he did so because *Frankenstein* casts doubt upon some tenets of the 'philosophical doctrine' we call Romanticism, a doubt that is expressed at the very opening of the novel as a hope, or more precisely, as a promise. The first letter that Walton writes his sister invokes a 'wind of promise', the 'cold northern breeze' that he feels as he walks in the streets of St Petersburg. To quiet his sister's evil forebodings, he assures her that he feels 'inspirited by this wind of promise' which 'play[s] upon my cheeks, ... braces my nerves, and fills me with delight' (p. 15). As he embarks on his journey, Walton feels the promise of the 'correspondent breeze', the gentle breeze that fans the cheek of Wordsworth as he begins the epic journey into his own mind, the wind that returns the Ancient Mariner to his 'own countree', and the wind that eventually brings the twin promises of spring and Revolution to Shelley. But Walton's wind blows from the cold, wintry north, not from the west; and the promise with which it frames the novel – the promise of reward for seeking glory and honour in filial, Promethean rebellion – like so many other promises in *Frankenstein*, is broken.

From *English Literary History*, 53 (1986), 141–61.

NOTES

[Beth Newman's deconstructive reading of the frame structure of the novel examines the way the text foregrounds processes of writing. Initially, in the novel, it is the writing that composes Walton's letters that comes between the reader and the telling of the story. Throughout the novel, Newman argues, spoken stories such as those of Frankenstein and the monster are framed by writing. These frames interrupt the process of direct communication between narrator and reader, undermining any assumption that there is a voice or presence in the text. Speech is preceded by writing, used in a textual, Derridean sense. For Derrida, Western language has presumed that speech is the model of human communication, even in written works. This tradition associates speech with the presence of another person and his/her meaning as the fixed point of origin to or a determining presence in the text. This model, however, depends on prior differentiations (to privilege speech over writing one must first have an idea of the difference between them) and these differentiations Derrida calls general writing. For Newman, *Frankenstein*'s frame structure discloses the indeterminacies of writing and subordinates characters in the text to the narratives that construct their identity and enable their speech. In this context the innocent character of Justine is framed as a murderous monster not only by the creature himself but by the stories narrated at her trial and by her confessor. Speech, intention and character are seen to be subordinate to the various narratives that compose the novel. Presented in the novel as speakers addressing and trying to seduce or persuade listeners, the narratives nonetheless depend on the frames of writing in which speech and character are given meaning and also displaced. The other texts included in the novel, the written journals and the letters in which Walton records the stories, defer any final resolution and emphasise the importance of the reading or interpretative context. Ed.]

1. Joseph Conrad, *Heart of Darkness,* ed. Robert Kimbrough (New York, 1971), p. 5.
2. Conrad, p. 69.
3. Conrad, p. 28.
4. While this conclusion is certainly true in the sense that every narrative, fictional or otherwise, has an author behind it, it is another matter to extend this by regarding every fictional narrative as an expression of a fictional character who narrates it. For a cogent exposition of the assumptions behind this argument and the limitations of it, see Jonathan Culler, 'Problems in the Theory of Fiction', *Diacritics*, 14 (Spring, 1984), 2–12. We might observe also that writers of fiction have deliberately and insistently developed techniques which aim to conceal or eliminate a particularised narrating subject, techniques like the so-called objective method sometimes employed by James and Hemingway, or the more radical effacements of narrating subject in the *nouveau roman*. No doubt students of narrative feel compelled to reiterate the credo that every narrative has a shaping intelligence behind it because the practice of so many writers – and the experience of reading their fiction – would deny it.
5. Though in *Turn of the Screw*, 'the story's written', as Douglas announces, it is part of an exchange of oral stories (Henry James, *The Turn of the Screw*, ed. Robert Kimbrough [New York, 1966], p. 2). Moreover, Douglas addresses the story particularly to the unnamed narrator, and does so in a frankly seductive manner, as the narrator is well aware.
6. Roland Barthes, *S/Z*, trans. Richard Miller (New York, 1974). See esp. p. 17.
7. Mary Shelley, *Frankenstein, or the Modern Prometheus*, ed. M. K. Joseph (London, 1969). Except where otherwise stated, all subsequent references are to this edition, which is based on the 1831 edition of the

text. *Frankenstein* was originally published in 1818; when it was reissued in 1831, Mary Shelley made some significant revisions.

8. *The Rime of the Ancient Mariner* – another frame narrative, we might observe – is obviously an important precursor text whose relation to *Frankenstein* has often been remarked. Peter Brooks makes an analogy between the two texts similar to my own, except that he suggests that what is spellbinding in *Frankenstein*, instead of being a 'glittering eye', is language itself. (See 'Godlike Science/Unhallowed Arts: Language, Nature and Monstrosity' in *The Endurance of Frankenstein*, ed. George Levine and U. C. Knoepflmacher, [Berkeley, 1974]). This is unquestionably so, but it seems to me that certain kinds of language seem more potent in *Frankenstein* than others. One of these is language put to narrative use; another, illustrated here, is language conveyed by the voice.
9. Germano Celant makes this the function of the frame in painting in 'Framed: Innocent or Gilt?' *Artforum*, 20 (Summer, 1982), 49–55. In particular, he explains that every individual painting may be thought of as 'a cut-out portion', 'a lesion, a wound, a tear, a slash, an action within the field of art ... The result is a scar or thickening – a frame – which functions as a defence, constructing a barrier which wards off and repels the isolation imposed by the cut' into 'art's body' (p. 49).
10. Oddly enough, Mary Shelley revised this part of the novel to make it more, not less awkward, and to make Elizabeth's breach of narrative convention more salient. In the 1818 text, this paragraph begins: 'After what I have said, I dare say you well remember the heroine of my little tale: for Justine was a great favourite of yours ....' See *Frankenstein, or the Modern Prometheus*, ed. James Rieger (Chicago, 1974), p. 22.
11. See, for example, James Hafley, 'The Villain in *Wuthering Heights*', *Nineteenth Century Fiction*, 13 (December, 1958), 199–215.
12. The idea that storytelling is often presented in fiction as a form of seduction is explored by Ross Chambers in *Story and Situation: Narrative Seduction and the Power of Fiction* (Minneapolis, 1984). Though he does not specifically discuss frame narratives (as such), his argument about why literary fictions, beginning with the nineteenth century, often present themselves as seductions bears some relation to framing in the broader sense of the term. He suggests that when literary texts began to undergo the process of reification, becoming specialised as *art* and autonomised as *text*, they ceased to have use value as conveyors of information and experience. To realise their own potential exchange value, Chambers argues, it became necessary for literary texts to exert powers of seduction to compensate for what they lost as direct acts of communication as they obtained their autonomy. (See esp. pp. 11–12.) It is as though the seductiveness of the text were

a result of the same process which, in Celant's argument, brought about pictorial framing. Perhaps that is one reason that frame narratives, in offering situational contexts for storytelling, often make seduction a crucial aspect of the situation.

13. When Mary Shelley set out to write her 'ghost story', according to her recollections in her 1831 Introduction, she found herself drawing a discouraging blank. It is likely that she mined her memories of earlier Gothic romances for inspiration, and Lewis would have loomed large in her mind. Both Shelleys had long been admirers of *The Monk*, which was published in 1796, when Lewis was only slightly older than Mary Shelley as she composed *Frankenstein*. We know that Mary Shelley read *The Monk* from the evidence of her journal (see *Mary Shelley's Journal*, ed. Frederick L. Jones [Norman, 1947], pp. 16, 32); and Judith Wilt has argued that the name Mathilda, which occurs in P. B. Shelley's *Zastrozzi* and as the title of one of Mary Shelley's stories, looks backward to Lewis's beautiful, diabolical seductress. See 'Frankenstein as Mystery Play' in *The Endurance of Frankenstein* (cited above, note 8), p. 34n.

Moreover, Lewis was practically there on the spot as she wrote, visiting Byron at the Villa Diodati soon after the friendly competition to write the grisliest ghost story had begun. While he was there he entertained Byron and Shelley by telling them his own ghost stories and tales of Gothic horror, which Shelley then wrote down in Mary Shelley's journal. But Lewis never surpassed his earlier efforts, and according to one of Mary Shelley's biographers, '[b]oth Shelley and Mary knew that her idea was far more effective than [the] insubstantial horrors' with which he regaled the circle of friends at the Villa Diodati. (See Jane Dunn, *Moon in Eclipse: A Life of Mary Shelley* [New York, 1978], p. 142.) If Mary Shelley was indeed trying consciously to surpass the famous Monk Lewis, it's not surprising that she would rewrite a scene from the novel that literally made his name.

14. Matthew Gregory Lewis, *The Monk* (New York, 1952), p. 65. All subsequent page numbers refer to this edition.

15. In expressing the idea that to be a woman is to be a monster, Mary Shelley is voicing an attitude about gender deeply rooted in Western culture, an idea underscored by some of the events in her own life from the time of *Frankenstein's* composition. One night at the Villa Diodati, Byron read Coleridge's 'Christabel' aloud. Shelley ran from the room shrieking, and did not calm down for a long time. He later told Mary that he looked at her and imagined that she had eyes instead of nipples. See Dunn, pp. 136–7.

For another view of the way 'Christabel' is inscribed in *Frankenstein*, see Marc A. Rubinstein, '"My Accursed Origin": The Search for the Mother in *Frankenstein*', *Studies in Romanticism*, 15 (1976), 184–6. Barbara Johnson offers an intriguing reading of the relation between woman and monster in 'My Monster/Myself', *Diacritics*, 12 (Summer, 1982), 2–12.

16. William Labov, *Language in the Inner City* (Philadelphia, 1972), p. 366.

17. This double logic operates in all framing. For different discussions of the way it works in painting, see Celant, cited above as well as Alfonso Procaccini, 'Alberti and the "Framing" of Perspective', *Journal of Aesthetics and Art Criticism*, 40, no. 1 (Fall, 1981), 29–39. Closer to home, Shoshana Felman finds a similar logic at work in Henry James's famous novella, which, she observes, 'pulls the outside of the story into its inside by enclosing what is usually outside it: its own readers. But the frame at the same time does the very opposite, pulling the inside outside ...' ('Turning the Screw of Interpretation', *Yale French Studies*, 55/56 [1977], 27). The most complicated analysis of the double logic of framing occurs in Jacques Derrida's discussion of 'The Parergon' in *La Vérité en peinture* which has been lucidly summarised by Jonathan Culler in *On Deconstruction: Theory and Criticism After Structuralism* (Ithaca, 1982), pp. 193–9.

18. In the context of the promise, a burlesque of *Frankenstein* that appeared on the London stage in 1824 offers some food for thought: it was called *Frank in Steam, or the Modern Promise to Pay*. Unfortunately history has not favoured us with a text of this play. It is mentioned by Christopher Small in *Ariel Like a Harpy: Shelley, Mary and Frankenstein* (London, 1972), p. 16.

19. This wording, too, exists only in the revised version of *Frankenstein*. The 1818 text puts it rather differently: the master 'has scarcely an idea beyond the rope and the shroud'. (A variant reading is 'beyond the ship and the crew'.) See Reiger, p. 15.

20. The quoted phrase is Gayatri Spivak's, who argues that *Frankenstein* 'does not deploy the axiomatics of imperialism' though 'there is plenty of incidental imperialist sentiment' in the text ('Three Women's Texts and a Critique of Imperialism', *Critical Inquiry*, 12:1 [Autumn, 1985], 254). This sentiment, manifesting itself in the text as the Western attitude towards the Middle East and Islam that Edward Said calls 'orientalism' (*Orientalism* [New York, 1978]), is most obvious in the representations of Safie and her father. Safie, the beautiful exotic on whom the text bestows a Christian mother and an abhorrence of 'Turkish' attitudes towards women, is referred to throughout ch.XIII as 'the Arabian' (or even the 'sweet Arabian'); her treacherous father is described throughout the next chapter as 'the Turk' in order to emphasise that he is Muslim (and so, after a fashion, 'explain' his treachery).

21. Robert Meister (ed.), *A Literary Guide to Seduction* (New York, 1963), pp. 15–16 (my emphasis). This is frankly an offensive book, an anthology dedicated to the proposition that 'it will do a maiden little

good to know *what* to do a bed if she was not properly bedded in the first place' (Afterword, p. 417).

22. Shoshana Felman, *The Literary Speech-Act: Don Juan with J. L. Austin, or Seduction in Two Languages* (Ithaca, 1983), p. 30. Felman, using Don Juan as the exemplary seducer, bases the rhetoric of seduction on too narrow a sample. Flipping through Meister's selections one turns up seductions that do not rely on promises. But her conclusions are suggestive all the same for many seductions. We might note that Matilda, in seducing Ambrosio in *The Monk*, exacts a promise from him:

    'Swear, that whatever be my secret, you will not oblige me to quit the monastery till my noviciate shall expire.'
    'I promise it faithfully.'

    (p. 85)

23. Peter Brooks discusses the Monster's use of the classical rhetorical tropes in 'Godlike Science/Unhallowed Arts', 206–7.

24. J. L. Austin's *How to Do Things With Words*, ed. I. O. Urmson and Marina Sbisa (Oxford, 1975); see esp. Lecture II (pp. 12–24).

25. In this connection see Tzvetan Todorov's remarks about narrative according to *The Arabian Nights*: 'Narrative equals life; absence of narrative, death. If Scheherazade finds no more tales to tell, she will be beheaded ... imperfect narrative also equals ... death.' See 'Narrative-Men' in *The Poetics of Prose*, Richard Howard, trans. (Ithaca, 1977), pp. 74–5.

26. Perhaps the conflict between domesticity and narrative is most clearly articulated in Charlotte Lennox's antiromance, *The Female Quixote* (New York, 1970, originally published 1752), where a young woman's readiness for marriage and domestic responsibility is signalled by her renouncing the desire to hear and to tell extravagant 'histories'.

27. This treatment of domestic life in *Frankenstein* has been read persuasively as a critique of the bourgeois family, an expression of a subversive attitude that Mary Shelley absorbed as she read and reread the works of her mother. See Kate Ellis, 'Monsters in the Garden', in *The Endurance of Frankenstein*, cited above, note 8. When we consider that Mary Shelley read these books in her favourite spot, atop her mother's grave, the subversiveness is given a twist toward the nostalgic and sentimental, and is perhaps mitigated by a longing for the stability of the conventional family that life had so far deprived her of.

28. Preface to *Frankenstein*, p. 14.

8

Frankenstein with Kant: A Theory of Monstrosity or the Monstrosity of Theory

BARBARA CLAIRE FREEMAN

The sort of interrogation I am proposing is neither philosophical nor literary but something in between these two. On the one hand, it is a testing out of the shifting boundary between philosophy, personified by Kant's *Critique of Judgment*, and literature, represented by Shelley's *Frankenstein*; on the other, it investigates what rebounds from these two texts: what comes back, or returns. If as Deleuze says, 'we have the *Critique of Judgment* as the foundation of Romanticism', perhaps *Frankenstein* is already encased in and anticipated by Kantian theory.[1] Correlatively, perhaps these texts, each the inverse of the other, predict and possibly even determine the shape of theory in the late twentieth century. If we are the heirs of *Frankenstein* and the third *Critique* – as much read *by* them as readers *of* them – what have we inherited, to whom are we indebted, and what are our debts? My thesis is that Victor Frankenstein's Monster is the third *Critique*'s heir, and that we are its inheritor.

First I argue that, in a philosophic register, Kant's depiction or construction of the sublime simultaneously portrays and defends itself against monstrosity; second that, in a literary register, *Frankenstein* makes explicit and dramatises what Kant's analytic contains but cannot say, demonstrating that the shape of the sublime, which fulfils the metaphysician's desire, is precisely that of monstrosity; and third, that Shelley's *Frankenstein* and Kant's *Critique of Judgment* together predict the form of contemporary theory – 'the as yet unnameable which is proclaiming itself in the terrifying form of monstrosity', as Derrida said when he brought Deconstruction (sometimes described as 'the French plague') to Baltimore in 1966. Through investigating the ways in which these two texts mutually inhabit and enact each other, I suggest that Kant's theory of the sublime is not only a form of the monstrous but also a figure of theory as such – perhaps even the paradigmatic form of it, and that theory in turn is itself monstrous or Frankensteinian. The romantic vision of the future prophesied by Shelley as monstrous and incarnated theoretically by the Kantian sublime is fulfilled in the present: specifically, by the terroristic effect produced by the missiles of contemporary French philosophy which, perhaps autobiographically reflecting upon the sublime, itself may be an instance of that which it purports merely to describe.

Kant's construction of the sublime is bound up in a system of encasements, injunctions, and imperatives that function to protect the sublime from the monstrous potential inherent in it. The identity of the sublime, itself 'a mere appendix'[2] to the concept of the beautiful and aesthetic judgement, is dependent upon a series of negations or appendages that constitute and frame it. Product of and produced by what it excludes, the sublime becomes what it is only by virtue of being distinguished from what it is not, and in every case that to which Kant opposes it is negative, dangerous, destructive.

From paragraphs 26 to 29, the principal sections in which Kant discusses the mathematical and dynamical sublime, four pairs of oppositions are presented, each of which is crucial to the definition of the sublime. Every couple functions to split the sublime in two, separating what is moral and good in it, on the right side of the Law, from what is illegal, marginal, on the outside. At stake is Kant's need to keep the sublime within its aesthetic encasement, so that, like the beautiful, it too may remain a symbol of 'the morally good'.

Sublime states of mind first must be produced by *colossal* but not *monstrous* representations of nature (par. 26, p. 91); second, they should provoke *religious* sentiments, giving rise to 'reverence', as opposed to *superstition*, which instils 'fear and apprehension' (par. 28, p. 103); third, the sublime can include *affection*, wherein the mind's freedom is merely hindered, but not *passion*, in which its freedom is abolished (par. 29, p. 113); last, sublime states of mind may involve *enthusiasm*, even though the latter carries with it the temporary risk of 'unbridled imagination', but not *fanaticism*, in which the imagination, as if diseased, becomes 'anomalous' or abnormal (par. 29, p. 116). In each case, Kant briefly represents the negative quality that might, if he did not quickly exclude it, become identified with the sublime and prevent it from being an aesthetic, hence legislatable, category.

Although each couple has its own fascination, here I will discuss only the distinction between the colossal and the monstrous, since it is perhaps most germane to a reading of *Frankenstein*. Kant defines the colossal as 'the presentation of concepts almost too great for any presentation' (par. 26, p. 91). The difference between the colossal and the monstrous is a matter of degree: the colossal, although it 'borders on the relatively monstrous', is never quite identical to it. Whereas the colossal involves 'the intuition of an object *almost* too great for our faculty of apprehension' (my emphasis), the monstrous object is defined by Kant as one that 'by its size, destroys the purpose which constitutes the concept of it' (par. 26, p. 91). By identifying the sublime exclusively with the colossal, then, Kant attempts to shield it from the monstrous object's 'destructive' force. Sensitive to the possibility of confusing 'things in nature the concepts of which bring with them a definite purpose' (e.g. animals with a 'known natural destination') with 'rude nature' (e.g. nonpurposive natural objects), Kant next cautions that the former, precisely because of its proximity to the monstrous, must never be allowed to 'exhibit the sublime'. But because 'rude nature', on the other hand, 'contains nothing monstrous (either magnificent or horrible)' and will thus always yield purely colossal representations, Kant insists that the sublime be exhibited only 'in rude nature merely as involving magnitude' (par. 26, p. 91). The negative and extrinsic, in this case identified with the 'monstrous', functions as a boundary line that shores up and gives definition to the positive, intrinsic, or 'colossal'. And although these divisions help to enclose the sublime within a theory of the beautiful that is encased by a theory of taste itself encased by a theory of judgement, an extremely fragile line divides the positive aspect of the sublime from its negative, destructive side. The sublime can never be contained because part of what has been removed and put outside still remains within, and what has been excluded may always return, as if from without. In this case, its name is *Frankenstein*, for between them Victor and his Monster stage everything Kant is careful to say the sublime isn't, but secretly is.

As Derrida remarked in another context, 'The frame doesn't fit.'[3] In the case of *Frankenstein*, his comment may be taken literally: as Victor observes, the first time he sees what has turned out to be a monster, 'His yellow skin scarcely covered the work of muscles and arteries beneath'.[4] The fit of the monster's skin is comparable to the encasement of the sublime within Kantian theory: *Frankenstein* demonstrates that the frame in which Kant encloses the sublime is too tight.[5]

Victor has tried expressly to create a 'being of gigantic stature', one whose size, 'about eight feet in height and proportionally large' (p. 49), would reflect Victor's lofty ambition and the magnitude of his task. It is supremely important that his creation be beautiful. Initially, the Monster's monstrosity is an effect of how he looks and not what he does. As soon as Victor sees the creature take its first breath and 'agitate its limbs', he can barely find words adequate to his distress at the creature's ugliness: 'How can I describe my emotions at this catastrophe, or how delineate the wretch whom with such infinite pains and care I had endeavoured to form? His limbs were in proportion, and I had selected his features as beautiful. Beautiful! Great God!' (p. 52). Victor proceeds to chronicle the Monster's various atrocities: 'his watery eyes, that seemed almost of the same colour as the sunken white sockets in which they were set, his shrivelled complexion, and straight black lips' (p. 52). Victor had intended to create something magnificent and instead gives birth to a 'catastrophe'. Indeed, *Frankenstein* can be read almost as a parody of the *Critique of Judgment*, for in it everything Kant identifies with or as sublime, including the products of sublimation, yield precisely what Kant prohibits: terror, monstrosity, passion, and fanaticism.

All the things Kant's sublime is supposed to be and do – for example, 'raise the energies of the soul above their accustomed height' (par. 28, p. 100) and produce a conviction of the mind's 'superiority to nature even in its immensity' (par. 28, p. 101) – the vision of the sublime in *Frankenstein* systematically inverts. Even the topography of the novel, full of mountain heights, elevated vistas, and crashing thunder, sounds like Kant's description of a sublime landscape. The reader might encounter the following topos, 'clouds piled up in the sky, moving with lightning flashes and thunder peals ... the dread and holy awe which seizes the observer at the sight of mountain peaks rearing themselves to heaven, deep chasms and streams raging therein, deep-shadowed solitudes that dispose one to melancholy meditation' (par. 28, pp. 101, 102) in one of Victor's accounts of a journey to Mont Blanc near his home in Geneva. But whereas in Kant 'the irresistibility of (nature's) might ... discloses to us a faculty of judging independently of and a superiority over nature' (par. 28, p. 101), in *Frankenstein* an identical geography produces neither peace of mind nor aesthetic pleasure, but rather a vision of and an encounter with monstrosity. Each time a sublime landscape is depicted, it is linked to the Monster's appearance. Indeed, after the Monster's birth at Ingolstadt, Victor's meetings with him take place only at the tops of mountains, on glaciers surrounded by fields of ice, or during violent storms, amidst echoing thunder and repeated, dazzling flashes of lightning. The landscape is the same as Kant's – that of Nature in all her might and majesty, but the effect (and affect) produced is not.

In Longinus, as in Kant, the lightning flash is one of the most privileged examples of the sublime. Longinus even posits an equivalence between them: sublime oratory, which exhibits a 'genuine power over language' is like 'a flash of lightning' in that both 'strike the hearer', 'rend everything before them' and in so doing 'reveal the full might of the orator'.[6] In *Frankenstein* lightning illuminates the sky and does indeed reveal the orator's full might, but the Monster is the one who possesses the gift of eloquence; and the sublime flash of lightning, even while it yields a moment of sheer luminosity, also brings with it utter devastation.

When Victor is fifteen he watches a 'terrible thunderstorm' in the security of his home 'with curiosity and delight'. But lightning strikes a nearby 'old and beautiful' oak, and a stream of fire issues from the tree that tears it to ribbons. Nature's sublime and dazzling lightning flash destroys the beautiful oak and in so doing foretells the future's shape: the lightning destroys the tree as the monster will destroy Victor and his family. Nothing remains but a 'blasted stump'. From the very outset, then, the sublime in *Frankenstein* lays waste to the beautiful and brings with it decimation. 'I never beheld anything so utterly destroyed' (p. 35), Victor says. The next flash of lightning in fact brings him face to face with monstrosity. Walking in the Alps on the way home after the murder of his brother William, Victor watches lightning 'play on the summit of Mont Blanc in the most beautiful figures' (p. 70), and continues the ascent while 'vivid flashes of lightning' dazzle his eyes and illuminate the lake, 'making it appear like a vast sheet of fire' (p. 71). But again a naturally beautiful form, or 'figure', is blasted away by the sublime, for here Victor meets the Monster for the first time. 'I perceived in the gloom a figure which stole from behind a clump of trees near me ... A flash of lightning illuminated the object and discovered its shape plainly to me; its gigantic stature, and the deformity of its aspect, more hideous than belongs to humanity, instantly informed me that it was the wretch, the filthy daemon, to whom I had given life' (p. 71). Moments of pure vision indeed illuminate 'the truth', but its shape is as monstrous as it is sublime.

What the lightning shows is that metaphysics' faith in vision as an adequate index to the truth is misplaced. Lightning in *Frankenstein* calls into question metaphysics' assumption that vision is an accurate judge of the truth, which is also presumed to be both good and beautiful. This belief, or bias, is reflected by Kant's conviction that beauty is the ultimate symbol of the good (par. 59 of the third *Critique* is titled 'Of Beauty as the Symbol of Morality'), and Victor's assumption that, because his progeny's shape is monstrous, so must be his spirit. The novel stages metaphysics' faith that truth is something that can be *seen*: no one questions the supposition that the true is identical to the good (which has a beautiful, or at least a pleasing, form), or that eyes and vision have a closer proximity to 'the truth' than ears and hearing. The only human who ever says a kind word to the Monster is the old, blind man De Lacey (whose name contains the word for what he cannot do, i.e. see), and even he trusts the evidence of his families' eyes rather than his own ears: when the family returns and see the Monster clinging to their father's knees, Agatha faints, Safie flees, and Felix beats him up. The Monster's voice is his only pleasing attribute: 'although harsh', it has 'nothing terrible in it' (p. 128), but his very eloquence makes him suspect. At the end Victor warns Walton not to be seduced by the Monster's rhetorical power when they meet: 'He is eloquent and persuasive; and once his words had even power over my heart: but trust him not ... hear him not' (p. 206). By aligning the lightning, the monster, and the sublime, the novel shows that Longinus's 'genuine power' – poetic or otherwise – may produce devastation as easily as beauty, and that the sublime has a power beauty does not have, one that has no necessary connection to the realms of ethics or aesthetics.

Romanticism's vision of itself, as of the future, is, with metaphysics, deeply implicated in the problematic of vision. In our tradition, as Heidegger has pointed out, the notions of vision and theory are closely linked.[7] 'Theory' comes from the Greek *theorein*, which combines *thea*, the visible aspect of things, and *horao*, which means to look at something closely or view it attentively. This rapport suggests that, at least in the West, the sense of sight has become a metaphor for knowledge itself. The etymology of the word 'theory' is particularly interesting because Victor calls natural philosophy 'the genius that has regulated my fate' (p. 32), while for Kant the provinces of natural philosophy and theory are almost identical: 'Philosophy', he tells us, 'is correctly divided into two parts quite distinct in their principles: the theoretical part, or *natural philosophy*; and the practical part, or Moral Philosophy' (Intro., p. 7). Victor, whose inquiries are 'directed to the metaphysical or, in the highest sense, the physical secrets of the world' (p. 32), may be said to personify metaphysics' desire for transparent meaning, showing the ways in which the theorist's very commitment to theory also leads to a certain blindness.

Victor represents Kant's 'natural philosopher' or 'theorist' to the letter. According to Kant, the province of theoretical philosophy is precisely the 'doctrine of nature': 'legislation through natural concepts is carried on by means of the understanding and is theoretical' (Intro., p. 10); and it is precisely to the study of natural philosophy, or metaphysics, that Victor, in his 'fervent longing to penetrate the secrets of nature' (p. 34), turns. From the day that he hears Professor Waldman lecture on the advancements that modern natural philosophy has made and the improvements it can be expected to accomplish, 'natural philosophy and particularly chemistry in the most comprehensive sense of the term' become nearly his 'sole occupation' (p. 45).

Victor, like Kant, wants knowledge of the foundations and ultimate causes of things. His belief that metaphysics can give access to 'the secrets of heaven and earth' (p. 32) is similar to Kant's faith that knowledge is built upon stable foundations that reason can locate, and, independently of experience, use 'to establish the unity of all empirical principles under higher ones and hence to establish the possibility of their systematic subordination' (Intro., p. 16). Kant's topographical, and territorialistic, view of knowledge as a geographical realm that reason can chart, divide, bridge, and then connect to other domains is of a piece with his faith in the stability of its foundations; his certainty that knowledge has an unchanging ground on which the theorist can construct an edifice reflects the extent to which metaphysics, albeit unconsciously, is committed to, if not constituted by, the thematics of sight. The desire that pervades the *Critique of Judgment*, that is, to demonstrate that 'the feeling of pleasure is determined by a ground a priori and valid for every man' (Intro., p. 23), and the utter confidence in the attainability of such an end is congruent with Victor's certainty that the acquisition of knowledge can give him insight into the nature of nature itself, and that metaphysics will yield a moment of pure, unmediated vision.

The way in which Victor provides a portrait of Kant, or a mirror of metaphysical desire, allows one to ask this crucial question: What is the logic that links the theorist's desire of truth, which Derrida has called 'the desire of reason as desire for a grounded structure', to a wish for the sublime and the construction of monstrosity?[8] Victor is to the Monster he creates and refuses to acknowledge what Kant is to the sublime he authors and will not admit. Today we are faced with or have inherited what Romanticism, envisioning the future, invented and then refused to see.

The twin meanings of the word 'monstrosity' help to explain the connection between the sublime on the one hand and theory, or the theorist, on the other. Just as Kant's most general definition of the sublime is bound up with magnitude ('We call that *sublime* which is *absolutely great* ... the sublime is that in comparison with which everything else is small' [par. 25, pp. 87, 88]), so the word 'monster' is defined most frequently as something of huge and often unmanageable proportions. An initial rapport between sublimity and monstrosity, then, consists in their enormity, their almost unnatural size. The affinity between them, however, not only pertains to magnitude, but resides in a certain relationship to theory: 'monster' also means something shown, proven, or demonstrated – like an idea or argument. From the Latin *monstrum*, 'monster' originally meant a divine portent or warning, so that from the outset it has borne a prophetic relationship to, or been a sign of, the future. What is important here, however, is that the French *monstre* (a relative of *montrer*, to show) was once in English a now obsolete form of monster, and meant both something huge or enormous, and a demonstration or proof, something shown or exhibited. A whole family of English words reflects this conjunction: *monstrable* means capable of being shown; *monstrance* means demonstration or proof; *to monstrate* is to prove; a *monstration* means a demonstration; and the archaic verb *to monster* meant to exhibit or point out. Theory, then, the showing or demonstrating of an argument or concept, is not only bound up with vision, but the very notion of showing is itself bound up with, indeed a synonym for, monstrosity: monstrosity is as involved with demonstrating and proving as proving is with monstrosity. This conjunction suggests that an investigation of monstrosity might yield a theory of theory and that, correlatively, an investigation of monstrosity might demonstrate something about demonstration, about that which purports to contain the sublime and prohibit the monstrous, while exhibiting the differences between them.

The etymology of 'monster' (or of the French *monstre*, since in *Frankenstein* the Monster's mother-tongue is French) allows an elaboration of theory as a form of monstrosity, and an exploration of sublimity as a form of, even a figure for, theory. The word monster also means 'a threatening force, an engulfing power', which describes both the movement of theory today and what the Monster in *Frankenstein* does. Just as in the last decade theory has acted like a monster by appropriating departments of Humanities and Letters and by blurring traditional distinctions between literature and philosophy (thereby confounding, or amalgamating, the study of beauty with that of truth), so the sublime, as if it personified theory itself, has lately become the principal subject of theoretical inquiry. In this regard it is perhaps worth noting that the word 'frank' once meant 'free from bondage or restraint', and that Kant's sublime 'is to be found in a formless object, so far as in it or by occasion of it *boundlessness* is represented' (par. 23, p. 82). If being 'free from bondage' is a condition for 'boundlessness', Frankenstein's name contains the word that is synonymous to, or one of the properties of, the sublime. Today the sublime, unbound, blasted out of its aesthetic encasement, has taken over, even dominates the realm of theory.

In the last decade, virtually every major French theorist – Deleuze, Derrida, Kristeva, Lacan, Lacoue-Labarthe, Lyotard, Marin, Nancy – and an increasing number of Americans – de Man, Chase, Ferguson, Hertz, Klein, Weber, Weiskel, to name but a few – have written about Kant, the sublime, or a combination thereof. Not only has there been an explosion of interest in the sublime but the rapid spread and proliferation of contemporary theory may be a version of the sublime, suggesting that theory today is also an instance of what it analyses and describes. Neil Hertz, for example, cites Kant's mathematical sublime to illustrate 'the current intellectual scene'. According to Hertz, the sheer magnitude and variety of theories produces a sublime effect:

> Kant alludes to 'the bewilderment or, as it were, perplexity which it is said seizes the spectator on his first entrance into St. Peters at Rome', but one needn't go to Rome to experience bewilderment or perplexity. They are available in quantity much closer to home. Professional explainers of literature have only to try to locate themselves in the current intellectual scene, to try to determine what is to be learned from the linguists or the philosophers or the pyschoanalysts or the political economists, in order to experience the requisite mental overload, and possibly even that momentary checking of the vital powers.[9]

Terror, for Burke 'in all cases whatsoever, either more openly or latently, the ruling principle of the sublime', is currently employed to describe the effect produced by the texts of contemporary French theorists, especially Derrida.[10] Geoffrey Hartman, for example, in a review of Christopher Norris's book on deconstruction, remarks that 'the contemporary critical essay often demands a knowledge that is highly specialised and uses a vocabulary drawn from various theorists. One can feel *terrorised* rather than instructed – let alone delighted' (emphasis added).[11] And according to John Searle, even Michel Foucault 'once characterised Derrida's prose style as an "*obscurantisme terroriste*"'.[12]

This international preoccupation perhaps reflects a resemblance between the sublime on the one hand and theory on the other. It is as if the sublime has become not only the privileged object of contemporary theory, but a figure for theory as such, illustrating the ways in which theory refers to, represents, or cites itself, and naming the kind of activity – that of incorporation – characteristic of and proper to theory. The very name *Frankenstein* is emblematic of this movement, for the title, once intended to name only the Monster's progenitor, now refers to the Monster instead. Indeed, 'frankenstein' is even a word in its own right: according to Webster's it means a monster in the shape of a man; a work or agency that proves troublesome to or destroys its creator; and a law unto itself, interested largely in its own perpetuation and expansion. 'Frankenstein', then, is an example of a word that monsterises, for the Monster has appropriated not only the novel's title, but his creator's very name.

Like Frankenstein's Monster, theory devours whatever it encounters, be it a discourse, text, individual, or institution. The terroristic effect of theory, as of monstrosity, resides in its capacity to incorporate and swallow up another entity without leakage or cessation of appetite. Lately, deconstructive theory in particular has infiltrated and then devoured departments of languages and literature, becoming the focus of attention, breaking down institutional divisions and domains. What terrorises those who oppose it – and even those who do not – is its totalising power and the rapidity with which it spreads, as if the university's immune system has no defence against it.[13] For this reason, Robert Con Davis and Ronald Schleifer, both sympathisers, call deconstruction 'a monster with an omnivorous appetite and the capability of devouring all opposition – virtually everything'.[14] It is as if the future of the so-called Sciences of Man has been, or is in the process of being, monsterised by theory.

Two of Derrida's early texts conclude by remarking upon the inability to envision the future other than with recourse to the notion of monstrosity. In the last paragraphs of 'Structure, Sign, and Play' (1966) and the exergue to part one of *Of Grammatology* (1967), Derrida attempts to imagine the future as 'a radical departure from the present' and is drawn, as if by necessity, to the metaphor of the monstrous, if metaphor indeed it is. At the end of 'Structure, Sign, and Play', after maintaining that there is no question of choosing between two interpretations of interpretation, Rousseauean nostalgia versus Nietzschean play, Derrida says that we are only beginning to glimpse 'the conception, formation, gestation, and labour of a kind of question', and then concludes with this now-famous sentence:

> I employ these words, I admit, with a glance toward the operation of child-bearing – but also with a glance toward those who, in a society from which I do not exclude myself, turn their eyes away when faced by the as yet unnameable which is proclaiming itself and which can do so, as is necessary whenever a birth is in the offing, only under the species of the non-species, in the formless, mute, infant, and terrifying form of monstrosity.[15]

Who or what is named by Derrida? Who indeed is Frankenstein's heir?

The same conjunction occurs in the last paragraph of the exergue to 'Writing before the letter'. As if anticipating *Glas*, the hybrid, multigenred parody of philosophy and literature, Derrida writes that 'the future which proclaims itself at present, beyond the closure of knowledge ... can only be anticipated in the form of an absolute danger. It is that which breaks absolutely with constituted normality and can only be proclaimed, *presented*, as a sort of monstrosity'.[16]

Why can the future be '*presented*' only 'as a sort of monstrosity'? The last sentence of the exergue, in which Derrida remarks that something 'within the future world ... will have put into question the values of sign, word and writing' offers a clue.[17] Perhaps the remainder of *Of Grammatology*, which Derrida's exergue anticipates, itself constitutes the extended putting into question Derrida associates with monstrosity.

Rosalind Krauss, in her influential essay 'Poststructuralism and the "Paraliterary"', speculates about a new genre she calls 'paraliterary', which is neither criticism nor fiction, philosophy nor literature, but something composed of both and identical to neither. The paraliterary, according to Krauss, 'cannot be called criticism, but it cannot, for that matter, be called non-criticism either. Rather, criticism finds itself caught in a dramatic web of many voices, citations, asides, divagations.' Krauss describes it as 'the space of debate, quotation, partisanship, betrayal, and reconciliation'.[18] Citing Derrida's work – 'aside from its rather terroristic reductiveness' – as exemplary of this genre, Krauss adds that the very creation of the paraliterary is 'the result of theory – their own theories in operation, so to speak'.[19] I submit that Romanticism's vision of the future was a vision of and is identical to theory itself, and that the practice of theory, theory in action, is itself the terrifying species or 'species of the non-species' Derrida finds unrepresentable. It is as if what Kant was barely able to contain and Shelley staged as monstrous already carried with it a prophecy or warning, predicting, or determining, the shape of theory's future as monstrous and sublime.

Fredric Jameson suggests that in the last generation a new kind of 'theoretical discourse' has emerged, that it is a manifestation, indeed the principal form of postmodernism, and that it 'marks the end of philosophy as such':

> A generation ago there was still a technical discourse of professional philosophy ... alongside which one could still distinguish the quite different discourse of the other academic disciplines ... Today, increasingly, we have a kind of writing simply called 'theory' ... this new kind of discourse, generally associated with France and so-called French theory, is becoming widespread and marks the end of philosophy as such.[20]

It may also mark, if not the end of literature, the end of any unproblematic distinction or stable demarcation between the genres of philosophy and literature. Theory in practice, as practice, threatens to displace the conjunction between 'philosophy' *and* 'literature', and replace it with a hyphen, the diacritical mark that both divides words and compounds them. In the place of a connection, or, to borrow one of Kant's favourite metaphors, a *bridge* between the domains of philosophy and literature, one may find instead the sign that indicates a merger has taken place – and that a birth still remains in the offing.

From *Substance*, 52 (1987), 21–31.

NOTES

[Barbara Freeman's essay enacts the disruptive and critical performance that it associates with the monster. Situating itself, in a deconstructive manner, between literary and philosophical discourse the essay, like the monster, occupies a marginal position that reflects on both discourses to question their assumptions and stability. The monster, undermining the binary oppositions, between nature and culture, life and death, human and inhuman, becomes an emblem of poststructuralist theory which also demonstrates the instability of the oppositions on which any discourse is based. As well as destabilising conventional oppositions, the figure of the monster also undermines the empirical and rational basis of any position. In Kant's philosophy the human subject occupies the central position in the system of empirical, rational and moral perceptions, judgements and laws. In Kant's theory of aesthetic judgements the sublime confronts the subject with something that appears beyond comprehension and reason, but is reinscribed as a mark of moral limits and law. Exceeding the framework of Kantian aesthetics, a figure more sublime than Kant's sublime could cope with, the monstrous figure that appears in *Frankenstein* enables a reading of Frankenstein as critical portrait of the Enlightenment philosopher and his untenable and misplaced metaphysical project. In linking the novel to issues of the present, the essay shows how the monster continues to be a disturbing and uncontrollable figure. Ed.]

1. Gilles Deleuze, *Kant's Critical Philosophy: The Doctrine of the Faculties*, trans. Hugh Tomlinson and Barbara Habberjam (Minneapolis, 1984), p. xii.
2. Immanuel Kant, *The Critique of Judgment*, trans. J. H. Bernard (New York, 1968), par. 23, p. 85. Subsequent citations are from this edition and included in the text.
3. Jacques Derrida, 'The Parergon', trans. Craig Owens, *October*, 9 (Summer 1979), 30.

4. Mary Shelley, *Frankenstein; or the Modern Prometheus*, ed. James Rieger (Chicago, 1982), p. 52. Subsequent citations in the text are to this edition of the 1818 version of the novel.

5. Frances Ferguson, discussing *Frankenstein's* relationship to nuclear thinking and discourse in her elegant article 'The Nuclear Sublime', also points out that the Monster's 'skin is too tight'. According to Ferguson, 'The monster ... is stretched too thin, as if his skin represented an unsuccessful effort to impose unity on his various disparate parts'. See 'The Nuclear Sublime', *Diacritics*, 14: 2 (Summer 1984), 8–9.

6. Longinus, *On Literary Excellence, Literary Criticism: Plato to Dryden*, ed. Allan H. Gilbert (Detroit, 1962), p. 174.

7. Martin Heidegger, *The Question Concerning Technology*, trans. W. Lovitt (New York, 1977), pp. 163–5.

8. Derrida, 'The Parergon', p. 8.

9. Neil Hertz, 'The Notion of Blockage in the Literature of the Sublime', *Psychoanalysis and the Question of the Text*, ed. Geoffrey H. Hartman (Baltimore, 1978), p. 62.

10. Edmund Burke, *A Philosophical Enquiry into the Origin of Our Ideas of the Sublime and Beautiful*, ed. James T. Boulton (Notre Dame, 1968), p. 58.

11. Geoffrey Hartman, 'Wild, Fierce Yale', *London Review of Books*, 21 Oct.–3 Nov. 1982, p. 26.

12. John R. Searle, 'The Word Turned Upside Down', *New York Review of Books*, 30, no. 16 (27 Oct. 1983), p. 77.

13. Avital Ronell, in 'Queens of the Night: Nietzsche's Antibodies', develops the idea that 'The dominant metaphors used to describe the defence and conservation, the immunity or decline of a body politic, or a given institutional body, derive primarily from physiology'. I am indebted to her suggestive reading of theories' relationship to 'immunodeficiency'. See 'Queens of the Night: Nietzsche's Antibodies', *Genre*, 16 (Winter 1983), 405.

14. Robert Con Davis and Ronald Schleifer, 'Introduction: The Ends of Deconstruction', *Rhetoric and Form: Deconstruction at Yale*, ed. R. C. Davis and R. Schleifer (Norman, 1985), p. 6.

15. Jacques Derrida, 'Structure, Sign and Play', trans. Alan Bass, *Writing and Difference* (Chicago, 1978), p. 293.

16. Jacques Derrida, *Of Grammatology*, trans. Gayatri Chakravorty Spivak (Baltimore, 1976), p. 5.

17. *Of Grammatology*, p. 5.

18. Rosalind Krauss, 'Poststructuralism and the "Paraliterary"', *October*, 13 (Summer 1980), 37.

19. Krauss, p. 38.

20. Fredric Jameson, 'Postmodernism and Consumer Society', *The Anti-Aesthetic: Essays on Postmodern Culture*, ed. Hal Foster (Port Townsend, 1983), p. 112.

9

Otherness in *Frankenstein*: The Confinement/ Autonomy of Fabrication

JERROLD E. HOGLE

> The universe is a monster of energy, without beginning or end; a fixed and brazen quantity of energy which grows neither bigger nor smaller, which does not consume itself, but only alters its face ... this, my Dionysian world of eternal self-creation, of eternal self-destruction....
>
> (Nietzsche, *The Will to Power*)

> We should begin by taking rigorous account of this *being held within* [prise] or this *surprise:* the writer writes *in* a language and *in* a logic whose proper system, laws, and life his discourse by definition cannot dominate absolutely. He uses them only by letting himself, after a fashion and up to a point, be governed by the system.
>
> (Derrida, *Of Grammatology*)

> The ignorance of the early philosophers on these and several other points served to decrease their credit with me: but I could not entirely throw them aside, before some other system should take their place in my mind.
>
> (Victor Frankenstein)

I

In the preface-after-the-fact by the author's author-husband, Mary Shelley's *Frankenstein* presents itself as a call for 'domestic affection' (p. 7).[1] And since the book's three narrators finish their stories in the loneliness of an ice-bound vessel, the call does go out: obsessive quests for Truth beyond the *domus* lead to the drift of alienation and the cold prison of self-involvement.[2] To say that, however, is not to uncover a moral presence or a presence of mind that clearly precede the language of the text. It is really to expose the novel's *denial* of presence in the face of its own fabrication and in the face of fabrication as the basis of human effort. For even as the narrators try to find the origins of things, the 'birthplace' of what they do is always a locus of writing that refers elsewhere, and the 'end' they apparently seek is always deferred as one production of signs gives way to another. Robert Walton's quest for the source of magnetism is spawned by 'a history of all the voyages made for the purpose of discovery' (p. 11); Frankenstein's lust for 'the causes of life' is engendered by the works of the best-known alchemists (pp. 32–3); and, at the famous midpoint of the novel's concentric arrangement (pp. 122–7), the creature's drive to locate his own genesis is rooted in Plutarch's *Lives,* Goethe's *Werther,* Milton's *Paradise Lost,* and his maker's laboratory journal, all of which are themselves 'rooted' in other narratives. Moreover, instead of arriving at the profound knowledge offered by some of their books, the narrators tell tales to one another that expand on their basic texts. The search for the origin is put off in new chains of language that supplement previous chains, with the 'central' chain grounding itself in a library of documents and honing in on the journal of a fabricator who admits his involvement in earlier fabrications. What the reader finally gets is an errant packet from a confused navigator, a group of letters cut off from a source already adrift on a surface of signs,[3] that repeats a *mélange* of rhetorical acts within its own act of rhetoric. The speakers are indeed alienated and imprisoned, but the movement of figuration is the ostraciser and keeper as it holds out a fulfilling completion that it also prevents. Whether it is called an 'origin', a 'cause', or a 'moral truth', the underlying presence in *Frankenstein* is nothing but a pretension within writing on top of writing, an absent objective lost from the start 'in darkness and distance' (the last phrase of the book).

So far, though, only Peter Brooks has taken on the rhetorical problem at the base of this novel.[4] He has aptly seen the monster as a sign of the non-meanings in Nature (human an otherwise), searching for community and coherence in a language that offers merely a play of differences. But even this view presumes an aberration, however ineffable, that somehow exists prior to composition. For me the monstrosity in *Frankenstein* is the very act of composition – be it a story, a charted voyage, or a fabricated man – as it confines itself within previous compositions that question the maker's authority and as it becomes autonomous from all authority in the drive of its own repetitions. Instead of an unmediated Nature, after all, what the novel offers primarily is a sequence of performances designed to persuade others on the basis of already conventional 'persuasions'. Morality and Human Nature are talked about, yet only as they are fathered by verbal patterns that the narrators have drawn from their reading; when Victor articulates his penchant for 'raising ghosts and devils' (pp. 34–5), his desire goes after 'a promise liberally accorded by my favourite authors... Cornelius Agrippa, Albertus Magnus, and Paracelsus, who have so long reigned the lords of my imagination'. Ultimately each of the narrators in the book enacts the machine of sign-production defined by Jacques Lacan: 'in the labour which [the speaker] undertakes to reconstruct [his Nature] *for another*, he finds again the fundamental alienation which made him construct it *like another one,* and which has destined [his construct] to be stripped from him *by another*.'[5] Thus fabrication throughout the novel is the making of an Imaginary Self, an 'other one', in configurations allowed by the Other (the intersubjective-intertextual ground of articulation). This process literally subjects the composer to the signs of a dead past that differs from him, divorcing him from a product that observers will decipher in terms of the Other and not the author. Mary Shelley seems to accept just that in her introduction to the 1831 version as she bids her 'hideous progeny go forth' into a world of readers having 'nothing to do' with her own life (p. 229). And so I want to follow out the purely performative gambits in *Frankenstein* as they insist, despite their pretensions, on their own ineffability and their own ways of giving birth to an aberration.

II

Among his several duties as the 'framing' figure in the book, Walton has the first chance to define the vocabularies that control the movement of the text. What he reveals in the process is the charting of his own course within a conflict of systems:

> [The North Pole that I seek] ever presents itself to my imagination as the region of beauty and delight. . .there snow and frost are forever

> banished; and sailing over a calm sea, we may be wafted to land surpassing in wonders and in beauty every region hitherto discovered on the habitable globe. Its productions and features may be without example, as the phenomena of the heavenly bodies undoubtedly are in those undiscovered solitudes. [Further,] I may there discover the wondrous power that attracts the needle: and may regulate a thousand celestial observations that may require only this voyage to render their seeming eccentricities consistent for ever.
>
> (pp. 9–10)

On the one hand, Walton can project what he does at this point because he accepts a rhetoric of *telos* or anagogy. Here every word presupposes an End, a final Revelation of Meaning, which lies beyond example and yet provides the standard for inadequate but visible pre-dictions of It. Mundane nature in these terms is simply a gallery of signs holding out 'a foretaste of those icy climes' (p. 9) in metaphoric emblems that mystify and promise all at once.[6] The mystery, in fact, is bound up with the promise, for the emblem resists the approach of investigation even as it vows to initiate the investigator. In any case, human perception and human action can only reach their goals under this inscription if they attain the primal space that completes and conflates all metaphors. Mary Shelley even cements these notions in her 1823 addenda to the novel, where the Pole is cited as proof that 'the aspect of nature differs essentially [or "at the essential level"] from anything of which we have experience' (p. 10). On the other hand, Walton also intones a rhetoric of *tabula* or representation, something like the *episteme* that Michel Foucault has found in major texts of the seventeenth and eighteenth centuries.[7] Now the ground of truth is not the Essential Sign but the capacity in language for charting the memory-traces of the mind. Under these conditions the explorer seeks meaning by recording and arranging names for his observations, trying always to dissolve 'eccentricities' by rendering old data consistent with new perceptions. The Transcendent Standard remains, but only as an assurance of the chart's emerging validity. As Descartes suggests, It provides a guarantee whereby the reason can claim an Origin (or God) as the prototype of itself, a Presence behind the self-presence that represents in a gradual process. There is, of course, some duplicity here; the desire that seeks the fullness of Nature in a developing table already assumes a Nature complete in itself. Yet, whatever the case, *telos* and *tabula* are very different ways of pursuing self-fulfilment.[8] In the former, power and value depend on the nearness of the self to the Essence. Representation demands little more than the progressive and consistent expansion of itself.

Still more to the point, as Walton continues to use both schemes for encoding himself and his voyage, his 'resolutions' become 'as fixed as fate' (p. 15), confining his account within their textual demands and their opposition to each other. While he plays the hero of a teleological quest, he has to see the Pole as a blend of established metaphors for the primal kingdom. Thus it combines elements of Hyperborea, Eden, Heaven itself, and even the Mount of the Muses. Walton can thereby talk of his failed poems as a groundless 'Paradise of my own creation' in need of that centre from which the inspired can draw the original Word (p. 11). At the same time, *Captain* Walton must plan his itinerary by way of 'St Petersburg' and 'Archangel' (pp. 9 and 13); he must give his crewmen places in such a scheme by describing them as noble savages (pp. 14–15); and, when he maps the route he will follow into the polar region, he has to arrive at 'plains of ice, which seem to have no end' (p. 17). He has made a prideful advance toward Heaven on his own power and must be cleansed from the guilt of presumption in Cocytus, the frozen core of Dante's *Inferno*. Naturally his only way out is a harrowing of Hell by a Christ-figure, so Victor is subjected to the role once he is taken on board. 'Such a man has a double existence', Walton says; 'he may suffer misery, and be overwhelmed by disappointments; yet when he is retired into himself, he will be like a celestial spirit, that has a halo around him, within whose circle no grief or folly ventures' (p. 23). But even as he proceeds through his own *Commedia*, Walton must undercut that vocabulary in the most obvious ways. Just as *telos* urges him to search for heat in the very extremes of the North, *tabula* leads him to note 'the southern gales' that 'breathe a degree of renovating warmth which I had not expected' (p. 16). He must also cite empirical grounds for his voyage that have nothing to do with the Muses, and so he lists his qualifications in 'mathematics, the theory of medicine, and those branches of physical science from which a naval adventurer might derive the greatest practical advantage' (p. 11). In this light the failure of his effort is caused, not by presumption, but by his miscalculations regarding the polar ice-cap. Even worse by the standards of *tabula*, these mistakes result from an interest in *telos* that is both antisocial in its mysticism and impractical in its methodology.[9]

Yet the real 'causes' of the failure are aporia (the hesitation between rhetorical modes) and the resulting parabasis (the foregrounding of articulation as mere performance). Within their own boundaries, first of all, *telos* and *tabula* make problematic assumptions about reference; one offers signs that indicate nothing but a privileged emblem, the metaphor at the apex, while the other represents mental associations that are themselves representations of other things. When the two clash openly they expose each other's duplicities, thereby shattering their own illusions of an accessible Truth beyond or before sign-ification. What appears instead is a return of the repressed: the primordial otherness, the deferral of meaning at the point of origin, that signifiers promise to mitigate and fail to mitigate by their very nature. For Walton, the truth about the Pole has to emerge as an absence the moment Victor asks if the ice will soon break. 'I could not answer', the Captain must say, 'with any degree of certainty' (p. 21). Walton's passions, the movement of his own mind, will not surface on paper, for writing 'is a poor medium for the communication of feeling' (p. 13). Because his voyage and his letters, then, are mere trackings of what is always somewhere else, the only goal that Walton can really pursue is verbal transmission for its own sake. 'You may deem me romantic', he writes to his sister, 'but I bitterly feel the want of a friend. I have no one near me, gentle yet courageous, possessed of a cultivated as well as of a capacious mind, whose tastes are like my own, to amend or approve my plans' (p. 13 again). In the words of Coleridge, one of Mary Shelley's favourite writers, 'my nature requires another nature for its support, [and] reposes only in another from the necessary indigence of its being'.[10] The 'I AM' is a lack in need of a mediator, its fabrication perceived by someone else, and everywhere in this dialectic the meaning is relational and deferred. The self is constituted by the other just as the other points back to the self, but without (in *Frankenstein,* at least) the *Aufhebung* that dissolves the Otherness in Hegel. By saying that he is 'romantic' in his desire for a friend, Walton may be hoping for the *telos* projected in quest-romances. Yet the exchange when it comes (with Victor Frankenstein) can only be an occasion for supplementing – 'approving' or 'amending' – what is already supplemental ('plans'). With his 'hopes blasted' and his 'purpose unfulfilled' (p. 213), Walton must finally be nothing but a signifier, the conduit of a dead man's tale and the catalyst of another's reaction. 'I will endeavour', he concludes, 'to detail these bitter circumstances to you, my dear sister; and while I am wafted towards England, and towards you, I will not despond.' In the end he is left with the very thing he has tried to escape: a production of writing as groundlessly grounded as the poems of his 'own creation'.

Perhaps the best figure for Walton's situation, however, appears in his second letter home. There he alludes in the most reckless way to another text by Coleridge: 'I am going to unexplored regions, to "the land of mist and snow", but I shall kill no albatross, therefore do not be alarmed for my safety' (p. 15). Now, granted, Walton keeps some of the details in his promise. Yet he speaks of the creature's arrival right at the juncture where the ice closes in (p. 17), the very point at which the Ancient Mariner sights his bane for the first time. From then on, again like his counterpart, Walton is 'lost in surprise and admiration' (p. 207), overwhelmed by symbols that destroy his self-assurance as they cry out for decipherment and recomposition. His future, too, is much like his predecessor's; he must return to England with a failure 'shamefully' on his mind (p. 213) and expiate this curse by telling his tale and nothing more. And the irony goes beyond a pattern of avoiding-and-resembling the Mariner. Walton is also repeating a text that obscures its own ground in concentric ripples of interpretation (the Mariner's, the Wedding-guest's, the narrator's, the reader's),[11] making it less a quest for knowledge and more a search for words. There is no uncovering of the 'prior causes' for the killing of the Albatross, nor does the Mariner behold the Spirit that supposedly inhabits the depths and drives the ship of fate. Instead the Mariner is mainly answering a question. 'wherefore stopp'st thou me?' (*Mariner,* l. 4), and articulating a moral after the fact to explain a sea of signifiers. Nonetheless, Walton takes on the sins of the Mariner anyway without even committing the deed that activates the torment in the poem. His guilt has no rationale besides the one in the *Rime;* a command displaced from Biblical writing to provide a basis for the self. In addition to the stain of presumption, Walton accepts the guilt of failing to love 'things both great and small' (*Mariner,* l. 615) simply because a text has a powerful hold on his psyche. Indeed Walton admits as much in the 1831 revision when he faces the vertigo of desire as both aroused and engulfed by a symbolic order. 'You will smile at my allusion', he says, 'but I will disclose a secret. I have often attributed my attachment to, my passionate enthusiasm for, the dangerous mysteries of ocean, to that production of the most imaginative of symbolic poets. There is something at work in my soul which I do not understand' (p. 231). What is at work, of course, is a pattern of desire and repression generating guilt, but all these 'motivations' are the results of the pre-text that encourages and denies exploration for the sake of confronting the self as a production of language.[12] Walton clearly projects himself 'like another one' in terms of a contradictory 'other' that is also other than itself, and if that is not frightening enough, he doubles that duplicity by playing the Wedding-guest to Frankenstein, who himself cites the *Rime* as one basis of his discourse (p. 54). Walton's 'self', if it emerges at all, is really dismembered and parcelled out in several aspects of composition. He is a repeater of other texts, an interpreter of existing symbols, a rhetorician in need of an audience, and an audience beholding a rhetorician – all of which replay the deferred status of the Mariner supplementing previous signs and waiting to be supplemented himself.

III

Victor embodies the same predicament even more, and not just because he mediates the creature's tale and is mediated by Walton's letters. He is the quintessential fabricator, carried away by methods of production beyond his control to the point of giving them a new life exceeding and threatening his own while claiming that life as 'his' nevertheless. His *exordium* to Walton points right to that paradox: 'I ardently hope that the gratification of your desires may not be a serpent to sting you, as mine has been' (p. 24). He takes his desire to be personal, yet here it repeats a version of Original Sin, a function from a teleological rhetoric that forces Victor to see himself as an eater of forbidden fruit. He is indeed a Faust-figure as many have said, but only because he believes the alchemical writers who reign as 'the lords of [his] imagination'. For Magnus, Agrippa, and Paracelsus, the 'natural magician' is not really free to find the *materia prima* in the mouldering depths of Mother Earth.[13] Though he holds out that very picture in his creation of a homunculus, Paracelsus outlaws his own effort. The source of life, he claims, is 'one of the greatest secrets, and it should remain a secret until the days approach when all the secrets will be known'.[14] The Christian language of *telos* is both the harbinger and the concealer of Revelation; any fabricator who violates the opacity of sacred signs will confront his own Satanic projection as the allegory of his guilt.

Consequently, when Victor sets out 'to mock the stupendous mechanism of the creator of the world' (Mary's introduction, p. 228), he must defile a sanctified region (the sepulchres of a church-yard) and raise a Devil who reduplicates the Lord of Cocytus Himself. 'Oh! no mortal could support that countenance', cries Victor; 'it became a thing such as even Dante could not have conceived' (p. 53). The creature is thus a repetition-with-a-difference who has to look as he does. The prescriptions of his maker demand a monster as the ritual-trace of a broken taboo, the echo of the Father's Word repressing unlicensed desire.

Victor even builds up this rhetorical masochism by styling his creation as the act of a 'modern Prometheus' (the subtitle of the novel), for just as he wonders if 'a new species would bless me as its creator and source' (p. 49), he enters another text of fated catastrophe, especially in its Christian refractions. The third Earl of Shaftesbury presents the Already-Written in *The Moralists* (1709): 'shall we mind the poets when they sing thy tragedy, Prometheus! Who with thy stolen celestial fire, mixed with vile clay didst mock heaven's countenance, and in the abusive likeness of the immortals madest the compound man: that wretched mortal, ill to himself and cause of ill to all.'[15] Victor, of course, carries out this figuration to the letter, all the way to the 'abusive likeness' at odds with itself and its parentage. And even as Hesiod shows how women and violence came to punish Promethean *hubris,*[16] Victor's presumption comes back to haunt him in the prospect of a female creature. Starting with only a vision of two monsters on the loose, Frankenstein imagines 'a race of devils' for which 'future ages might curse me as their pest' (p. 163), a wrenching yet built-in reversal of the self-image that he had once projected beyond his own death. As the arche-text demands, the Promethean act has made the new creator an outcast from Paradise yet again. But now the sentence is passed by some constructs at the base of Victor's effort, by his confinement in verbal chains that make his fabrications painfully his and painfully other at the same time.

On top of all that, too, Victor has to see 'the Modern Prometheus' as a contradiction in terms. 'It may appear very strange', he admits, that a student of ancient mythology 'should arise in the eighteenth century' (p. 34), since the age-old metaphors defining the causes of man stand 'entirely exploded' by a 'system of science' that is 'real and practical' by contrast. The exploding mechanism, naturally, is *tabula,* and Professor Waldman explains that to

Victor at the University of Ingolstadt. There the Moderns respect the Ancients just enough 'to give new names and arrange in connected classifications, the facts which [our Fathers] in a great degree had been the instrument of bringing to light' (p. 43). Only by making the shift himself can Victor speak to Walton of 'a scientific pursuit [that offers] continual food for discovery and wonder' (p. 46). This is hardly the *telos* view of time, after all; repetitive sin and the Gift of Revelation are here covered over by an accumulation of data that is, by definition, never complete. Now Victor's road to the origin has entered the texts of Erasmus Darwin and Sir Humphrey Davy, where the source of life is never beheld as a singular essence and is yet available in the emerging laws of attraction that pull disparate elements into living wholes. These laws, in turn, are based on the symbolic relation of chemical affinities and electrical polarities, a system of differences that underwrites the experimental galvanising of dead tissue.[17] Once into this scheme Victor strives 'to infuse a spark of being' into 'a lifeless thing' (p. 52) and thereby grants all powers of decision to a *programme* (or proscription) that dismantles the early codes of his desire. First, instead of the primal seed in the primal Mother, he is 'led to examine the cause and progress of decay' in specimens from a crypt (p. 47). Then, when he tries to reverse this progress in an act of representation, he is only 'encouraged to hope that my present attempts would at least lay the foundations of future success', and he is really kept from perfection under empirical *dicta* by 'the minuteness of parts' that he must confront in making the body of a man (p. 49). Again the creature has to be ugly, but the grounds are different. *Tabula* forces Victor to make something rough, oversized, and deferred, transforming a brave new world into a demonstration that requires improvement at some other time. Aporia reigns once more as the Promethean dream dissolves in the face of a laboratory patchwork and as Victor recoils from the patchwork in the name of his dream.

At the same time, because of this nexus, the well-known 'lessons' of Victor's story break apart to reveal the poses of the schemes that generate them. Indeed his most famous pronouncement is a blatant mix of inconsistent postures. 'If the study to which you apply yourself has a tendency to weaken your affections', he tells Walton, 'then that study is certainly unlawful, that is to say, not befitting the human mind' (p. 51). Here of course is a repetition of the most eternal Law, the Injunction at the Tree of Knowledge. Here too is an echo of John Locke, for whom the proper training of the young is easily clouded by a strange 'Connexion of Ideas wholly owing to Chance or Custom' that 'fills their heads with false views, and their Reasonings with false consequences'.[18] Victor, in fact, has already placed himself in this pattern when he recalls finding 'a volume of Cornelius Agrippa' during a storm at Thanon (p. 32). Except for this circumstance, he says, 'the train of my ideas would never have received the fatal impulse that led to my ruin' (p. 33). It seems the psyche composes tables because the table is its given method, and if an aberrant sign infects the matrix started by Nature, a disease has begun that has to pervert the expansion of the mind thereafter. But the development of chance impressions is not a primordial Fall, so Victor can keep the two together only by leaps of rhetoric. The supreme indication, as we might expect, comes when he remembers his ultimate discovery: 'I paused, examining all the minutiae of causation... until from the midst of this darkness a sudden light broke in upon me' (p. 47). All at once Revelation appears to dissipate the metonymic table and carry the soul to forbidden regions beyond the powers of representation. Though he ascribes his downfall to a ruined education much of the time, Victor never speaks of his greatest secret as a mistaken association. It is always as 'impenetrable' as the Mysteries of Heaven (p. 207). Thus it is no surprise when Victor's final speech becomes an oxymoronic dance; with the proper name of his goal always and already supplanted by the initial repressions of his own languages, he urges Walton to 'avoid ambition' under the standards of *telos*, yet he hopes that 'another may succeed' in filling out the table that he has helped to augment (p. 215). By this point , though, his term have called more attention to themselves than they have to their 'contents', leading Walton to take his visitor's words as more often purely persuasive than strictly informative. Victor's 'eloquence is forcible and touching', we find, and, especially when he recounts a dream, he 'gives solemnity to his reveries that render them to me almost as imposing and as interesting as truth' (p. 208).

Hence, despite the continuing fiction that a 'truth' which never appears is somehow the sine qua non, Victor's tale can be thrown open to a reading of its fabrications as empty reinscriptions. The monster, as a case in point, is a metaphor for the origin in the most radical sense. He condenses in his own visage a panoply of metaphors that are themselves alluding to metaphors of the origin, and Victor beholds that process in the dream that follows his act of creation:

> I saw Elizabeth [his fiancée] walking in the streets of Ingolstadt. Delighted and surprised, I embraced her; but as I imprinted the first kiss on her lips, they became livid with the hue of death; her features appeared to change, and I thought that I held the corpse of my dead mother in my arms; a shroud enveloped her form, and I saw the grave-worms crawling in the folds of the flannel. I started from my sleep with horror [and] beheld the wretch – the miserable monster whom I had created.
>
> (p. 53)

As the Freudian critics have noted, the figures for love and decay in this passage are blended into one icon by the end of the dream, a single face that incarnates both the desire and the repulsion that Victor feels in his approach to the 'original' states of non-difference (sexual union and death).[19] Clearly enough, the creature's image is an outgrowth of memory-traces that displace and subsume each other in Victor's psyche as he seeks to join himself to the most fundamental Other he can find. But that machinery only makes the monster's conception a play of textual surfaces. Once he confronts fabrication as related to generation, Victor recalls the already-written script of his marriage to Elizabeth, and that recollection is linked to the moment of death in which that script was composed. He promises to marry Elizabeth, after all, in spite of her adoption as his sister when his mother appoints the girl as a surrogate for herself and then joins the hands of her two 'children' in the final statement of her life (p. 38). As a result, to embrace his primary (and partially forbidden) symbol of love is also to reach out for the traces of his lost origin (his buried mother). Yet the Signs of the Mother have already been offered by the alchemists *without* the tainted mediation of Elizabeth if Victor will simply plumb the depths of the earth. The actual digging, in turn, comes when the table of minute observation – a close look at the features of death – has repressed alchemy as Victor's standard discourse. So the excavation (or penetration) that leads to the creature is a kind of sexual climax, a return to the womb, a grasping for an absent wholeness, a wish for death, a gathering of data, a journey to the *logos*, a violation of Sacred Mysteries, a bid for immortality, and a search for some alternative to the lack of finality in life, but all these are performed only in figurative ways and only on the basis of other figural patterns that reveal no Formal Cause prior to figuration. When he is finally put together out of vestiges from the grave, themselves already signs of an absence at the beginning, the monster is a 'cryptic' production in every conceivable way: a simulacrum of the body composed of decomposed tissues, a figure of many other faded figures, and an interweaving, fabrication, or *textus* of the conflicting rhetorics engulfing his maker. The real horror is not so much his sewn-up appearance as what his face reveals about Victor's main objective. The primal Other is now discovered as nothing but a symbolic order, a plethora of fragments referring to themselves, where the source remains forever lost and yet where the origin always beckons within the multiplicity of signs as the dark and distant object of desire.[20]

If Victor admits this Otherness in his narrative, though, he does it only indirectly. Most of the time he strives to place the supporting cast in roles that suit his tropologies, turning his parents into the monarchs of a Paradise regained (pp. 27–8), Elizabeth into a Beatrice who sheds 'radiance from her looks' (p. 235), and Henry Clerval, 'the brother of soul' (p. 31), into a young Amadis and a sympathetic expert on 'the sensations of others' (p. 63). All of these serve Frankenstein as elements in a 'sacred' Beginning (p. 31), as synecdoches whose progressive deaths incarnate a Paradise lost and an education gone wrong. Still, on those occasions when Victor relaxes his rhetoric, he grants these characters some freedom from the schemes he provides and even allows them to define their own abilities as supplementers of an absence. While 'the world was to me a secret which I desired to discover', Elizabeth takes life as 'a vacancy, which she sought to people with imaginations of her own' (p. 30). She finally becomes so acquainted with the groundless nature of fabrication that she can dissect the posturings of the law at the trial of the maid Justine: 'Oh! How I hate its shews and mockeries! When one creature is murdered, another is immediately deprived of life in a slow, torturing manner... They call this *retribution*' (p. 83).[21] Clerval, for his part, is most at home in the endless play of empty symbols. He finds 'consolation in the works of the orientalists', based as they are on the deferral of desire ('the fire that consumes your own heart'), and he takes on 'languages [as] his principal study' merely 'to open a field for self-instruction' (p. 64). Thus, by joining in a celebration of sign-production as radically other and never complete, Victor gives in here and there to fabrication as a freedom confined only within its methods of operation. For those few moments he accepts Percy Shelley's call for the 'abolition of personal slavery';[22] he becomes 'a portion of that beauty which we contemplate' and permits an other to be locus of his changeable significance without insisting on the presence of an Absolute as the basis of his self-definition.

When he confronts himself alone, however, he cannot accept significance as deferred. At such times the fear of non-meaning, the terror of a possible vacancy at the centre of existence, begets a vertigo that only an eschatology can alleviate. 'Alas!' he exclaims in recalling his journey to the Mer de Glace, 'why does man boast of sensibilities superior to those apparent in the brute; it only renders them more necessary beings. If our impulses were confined to hunger, thirst and desire, we might nearly be free; but now we are moved by every wind that blows, and a chance word or scene that word may convey to us' (pp. 92–3). He also quotes Shelley in the same breath: 'We feel, conceive, or reason; laugh or weep, / Embrace fond woe, or cast our cares away; / It is the same: for, be it joy or sorrow, / The path of its departure still is free' (lines 11–14 of 'Mutability'). None of these figurations will grant him an absolute presence; in fact, that problem is their subject. All they can show is the distance of man from any 'necessary' basis save the movement of desire, and that movement is a constant irony where even the mind is as different from itself as any sign that seems to describe it. Actually symbols have more justification than those who use them, since people insist on being swayed by a 'chance word' and what it claims to project. Whence Victor, seeking some permanence in contemplation at least, rushes into a conventional plea for union with the cosmos by asking 'wandering spirits [to] allow me this faint happiness or take me, as your companion, away from the joys of life' (p. 93). Again, as in Victor's dream, a love of beauty and a lust for death appear as sides of the same coin, both offering an end to the self's continual otherness in figures that promise a non-difference they cannot really grant. Even so, in the face of perceptions that are never more than signifiers of his own finitude, Victor sees only two means of transcendence as he beholds the opaque surface of Montanvert. Either he can try to dissolve into Nature and be a part of what is curtained from his sight, or he can force the closure of self-consciousness by seeking his own demise.

Yet the answer to this prayer is what it has to be: a revelation of difference instead of union. As if responding directly to Victor's plea, the monster emerges from his Alpine retreat as a shocking emblem of what occurs when apotheosis is attempted with the aid of mere signs (p. 94). Victor has tried to call forth the object of his heart's desire, but instead he is placed in the hands of the machine he has made for that very purpose, the engine of his autoeroticism that has taken on a life of its own. Indeed, from the start, Frankenstein's effort has been a masturbational strategy designed to bypass mortal insemination for the sake of disseminating ultimate causes in a rhetorical display. Now the product of his phallic push for a metaphoric child has become so autonomous from the 'father' that it renders Victor helpless (in a way, castrated) in the face of the patterns built into it. It carries out unconscious aggression while the conscious mind is passive, yet only in pursuit of the schemes that Victor has espoused to constitute a symbol for the source. The creature is the agent, after all, who works through the *telos* and *tabula* plots that Victor has claimed for himself, completing a tragedy and a perversion of ideas by killing those who offer mediation instead of the origin. In doing so the monster obscures his proximity to causes by aping the systems that compose him against the will of the maker who has set him into motion. As a presence in his creation Victor is emasculated, drained of personal power, cut up into his pre-texts, and finally effaced altogether; the 'child', in turn, is cut off from the parent to find his own way as a supplement of rhetorical chains. No wonder Victor oscillates among sympathy, rejection, and self-abuse in reacting to what he has made. The creature is so much an extension of his creator, so entirely the incestuous product of a self-centred desire, that he appears as another self looking back at the self.[23] On the other hand, he is manifestly different as he acts out the scripts that have torn Victor apart even while they have spawned the act of composition. The author creator must be punished – by himself, if necessary – for repeating the desire of his progenitor-texts in spite of their warnings against repetition, and the symbol of this violation must have its own compulsion to repeat that grinds down and supersedes the fabricator in the very fulfilment of his fabrication.[24]

Soon, with this realisation pressing upon him, Victor begins to welcome death as more than a closure of consciousness. 'This hour', he says to Walton, 'when I momentarily expect my release, is the only happy one which I have enjoyed for several years. The forms of the beloved dead flit before me, and I hasten to their arms' (p. 215). Of course his necrophilia is still a craving for lost plentitude and a lust for non-difference, but all of this makes death at the same time the foundation and ultimate 'truth' of fabrication. By projecting self-completion into the future of his own absence, Victor is admitting how every production of desire presupposes the death of the producer. To be sure, he has always assumed as much, for he has constantly worked through dead letters to get beyond the level of signs, and that process demands that he be somewhere else when his composition presents itself. The creature is the prime example, since he is made to reveal the sources of life to future generations in a body made from fragments that point to the death of their sources. And Victor's last words carry that effort on by proposing an ultimate union in phrases that deny the permanent presence of the self within them. Signs of love and decay come together once again, but only because they hold out the fulfilment of the speaker and then defer it to a point when the 'I' will signify the living death of a textual function. Thus Victor is pleased in the end when his fabrication leads him to the real 'basis' of monstrosity: the erasing of the fabricator from the product of his aspirations, from the text of his immortality that is also his epitaph. When all is said and done, Victor has located what he seeks, and yet he has merely beheld the hollow ground (the original 'crypt') of a performance that reveals nothing besides the nature of performance.

IV

The monster's story, in its turn, is a highly appropriate centre for *Frankenstein.* It apparently shows the coming-to-awareness of a primitive mind, the dawning of a seminal man (the progeny of a Prometheus). As a result, it becomes a thematic core for the life surrounding it, unfolding the origin on a sea of ice that prefigures the apex of the world and the outskirts of the novel. Yet with all its focus on beginnings, it is only (as Edward Said would say) a 'gift inside language',[25] a reproduction of beginnings in words that are after the fact and already circumscribed by other words. If the monster is the most original of all the narrators, he is also the most derived and displaced. He is first a point of departure composed by another rhetorician, and then he is a victim of succeeding narrators, dispossessed of a statement that comes to the reader at least twice refracted by different voices. The creature can be an origin only as a representation re-presented by other representations. He 'begins' for himself as a lack, a set of signs, which needs additional signs in order to mean at all. And he 'ends' as a fabrication of beginnings that owe their existence to fabrications already begun. The concept that comes closest to his 'essence' is Jacques Derrida's monstrous (non)concept the *supplément*, for the creature centres his text by looming as a violent exorbitance, an initial figure that is secondary to start with, and by holding out his transcendent origin as a myth to be imposed by signs that both repeat and supplant him.

Within itself, moreover, the creature's tale is an allegory of selfhood-as-language. The monster occupies the place of the source by composing his youth entirely out of the rhetorics he learns to speak, so much so that everything he says can be removed from him and traced back to a single text or a textual system in his 'library'. His growing self-awareness, for example (pp. 97–100), is recalled in the patterns of the first book he discovers, the Comte de Volney's *Ruins of Empires* (1791; noted initially on p. 114). Volney himself begins with pre-scriptions from Diderot, Rousseau, and Condillac among others,[26] and thus he renders the first man as a figure 'like animals, without experience of the past [or] foresight of the future'. The archetypal person comes to himself in 'the forest, guided only and governed by the affections of his nature' including 'the pain of hunger' and the need to 'cover his body'.[27] The creature, when he remembers with 'difficulty' the 'original area of my being' (p. 97), therefore starts with 'the forest near Ingolstadt' and with the anguish of 'hunger and thirst' (p. 98). He then adds at this point (not before) how a 'sensation of cold' drove him to find clothing in Victor's apartment. This representation is blatant reinscription, as it determines temporality by a pretext and not by 'what actually happened'. In a wider vein, too, the creature accounts for his moral inclinations partly by accepting Volney's main rhetorical mode. This allows him to encipher his entire journey as a tabulation of perceptual growth that demands certain results to complete its operation. Hence the De Lacey cottage becomes the schoolroom where the creature learns first to link actions with his own sensations and later to repeat 'the names that were given [to] familiar objects of discourse' (p. 107). After that, when the early steps have been organised by a symbolic order, the creature can represent to himself the motives, routines, histories, and possibilities that constitute a life with a meaningful logic, even though his representations may generate this logic as a way of justifying themselves. He can now produce a *topos* in which to encode the mystery of his own appearance and the revulsion of human beings, thereby spawning a set of decisions based more on the mechanics of *tabula* than a knowledge of his own mind. He concludes, for one thing, that circumstances make the soul, that it feels only what impressions and physical needs have allowed it to produce. If a world that once seemed worthy of love is altered by acts of rejection and abuse, then the responder is bound to cultivate the new propensities himself (as Volney specifically teaches the monster on p. 115). Concurrently, though, the monster projects a cure in the interlaced community that representation is always pursuing. 'It was in intercourse with man alone', he cries, 'that I could hope for pleasurable sensations' (p. 114). Consequently he can say to Victor, 'make me happy, and I will be virtuous' (p. 95); then he can ask for a counterpart as a means of securing that virtue. With her 'I can live in the interchange of those sympathies necessary to my being' (p. 140) and there develop the list of relations that all men can attain if they fulfil the ethics of empirical-tabular language.

Not surprisingly, however, the creature makes just as many claims in the rhetoric of *telos*, which he encounters in *Paradise Lost* and which he readily adopts as the basis of 'true history' (p. 125). Here he can take on a meaning that is constant instead of additive.

> I often referred [Milton's characters], as their similarity struck me, to [myself]. Like Adam, I was created apparently united by no link to any other being in existence; but his state was far different from mine in every other respect. He had come forth from the hands of God a perfect creature, happy and prosperous, guarded by the especial care of his Creator; he was allowed to converse with, and acquire knowledge from beings of a superior nature; but I was wretched, helpless, and alone. Many times I considered Satan as the fitter emblem of my condition; for often, like him, when I viewed the bliss of my protectors, the bitter gall of envy rose within me.
>
> (p. 125)

Naturally the creature regards this 'emblem' as a belated sign of what he has already become. Yet the sign really directs him to adopt it as a beginning, a fated excuse for what he is and does at all times. And so it describes his status well before his account of *Paradise Lost*, especially when a prospect of shelter looks 'as Pandemonium appeared to the demons of hell' (p. 101). The monster sees himself as damned from the start, foredoomed in the absence of Creator and community to assume a metaphoric origin that confronts him by chance. He actually starts, of course, with his own non-meaning, but Milton provides an Expulsion by the Father to explain even that; the poem thereby engenders a lust for primal chaos (since the Father is not there) as a fitting response to the terror of primordial separation. 'I, like the arch fiend, bore a hell within me', the creature decides, 'and finding myself unsympathised with, wished to tear up the trees, spread havoc and destruction around me; and then to have sat down and enjoyed the ruin' (p. 132). At the same time, since the feelings in this outcry are only the projected desires of a text, an upending of that text generates a reverse kind of anticipation. The monster upends it himself, in fact, by composing the history of the De Laceys in a teleological fashion (p. 117–22). He sees the heroism of Felix De Lacey as rewarded by his reunion with Safie, who flees the chaos of the pagan east for the Christian world of her mother's line, thus recovering her lost origin and her predestined other. Aided in this fabrication by Milton's picture of prelapsarian love, the monster now has a construct to offer as a scheme for dissolving his Satanic posture. When he finally delivers his story to his creator, then, he asks for a Paradise regained complete with a new Eve and a new Eden for a would-be Adam longing for the pleasure of the text. Nothing could be more completely rhetorical, for this appeal is not only a reference to mere figures. It is also a crafty sliding from a language of need to a language of destiny. Victor has every reason, it would seem, both to admire his creature's eloquence (p. 144) and to suspect its inconsistencies as 'treachery' against mankind (p. 206).

Yet Victor is not really being fair. Like his maker, the monster persuades others only insofar as he is persuaded himself on the best methods of self-construction. He decides on his Satanic argument, we discover, only after debating the varied alternatives that he confronts in one place at the midpoint of his tale. In addition to *Paradise Lost* and its offer of a *mythos* with Beginnings and Ends, the creature beholds the textual 'selves' of Plutarch, Goethe, and Frankenstein, though only as they are verbal matrices naming an absence and only as they hold out different promises of meaning with no foundations aside from linguistic assumptions. The offer closest to Milton's is presented in the *Parallel Lives*, where ancient leaders are compared across enormous gulfs of time on the basis of moral absolutes that transcend temporality; any monarch 'who remits or extends his authority', Plutarch claims, 'is no longer a king or ruler [but in fact] a demagogue or despot.'[28] To statements of such surety, where the sign claims to 'let you in' on a Permanence, Goethe's hero has to retort with questions: 'Can you say "this is", when everything is transitory, when everything rolls by with the speed of a tempest [?]...What is man, that vaunted demigod?...When he soars in joy or sinks in suffering, is he not arrested in both, brought back to dull, cold consciousness at the very moment when he yearns to lose himself in the infinite?'[29] This time the creature opens up a tabulation of passions, but one cut off from constant referents, indeed from anything except death and the sliding of signifiers over signifieds that are not really present to themselves. Humanity exists merely as different from a fullness that exists merely as different from the finite. And Victor's journal, no surprise, presents a variation on the same problem. Even as it gives the monster his 'accursed origin', it also makes him nothing but a repetition that is different, a 'filthy type' of his author 'more horrid from its very resemblance' (p. 126). Worse yet, the exact nature of the (dis)connection is unclear, for the journal is replete with rhetorical shifts from the 'language which, painted [Victor's] horrors' to 'accounts of domestic occurrences'. If the maker's disgust renders the monster's disgust 'ineffaceable', it is mainly because the creature is a mangled reflection of an entangled text (the patchwork of a patchwork). In the end the journal only provides its reader with an unanswered question, 'Why did you form a monster so hideous that even you turned from me in disgust?' (p. 126 again), restating the very lack that the creature has been searching to fill. Since Werther offers nothing more secure, the monster must fall back on the guarantees of Plutarch, who takes 'a firm hold on my mind' (p. 125), and the emblems of Milton, who turns lack into an affront. 'I remembered Adam's supplication to his Creator', the monster says, 'but where was mine? He had abandoned me, and in the bitterness of my heart, I cursed him' (p. 127). From here on, because he is committed to the absolutes of rhetorical choices and because the Creator 'remits his authority' by denying a new Paradise, evil becomes the creature's good in the drive of a language that comes to underlie his every act.

Still, for all that, the monster does acknowledge the nature and the ground of his longings. Just before he recounts the subscription to Milton, he provides a sense of his 'real' beginnings by quoting his author's quotation of another author and finding the significance that such a (non)origin reveals. 'I was dependent on none, and related to none', he concludes, for "the path of my departure was free"; and there was none to lament my annihilation. [Then] who was I? Whence did I come? What way my destination? These questions continually recurred, but I was unable to resolve them' (p. 124). He has not read Victor's journal at the time these queries appear to surface, but he has when he raises them before his maker; the result establishes the 'past' as the present of his citations, the 'present' as the defer-ence of his lamentation, and the 'future' as an answer-on-the-way full of previous figurations. His argument for a mate, then, is actually circular. In the unguarded moment when he sees the fictionality of his *telos* and *tabula* projections, he holds out his counterpart as a near-duplicate of his own nature: 'I now indulge in dreams of bliss that cannot be realised. [Therefore] I demand a creature of another sex, but as hideous as myself; the gratification is small, but it is all I can receive, and it shall content me' (pp. 141–2). The road to a meaningful self for the creature must look forward as well as backward to repetition, since a mind without a presence to ground it has to defer its significance to a self-reflecting image yet to be completed. Now even his own questions about his identity manifest the peculiar 'spacing' of the fabricated 'I'. The self-composer is always in search of a founding past, and yet that quest is the making of a rhetoricised future, where difference can only operate as repetition and repetition can only operate as part of the play of differences.

Consequently, the novel's readers are more incisive than they know when they see the monster as 'uncanny' to himself and to others. Freud defines the *Unheimlich*, after all, as the looming of repressed otherness, the confrontation of man with his own compulsion to repeat and his own sense of death (or imminent castration) at the heart of differential desire.[30] The monster, clearly enough, incarnates this ugly secret precisely because he embodies fabrication. First he is created in a 'primal scene' of multiple repetitions that exposes its ground as fragments of death at every turn. After that he differs from people as they are thought to be while resembling them as products of a symbolic order, and so he is held at a distance by acts of repression and names that are not specific. Soon his difference, however, begins to reflect the same thing in everyone else. Standing as he often does for the systems that others pursue, he mirrors the rhetorics of characters who use him – and need him – to finish their own deferred histories. He is the father of a new race to Victor, a fabulous savage to Walton, a beneficent spirit to the De Laceys, and later a demon to each of these, constantly doubling in his own duplicity the lack of permanent value in all of his detractors. He beckons his observers and himself, in fact, toward the prospect they most fear: a vision of man effaced by his own fabrications and forced to accept continual displacement, a Nietzschean energy of repetition that kills, as the only basis of a selfhood that will never be fully present. As Derrida has said, 'the future can only be anticipated in the form of absolute danger. It is that which breaks absolutely with constituted normality and can only be proclaimed, *presented*, as a sort of monstrosity.'[31] The creature therefore answers his own questions about himself when he starts the drift toward absence at the close of the book. Once he can burn himself to ashes, he decides, 'my spirit will sleep in peace; or if it thinks it will not surely think thus' (p. 221). This in itself is a quest for non-difference that is monstrously different from its own claims, for not only is it split in half by a blatant aporia and headed for the signs (the ashes) of lack instead of transcendent thought; it also is a tearing of existing figures out of the religious text that holds them, a violent displacement of a 'constituted normality' resulting in the salvation of mere rhetoric. The creature may be projecting a recovery of his own origins in the finality of dead tissue, but all he can really do is produce a set of signifiers by being a signifier repeating other signifiers. What remains of him is chiefly a pre-figure for the later displacement of readings and rewritings, some of them in the novel and some after its publication. Monstrosity by definition is never finished, even with itself. As the uncanny 'basis' of fabrication – or as an endless remaking of *Frankenstein* films – it always demands the confinement of reproductions within its frightening difference even while it has to give way to the autonomy of different reproductions.

V

Some of my readers, of course, will attack the erasure of Mary Shelley from much of what I say here. And naturally I can retort with the example of Victor Frankenstein, who exposes authorship as a self-involvement that only disperses and effaces the self involved. Yet I cannot deny the worth of the recent studies that see *Frankenstein* as the product of a birth-anxiety.[32] For if Mary Shelley was always afraid that birth was the prelude to an inscription in stone, then she confronted the same terrors in the act of writing. Indeed in the 1831 preface, the essay that calls her fictional 'progeny' something 'hideous', she reflects in revealing ways on how fabrication is like reproduction. One parallel is the 'anxiety of influence'; she speaks of Shelley 'inciting' her to 'prove myself worthy of my parentage, and enrol myself on the page of fame' (p. 223).

The progenitor always has his or her progenitors, be they actual ancestors or inspiring writer-husbands, and the achievements of those who come before may suffocate the one who follows in operations (or pages) that have already been produced. The moment conception is considered, in fact, all sorts of prior-ities are inescapable: 'invention', Mary adds, 'does not consist in creating out of a void, but out of chaos; the material must in the first place be afforded: it can give form to dark, shapeless substances, but it cannot bring into being the substance itself' (p. 226). For the woman especially, the inseminator is generally thought of as someone else, and so in this passage where she tries to develop something already begun by Cicero's *inventio* and the Book of Genesis, Mary Shelley is obviously in the situation of her own narrators, subsumed as they all are in an onslaught of predecessors who deny original meaning and offer only prefigurations.[33] Worse still, the ensuing 'child' is always duplicitous in aping previous authorities and yet keeping the new parent from possessing what is forever other ('the substance itself'). The ultimate loss of child-possession and work-possession, then, is another similarity in the creative trauma of both. What comes forth can be regarded as 'yours', but it is also not 'yours' when it finally supersedes the maker's control and the maker's life. As it happens, Mary Shelley sees the autonomy of *Frankenstein* well before her son (the namesake of her dead husband) is independent of her. In 1823 she writes to Leigh Hunt from London on the stage production of her novel at The English Opera House. 'The story is not well managed', she finds, and what remains most vividly from the book is 'the nameless way of naming the unnameable' when the creature is listed as a blank on the playbill.[34] Even that, in point of fact, supplants the shifting nomenclature of the monster and thus underlines primarily the eliding of the author by her interpreters, the covering up (nay, interring) that she readily faces when she resigns her 'offspring' to her readers in 1831 (p. 228). Whatever she may claim elsewhere, the Mary Shelley who appears in connection with her product understands only too well the entirely consuming and entirely separate memorial that the spawning of a fabrication must finally produce.

Conversely, she also sees the breach between fabrication and insemination. The first disseminates the signs of the something deferred, while the second offers at least the hope of an emerging presence. And that disparity, if anything, is the most constant 'theme' in Frankenstein in spite of – and because of – its deconstruction of itself. Even though the author cannot unite the *telos* and *tabula* schemes that confine her, both of them agree on mediation, the operation of the signifier, as more pressing and more attainable than the ultimate 'presence within'. The narrators are frustrated and destructive only because their drive for an Absolute leads them to reject the mediators that hold It out and keep It hidden at the same time. If Victor's avoidance of Elizabeth and Walton's absence from Margaret Saville have often been stretched into Mary's attack on a preoccupied Shelley, it is no stretch to see that avoidance as a flight from the mere otherness (the incompleteness of 'domestic affection') that constitutes much of human life. Victor ought to love his monster on the same grounds, the grounds of desire as always different from its objectives and from itself, always aroused by an Other that denies fulfilment even as it offers the pleasure of symbolic exchange. The supreme locus of this moral non-presence, though, is the poet Henry Clerval, who stands as a reinscription of the uncorrupted self in Wordsworth's 'Tintern Abbey':

> The sounding cataract
> Haunted *him* like a passion: the tall rock,
> The mountain, and the deep and gloomy wood,
> Their colours and their forms, were then to him
> An appetite: a feeling, and a love,
> That had no need of a remoter charm,
> By thought supplied, or any interest
> Unborrowed from the eye,
> (11. 76–83 of the poem; p. 154 of the novel)

The signs on every line of this passage are always and only mediators, announcing their difference not only from themselves and the desiring self (the locus of an 'appetite' directed elsewhere), but also from a 'remoter charm', a presence 'far more deeply interfused' that announces its absence the moment it is signified. The poet and his repetition in Clerval, both of whom start as figures for a previous text, thereby present their focus as the attempted but fragile 'likeness' of themselves and what differs from them. They offer a world of mere signs displacing other signs and calling for a rhetorical communion, all of which looks out for a lost origin without any attempt to recover it.[35] Victor follows this citation, not surprisingly, with a verbal attempt to recover Clerval, who has now been killed by the mediating engine that is made to push mediators aside. Yet the resulting eulogy is another fabrication of an absent presence and a fragmentation of the speaking self into a desire for another text beyond the one in progress, a vivid example of the angle I suggest for approaching the entire novel that is *Frankenstein*. As a further result, too, I cannot really offer this suggestion as any sort of absolute. It is only, like the novel that it displaces and re-enciphers, a sub-scription to a group of signs. It is working out its own confinement and its own autonomy from the author in the pursuit of desires generated by other texts, and its only goals are the energising exchange of another's reading and the possible understanding of its own monstrosity.

From *Structuralist Review*, 2 (1980), 20–45.

NOTES

[Jerrold Hogle's essay draws on the work of four major poststructuralist writers: Lacan, Foucault, Derrida and de Man. It looks at the way that Frankenstein attempts to affirm an absolute and imaginary creative presence, a plenitude of selfhood, in which the divinity is the mirror of complete unity and authority. This project is displaced by the otherness, the monstrous textual differences highlighted in deconstructive criticism and identified as a conflict of two discursive formations. For Foucault, discursive formations are historically specific systems of knowledge and practice. The conflict in *Frankenstein*, according to Hogle, is between a rational discursive formation which insists on scientific classification and a religious framework which depends on divine revelation. Frankenstein's act of creation is caught between the two, a failed attempt to author himself as a fully human and enlightened being by means of a narrative that delivers only textual monsters. It is an act of self-fabrication, moreover, that finds itself bound up in the movements of the texts it tries to transcend. These texts, the various literary, philosophical and scientific writings preceding and alluded to in and composing the novel, disclose Frankenstein's project and ideal of self to be effects of previous systems of knowledge and practice rather than of his own invention. Rather than being beyond textuality, Frankenstein occupies a world fabricated and displaced by signs. Ed.]

1. All my citations from the novel and its prefaces come from *Frankenstein; or the Modern Prometheus,* ed. James Rieger (Indianapolis, 1974), the only version to date that includes the text of 1818, the addenda of 1823, and the substantial revisions of 1831.
2. Several studies have argued this conclusion as evidence of a moral presence in the novel. See especially M. A. Goldberg, 'Moral and Myth

in Mrs. Shelley's *Frankenstein'*, *Keats–Shelley Journal,* 8 (1959), 27–38, and James Rieger, *The Mutiny Within* (New York, 1967), pp. 81–9.

3. On the absence and drift of letters and epistolary fiction, see Homer Obed Brown, 'The Errant Letter and the Whispering Gallery', *Genre,* 10 (1977), 573–99; on 'the necessary *Nachträglichkeit* of voyaging', see John Carlos Rower, 'Writing and Truth in Poe's *The Narrative of Arthur Gordon Pym'*, *Glyph II* (Baltimore, 1977), pp. 102–21.

4. See '"Godlike Science/Unhallowed Arts": Language, Nature and Monstrosity', in George Levine and U. C. Knoepflmacher (eds), *The Endurance of* Frankenstein: *Essays on Mary Shelley's Novel* (Berkeley, 1979), pp. 205–20. I am grateful to Professor Brooks for sending me a copy of his article prior to publication. Something in this direction is also attempted by L. J. Swingle in 'Frankenstein's Monster and Its Romantic Relatives: Problems of Knowledge in English Romanticism', *Texas Studies in Literature and Language,* 15 (1973–4), 51–65, but this effort ignores the inherent mystery of rhetoric itself.

5. Jacques Lacan, 'The Function of Language in Psychoanalysis', trans. Anthony Wilden, in *The Language of the Self* (Baltimore, 1968), p. 11.

6. For the best study yet of the Puritan emblematics that Mary Shelley draws from her father, see J. Paul Hunter, *The Reluctant Pilgrim: Defoe's Emblematic Method and Quest for Form in* Robinson Crusoe (Baltimore, 1966). I am also indebted personally to Professor Hunter for comments on *Frankenstein* and on my present effort.

7. Michel Foucault, *The Order of Things: An Archeology of the Human Sciences,* trans. anon. (New York, 1970), esp. pp. 50–77.

8. Some intimations of this conflict (though not in rhetorical terms) appear in John A. Dussinger, 'Kinship and Guilt in Mary Shelley's *Frankenstein'*, *Studies in the Novel,* 8 (1976), 38–55; Irving H. Buchen, '*Frankenstein* and the Alchemy of Creation and Evolution', *The Wordsworth Circle,* 8 (1970), 103–12; David Ketterer, *Frankenstein's Creation: The Book, The Monster, and Human Reality,* ELS Monograph No. 16 (Univ. of Victoria, 1979) pp. 9–44; and George Levine, 'The Ambiguous Heritage of *Frankenstein'*, *The Endurance of Frankenstein,* pp. 3–30.

9. For an attack on 'Polar fantasies' using these very standards, see the anonymous 'Polar Ice and the North-West Passage' in *The Edinburgh Review,* 30 (J[illegible]–Sept, 1818), 1–59.

10. *The Notebooks of Samuel Taylor Colridge,* ed. Kathleen Coburn (New York, 1957–61), I, no. 1679. For more on the place of Coleridge in *Frankenstein* see Robert Kiely, *The Romantic Novel in England* (Cambridge, Mass., 1972), pp. 166–73.

11. This succession of displacements also includes the gloss, though *Frankenstein* probably does not quote the poem from the 1817 text. See Lawrence Lipking, 'The Marginal Gloss', *Critical Inquiry,* 3 (1977), 609–21. I cite the *Rime*, by the way, from the 1798 version in *The Annotated Ancient Mariner,* ed. Martin Gardner (New York, 1965).

12. For a wider discussion of guilt as the consequence of textuality, see Paul de Man, 'The Purloined Ribbon', *Glyph, 1* (Baltimore, 1977), pp. 28–49, an essay to which I owe much.

13. For the best statement of the promise, see Henry Cornelius Agrippa, *Three Books of Occult Philosophy or Magic: Book One – Natural Magic*, ed. Willis F. Whitehead (1897; rpt. London, 1971), p. 34. For the interdiction of what he has just said, see Agrippa again, *Of the Vanitie and Uncertaintie of Artes and Sciences*, ed. Catherine M. Dunn (Northridge, 1974).

14. Quoted in translation by Radu Florescu, *In Search of Frankenstein* (Boston, 1976), p. 227. In addition to the homunculus, there is a pre-text for Victor's work in the mechanical figure by Albertus Magnus that points to the same warning. See William Godwin (Mary Shelley's father) in *Lives of the Necromancers* (London, 1834), pp. 260–3 and 359–61.

15. Included in *Characteristics of Men, Manners, Opinions, Time*, ed. John M. Robertson (Indianapolis, 1964), II, 10.

16. See the *Theogony in Hesiod, The Homeric Hymns, and Homerica,* trans. Hugh G. Evelyn-White (New York, 1914), pp. 122–23 Z11, 585–612.

17. The clearest exposition of Darwin's approach to spontaneous generation appears in the Additional Notes to *The Temple of Nature* (1803; rpt. London, 1973), esp. pp. 1–13 and 46–79. Indeed on p. 3 of these mini-essays he describes how 'microscopic animals are produced' through 'infusions [of] vegetable or animal matter' by 'electrical scientists'. And it is just such experiments that Mary Shelley connects with Darwin in her introduction to *Frankenstein* (p. 228). Davy pursues 'the dependence of electrical and chemical action' during the *Elements of Chemical Philosophy* (1812) in *The Collected Works*, ed. John Davy (1840; rpt. New York, 1972), IV, esp. 91–131. This book also prefigures Waldman by arguing the displacement of alchemy through 'observation, experiment, and analogy' (IV, 2). For her reading of this very section, see *Mary Shelley's Journal*, ed. Frederick L. Jones (Norman, 1947), p. 73.

18. *An Essay Concerning Human Understanding*, ed. Peter H. Nidditch (Oxford, 1975), pp. 395 and 397. Mary even notes a reading of this text while she composes *Frankenstein* in the *Journal*, pp. 74–5.

19. A good summary of the usual Freudian readings appears in Martin Tropp, *Mary Shelley's Monster: The Story of* Frankenstein (Boston, 1976), pp. 11–83. The most often used (though uncited) ground for such responses, of course, is *Beyond the Pleasure Principle* in *The Standard Edition of the Complete Psychological Works of Sigmund Freud*, trans. and ed. James Strachey et al. (London, 1953–66), XVII, 7–64.

20. Lacan even regards this kind of discovery as an unmasking of 'the true *monstrum horrendum*', a divulging of 'what is destined by nature to signify the annulment of what it signifies'. See the 'Seminar on "The Purloined Letter"', trans. Jeffrey Mehlman, *Yale French Studies*, 48 (1972), 63 and 71.

21. Such a statement, of course, is not original with Elizabeth. It is one of several allusions to Godwin's *Enquiry Concerning Political Justice*, 3rd edn, ed. F. E. L. Priestly (Toronto, 1946), this one echoing volume 1, 322–46. Yet it also reflects the concern of Mary Shelley's father that existing systems have no basis in anything except their own rhetoric. *Frankenstein*, after all, does resemble *Caleb Williams* (1794), Godwin's tale of a servant pursued by a fiendish master, both of whom have created themselves in textual images. By the end of that novel the speaker is led to wonder if a solid definition of self is possible at all in the modern world. See *Caleb Williams*, ed. David McCracken (London, 1970), p. 326, and Jerrold E. Hogle, 'The Texture of the Self in Godwin's *Things as They Are*', *boundary* 2, 7, No. 2 (Winter 1979), 261–81.

22. See 'A Defence of Poetry' in *Shelley's Poetry and Prose*, ed. Donald H. Reiman and Sharon B. Powers (New York, 1977), pp. 496–7. Further citations from Shelley's work have been checked against this book.

23. Too many critics, however, have stopped at this point in assessing the creature as a *Doppelgänger*. The group even includes Harold Bloom in '*Frankenstein; or the Modern Prometheus*', *Partisan Review*, 32 (1965), rpt. in Bloom's *The Ringers in the Tower* (Chicago, 1971), pp. 118–29. This essay neatly shows how Victor voids himself by giving all powers of desire to his creature, yet it does not see how Victor pursues creation expressly to achieve a definition of self that needs fabrication to ground it. For me the monster is a double for something already double, a second other that embodies Victor's complex relation to the Other of his textual options.

24. On these problems of 'authorship' I am much indebted to John T. Irwin, *Doubling and Incest/Repetition and Revenge: A Speculative Reading of Faulkner* (Baltimore, 1975), pp. 158–72.

25. A notion developed out of Nietzsche in *Beginnings: Intention and Method* (New York, 1975), p. 43.

26. These authors guide the epistemology of Mary Shelley in Burton R. Pollin, 'Philosophical and Literary Sources of *Frankenstein*', *Comparative Literature*, 17 (1965), 97–108. Pollin does cite some persuasive parallels, without a doubt; but in concentrating on these writers as 'influences' (forces flowing into Mary Shelley's mind as presences of thought), he misconstrues their relation to *Frankenstein*. I find Mary entering into the verbal possibilities of their texts, and this view is supported by the creature's own 'entrance' into Volney, a writer whom Pollin scarcely mentions.
27. Comte de Volney, *Les ruines, ou meditation sur les révolutions des empires*, in *Oeuvres completes de C. F. Volney* (Paris, 1821), I, 29–30. The translation is mine.
28. From 'Theseus and Romulus' in *Parallel Lives*, trans. Bernadette Perrin (Cambridge, Mass, 1914), I, 193. This is one of the *Lives*, incidentally, mentioned in the creature's tale.
29. *The Sufferings of Young Werther*, trans. Harry Steinhauer (New York, 1970), pp. 38 and 72.
30. See 'The "Uncanny"' in *Standard Edition* XVII, 219–52, plus Derrida, 'La double séance', in *La Dissémination* (Paris, 1972), pp. 300–1.
31. *Of Grammatology*, trans. Gayatri Chakravorty Spivak (Baltimore, 1976), p. 5. Frances Ferguson also connects this statement with *Frankenstein* (though briefly) in 'Reading Heidegger: Paul de Man and Jacques Derrida', *boundary* 2, 4 (1976), 605.
32. See especially Ellen Moers, 'Female Gothic: The Monster's Mother', *New York Review of Books*, 21 March 1974, 24–8, and Marc A. Rubenstein, '"My Accursed Origin": The Search for the Mother in *Frankenstein*', *Studies in Romanticism*, 15 (1976), 165–94.
33. See Mary Poovey, '"My Hideous Progeny": Mary Shelley and the Feminization of Romanticism', *PMLA*, 95 (1980), 332–47.
34. *The Letters of Mary W. Shelley*, ed. Frederick L. Jones (Norman, 1994), I, 259.
35. See Paul de Man, 'Intentional Structure of the Romantic Image', in Harold Bloom (ed.), *Romanticism and Consciousness* (New York, 1970), pp. 65–77, and Frances Ferguson, *Wordsworth: Language as Counter-spirit* (New Haven, 1977), pp. 126–54.

10

Three Women's Texts and a Critique of Imperialism

GAYATRI CHAKRAVORTY SPIVAK

It should not be possible to read nineteenth-century British literature without remembering that imperialism, understood as England's social mission, was a crucial part of the cultural representation of England to the English. The role of literature in the production of cultural representation should not be ignored. These two obvious 'facts' continue to be disregarded in the reading of nineteenth-century British literature. This itself attests to the continuing success of the imperialist project, displaced and dispersed into more modern forms.

If these 'facts' were remembered, not only in the study of British literature but in the study of the literatures of the European colonising cultures of the great age of imperialism, we would produce a narrative, in literary history, of the 'worlding' of what is now called 'the Third World'. To consider the Third World as distant cultures, exploited but with rich intact literary heritages waiting to be recovered, interpreted, and curricularised in English translation fosters the emergence of 'the Third World' as a signifier that allows us to forget that 'worlding', even as it expands the empire of the literary discipline.[1]

It seems particularly unfortunate when the emergent perspective of feminist criticism reproduces the axioms of imperialism. A basically isolationist admiration for the literature of the female subject in Europe and Anglo-America establishes the high feminist norm. It is supported and operated by an information-retrieval approach to 'Third World' literature which often employs a deliberately 'non-theoretical' methodology with self-conscious rectitude.

In this essay, I will attempt to examine the operation of the 'worlding' of what is today 'the Third World' by what has become a cult text of feminism: *Jane Eyre*.[2] I plot the novel's reach and grasp, and locate its structural motors. I read *Wide Sargasso Sea* as *Jane Eyre*'s reinscription and *Frankenstein* as an analysis – even a deconstruction – of a 'worlding' such as *Jane Eyre*'s.[3]

I need hardly mention that the object of my investigation is the printed book, not its 'author'. To make such a distinction is, of course, to ignore the lessons of deconstruction. A deconstructive critical approach would loosen the binding of the book, undo the opposition between verbal text and the biography of the named subject 'Charlotte Brontë', and see the two as each other's 'scene of writing'. In such a reading, the life that writes itself as 'my life' is as much a production in psychosocial space (other names can be found) as the book that is written by the holder of that named life – a book that is then consigned to what *is* most often recognised as genuinely 'social': the world of publication and distribution.[4] To touch Brontë's 'life' in such a way, however, would be too risky here. We must rather strategically take shelter in an essentialism which, not wishing to lose the important advantages won by US mainstream feminism, will continue to honour the suspect binary oppositions – book and author, individual and history – and start with an assurance of the following sort: my readings here do not seek to undermine the excellence of the individual artist. If even minimally successful, the readings will incite a degree of rage against the imperialist narrativisation of history, that it should produce so abject a script for her. I provide these assurances to allow myself some room to situate feminist individualism in its historical determination rather than simply to canonise it as feminism as such.

Sympathetic US feminists have remarked that I do not do justice to Jane Eyre's subjectivity. A word of explanation is perhaps in order. The broad strokes of my presuppositions are that what is at stake, for feminist individualism in the age of imperialism, is precisely the making of human beings, the constitution and 'interpellation' of the subject not only as individual but as 'individualist'.[5] This stake is represented on two registers: childbearing and soul making. The first is domestic-society-through-sexual-reproduction cathected as 'companionate love'; the second is the imperialist project cathected as civil-society-through-social-mission. As the female individualist, not-quite/not-male, articulates herself in shifting relationship to what is at stake, the 'native female' as such (*within* discourse, *as* a signifier) is excluded from any share in this emerging norm.[6] If we read this account from an isolationist perspective in a 'metropolitan' context, we see nothing there but the psychobiography of the militant female subject. In a reading such as mine, in contrast, the effort is to wrench oneself away from the mesmerising focus of the 'subject-constitution' of the female individualist.

To develop further the notion that my stance need not be an accusing one, I will refer to a passage from Roberto Fernández Retamar's 'Caliban'.[7] José Enrique Rodó had argued in 1900 that the model for the Latin American intellectual in relationship to Europe could be Shakespeare's Ariel.[8] In 1971 Retamar, denying the possibility of an identifiable 'Latin American Culture', recast the model as Caliban. Not surprisingly, this powerful exchange still excludes any specific consideration of the civilisations of the Maya, the Aztecs, the Incas, or the smaller nations of what is now called Latin America. Let us note carefully that, at this stage of my argument, this 'conversation' between Europe and Latin America (without a specific consideration of the political economy of the 'worlding' of the 'native') provides a sufficient thematic description of our attempt to confront the ethnocentric and reverse-ethnocentric benevolent double bind (that is, considering the 'native' as object for enthusiastic information-retrieval and thus denying its own 'worlding') that I sketched in my opening paragraphs.

In a moving passage in 'Caliban', Retamar locates both Caliban and Ariel in the postcolonial intellectual:

> There is no real Ariel–Caliban polarity: both are slaves in the hands of Prospero, the foreign magician. But Caliban is the rude and unconquerable master of the island, while Ariel, a creature of the air, although also a child of the isle, is the intellectual.
>
> The deformed Caliban – enslaved, robbed of his island, and taught the language by Prospero – rebukes him thus: 'You taught me language, and my profit on't / Is, I know how to curse'.
>
> (pp. 28, 11)

As we attempt to unlearn our so-called privilege as Ariel and 'seek from [a certain] Caliban the honour of a place in his rebellious and glorious ranks', we do not ask that our students and colleagues should emulate us but that they should attend to us (p. 72). If, however, we are driven by a nostalgia for lost origins, we too run the risk of effacing the 'native' and stepping forth as 'the real Caliban', of forgetting that he is a name in a play, an inaccessible blankness circumscribed by an interpretable text.[9] The stagings of Caliban work alongside the narrativisation of history: claiming to *be* Caliban legitimises the very individualism that we must persistently attempt to undermine from within.

Elizabeth Fox-Genovese, in an article on history and women's history, shows us how to define the historical moment of feminism in the West in terms of female access to individualism.[10] The battle for female individualism plays itself out within the larger theatre of the establishment of meritocratic individualism, indexed in the aesthetic field by the ideology of 'the creative imagination'. Fox-Genovese's presupposition will guide us into the beautifully orchestrated opening of *Jane Eyre*.

It is a scene of the marginalisation and privatisation of the protagonist: 'There was no possibility of taking a walk that day.... Out-door exercise was now out of the question. I was glad of it', Brontë writes (p. 9). The movement continues as Jane breaks the rules of the appropriate topography of withdrawal. The family at the centre withdraws into the sanctioned architectural space of the withdrawing room or drawing room; Jane inserts herself – 'I slipped in' – into the margin – 'A small breakfast room *adjoined* the drawing room' (p. 9; my emphasis).

The manipulation of the domestic inscription of space within the upwardly mobilising currents of the eighteenth- and nineteenth-century bourgeoisie in England and France is well known. It seems fitting that the place to which Jane withdraws is not only not the withdrawing room but also not the dining room, the sanctioned place of family meals. Nor is it the library, the appropriate place for reading. The breakfast room 'contained a book-case' (p. 9). As Rudolph Ackerman wrote in his *Repository* (1823), one of the many manuals of taste in circulation in nineteenth-century England, these low bookcases and stands were designed to 'contain all the books that may be desired for a sitting-room without reference to the library'.[11] Even in this already triply off-centre place, 'having drawn the red moreen curtain nearly close, I [Jane] was shrined in double retirement' (pp. 9–10).

Here in Jane's self-marginalised uniqueness, the reader becomes her accomplice: the reader and Jane are united – both are reading. Yet Jane still preserves her odd privilege, for she continues never quite doing the proper thing in its proper place. She cares little for reading what is *meant* to be read: the 'letter-press'. *She* reads the pictures. The power of this singular hermeneutics is precisely that it can make the outside inside. 'At intervals, while turning over the leaves of my book, I studied the aspect of that winter afternoon.' Under 'the clear panes of glass', the rain no longer penetrates, 'the drear November day' is rather a one-dimensional 'aspect' to be 'studied', not decoded like the 'letter-press' but, like pictures, deciphered by the unique creative imagination of the marginal individualist (p. 10).

Before following the track of this unique imagination, let us consider the suggestion that the progress of *Jane Eyre* can be charted through a sequential arrangement of the family/counter-family dyad. In the novel, we encounter, first, the Reeds as the legal family and Jane, the late Mr Reed's sister's daughter, as the representative of a near incestuous counter-family; second, the Brocklehursts, who run the school Jane is sent to, as the legal family and Jane, Miss Temple, and Helen Burns as a counter-family that falls short because it is only a community of women; third, Rochester and the mad Mrs Rochester as the legal family and Jane and Rochester as the illicit counter-family. Other items may be added to the thematic chain in this sequence: Rochester and Céline Varens as structurally functional counter-family; Rochester and Blanche Ingram as dissimulation of legality – and so on. It is during this sequence that Jane is moved from the counter-family to the family-in-law. In the next sequence, it is Jane who restores full family status to the as-yet-incomplete community of siblings, the Riverses. The final sequence of the book is a *community of families*, with Jane, Rochester, and their children at the centre.

In terms of the narrative energy of the novel, how is Jane moved from the place of the counter-family to the family-in-law? It is the active ideology of imperialism that provides the discursive field.

(My working definition of 'discursive field' must assume the existence of discrete 'systems of signs' at hand in the socius, each based on a specific axiomatics. I am identifying these systems as discursive fields. 'Imperialism as social mission' generates the possibility of one such axiomatics. How the individual artist taps the discursive field at hand with a sure touch, if not with transhistorical clairvoyance, in order to make the narrative structure move I hope to demonstrate through the following example. It is crucial that we extend our analysis of this example beyond the minimal diagnosis of 'racism'.)

Let us consider the figure of Bertha Mason, a figure produced by the axiomatics of imperialism. Through Bertha Mason, the white Jamaican Creole, Brontë renders the human/animal frontier as acceptably indeterminate, so that a good greater than the letter of the Law can be broached. Here is the celebrated passage, given in the voice of Jane:

> In the deep shade, at the further end of the room, a figure ran backwards and forwards. What it was, whether beast or human being, one could not ... tell: it grovelled, seemingly, on all fours; it snatched and growled like some strange wild animal: but it was covered with clothing, and a quantity of dark, grizzled hair, wild as a mane, hid its head and face.
>
> (p. 295)

In a matching passage, given in the voice of Rochester speaking *to* Jane, Brontë presents the imperative for a shift beyond the Law as divine injunction rather than human motive. In the terms of my essay, we might say that this is the register not of mere marriage or sexual reproduction but of Europe and its not-yet-human Other, of soul making. The field of imperial conquest is here inscribed as Hell:

> 'One night I had been awakened by her yells ... it was a fiery West Indian night. ...
>
> '"This life," said I at last, "is hell! – this is the air – those are the sounds of the bottomless pit! *I have a right* to deliver myself from it if I can. ... Let me break away, and go home to God!"...
>
> 'A wind fresh from Europe blew over the ocean and rushed through the open casement: the storm broke, streamed, thundered, blazed, and the air grew pure. ... It was true Wisdom that consoled me in that hour, and showed me the right path. ...
>
> 'The sweet wind from Europe was still whispering in the refreshed leaves, and the Atlantic was thundering in glorious liberty. ...
>
> '"Go," said Hope, "and live again in Europe. ... You have done all that God and Humanity require of you."'
>
> (pp. 310–11; my emphasis)

It is the unquestioned ideology of imperialist axiomatics, then, that conditions Jane's move from the counter-family set to the set of the family-in-law. Marxist critics such as Terry Eagleton have seen this only in terms of the ambiguous *class* position of the governess.[12] Sandra Gilbert and Susan Gubar, on the other hand, have seen Bertha Mason only in psychological terms, as Jane's dark double.[13]

I will not enter the critical debates that offer themselves here. Instead, I will develop the suggestion that nineteenth-century feminist individualism could conceive of a 'greater' project than access to the closed circle of the nuclear family. This is the project of soul making beyond 'mere' sexual reproduction. Here the native 'subject' is not almost an animal but rather the object of what might be termed the terrorism of the categorical imperative.

I am using 'Kant' in this essay as a metonym for the most flexible ethical moment in the European eighteenth century. Kant words the categorical imperative, conceived as the universal moral law given by pure reason, in this way: 'In all creation every thing one chooses and over which one has any power, may be used *merely as means*; man alone, and with him every rational creature, is an *end in himself*.' It is thus a moving displacement of Christian ethics from religion to philosophy. As Kant writes: 'With this agrees very well the possibility of such a command as: *Love God above everything, and thy neighbour as thyself*. For as a command it requires respect for a law which *commands love* and does not leave it to our own arbitrary choice to make this our principle'.[14]

The 'categorical' in Kant cannot be adequately represented in determinately grounded action. The dangerous transformative power of philosophy, however, is that its formal subtlety can be travestied in the service of the state. Such a travesty in the case of the categorical imperative can justify the imperialist project by producing the following formula: *make* the heathen into a human so that he can be treated as an end in himself.[15] This project is presented as a sort of tangent in *Jane Eyre*, a tangent that escapes the closed circle of the *narrative* conclusion. The tangent narrative is the story of St John Rivers, who is granted the important task of concluding the *text*.

At the novel's end, the *allegorical* language of Christian psychobiography – rather than the textually constituted and seemingly *private* grammar of the creative imagination which we noted in the novel's opening – marks the inaccessibility of the imperialist project as such to the nascent 'feminist' scenario. The concluding passage of *Jane Eyre* places St John Rivers within the fold of *Pilgrim's Progress*. Eagleton pays no attention to this but accepts the novel's ideological lexicon, which establishes St John Rivers' heroism by identifying a life in Calcutta with an unquestioning choice of death. Gilbert and Gubar, by calling *Jane Eyre* 'Plain Jane's progress', see the novel as simply replacing the male protagonist with the female. They do not notice the distance between sexual reproduction and soul making, both actualised by the unquestioned idiom of imperialist presuppositions evident in the last part of *Jane Eyre*:

> Firm, faithful, and devoted, full of energy, and zeal, and truth, [St John Rivers] labours for his race. ... His is the sternness of the warrior Greatheart, who guards his pilgrim convoy from the onslaught of Apollyon. ... His is the ambition of the high master-spirit[s] ... who stand without fault before the throne of God; who share the last mighty victories of the Lamb; who are called, and chosen, and faithful.
>
> (p. 455)

Earlier in the novel, St John Rivers himself justifies the project: 'My vocation? My great work? ... My hopes of being numbered in the band who have merged all ambitions in the glorious one of bettering their race – of carrying knowledge into the realms of ignorance – of substituting peace for war – freedom for bondage – religion for superstition – the hope of heaven for the fear of hell?' (p. 376). Imperialism and its territorial and subject-constituting project are a violent deconstruction of these oppositions.

When Jean Rhys, born on the Caribbean island of Dominica, read *Jane Eyre* as a child, she was moved by Bertha Mason: 'I thought I'd try to write her a life'.[16] *Wide Sargasso Sea*, the slim novel published in 1965, at the end of Rhys' long career, is that 'life'.

I have suggested that Bertha's function in *Jane Eyre* is to render indeterminate the boundary between human and animal and thereby to weaken her entitlement under the spirit if not the letter of the Law. When Rhys rewrites the scene in *Jane Eyre* where Jane hears 'a snarling, snatching sound, almost like a dog quarrelling' and then encounters a bleeding Richard Mason (p. 210), she keeps Bertha's humanity, indeed her sanity as critic of imperialism, intact. Grace Poole, another character originally in *Jane Eyre*, describes the incident to Bertha in *Wide Sargasso Sea*: 'So you don't remember that you attacked this gentleman with a knife? ... I didn't hear all he said except "I cannot interfere legally between yourself and your husband". It was when he said "legally" that you flew at him' (p. 150). In Rhys' retelling, it is the dissimulation that Bertha discerns in the word 'legally' – not an innate bestiality – that prompts her violent *re*action.

In the figure of Antoinette, whom in *Wide Sargasso Sea* Rochester violently renames Bertha, Rhys suggests that so intimate a thing as personal and human identity might be determined by the politics of imperialism. Antoinette, as a white Creole child growing up at the time of emancipation in Jamaica, is caught between the English imperialist and the black native. In recounting Antoinette's development, Rhys reinscribes some thematics of Narcissus.

There are, noticeably, many images of mirroring in the text. I will quote one from the first section. In this passage, Tia is the little black servant girl who is Antoinette's close companion: 'We had eaten the same food, slept side by side, bathed in the same river. As I ran, I thought, I will live with Tia and I will be like her. ... When I was close I saw the jagged stone in her hand but I did not see her throw it. ... We stared at each other, blood on my face, tears on hers. It was as if I saw myself. Like in a looking glass' (p. 38).

A progressive sequence of dreams reinforces this mirror imagery. In its second occurrence, the dream is partially set in a *hortus conclusus*, or 'enclosed garden' – Rhys uses the phrase (p. 50) – a Romance rewriting of the Narcissus topos as the place of encounter with Love.[17] In the enclosed garden, Antoinette encounters not Love but a strange threatening voice that says merely 'in here', inviting her into a prison which masquerades as the legalization of love (p. 50).

In Ovid's *Metamorphoses*, Narcissus' madness is disclosed when he recognises his Other as his self: 'Iste ego sum'.[18] Rhys makes Antoinette see her *self* as her Other, Brontë's Bertha. In the last section of *Wide Sargasso Sea*, Antoinette acts out *Jane Eyre*'s conclusion and recognises herself as the so-called ghost in Thornfield Hall: 'I went into the hall again with the tall candle in my hand. It was then that I saw her – the ghost. The woman with streaming hair. She was surrounded by a gilt frame but I knew her' (p. 154). The gilt frame encloses a mirror: as Narcissus' pool reflects the selfed Other, so this 'pool' reflects the Othered self. Here the dream sequence ends, with an invocation of none other than Tia, the Other that could not be selfed, because the fracture of imperialism rather than the Ovidian pool intervened. (I will return to this difficult point.) 'That was the third time I had my dream, and it ended. ... I called "Tia" and jumped and woke' (p. 155). It is now, at the very end of the book, that Antoinette/Bertha can say: 'Now at last I know why I was brought here and what I have to do' (p. 155–6). We can read this as her having been brought into the

England of Brontë's novel: 'This cardboard house' – a book between cardboard covers – 'where I walk at night is not England' (p. 148). In this fictive England, she must play out her role, act out the transformation of her 'self' into that fictive Other, set fire to the house and kill herself, so that Jane Eyre can become the feminist individualist heroine of British fiction. I must read this as an allegory of the general epistemic violence of imperialism, the construction of a self-immolating colonial subject for the glorification of the social mission of the coloniser. At least Rhys sees to it that the woman from the colonies is not sacrificed as an insane animal for her sister's consolidation.

Critics have remarked that *Wide Sargasso Sea* treats the Rochester character with understanding and sympathy.[19] Indeed, he narrates the entire middle section of the book. Rhys makes it clear that he is a victim of the patriarchal inheritance law of entailment rather than of a father's natural preference for the firstborn: in *Wide Sargasso Sea*, Rochester's situation is clearly that of a younger son dispatched to the colonies to buy an heiress. If in the case of Antoinette and her identity, Rhys utilises the thematics of Narcissus, in the case of Rochester and his patrimony, she touches on the thematics of Oedipus. (In this she has her finger on our 'historical moment'. If, in the nineteenth century, subject-constitution is represented as childbearing and soul making, in the twentieth century psychoanalysis allows the West to plot the itinerary of the subject from Narcissus [the 'imaginary'] to Oedipus [the 'symbolic']. This subject, however, is the normative male subject. In Rhys' reinscription of these themes, divided between the female and the male protagonist, feminism and a critique of imperialism become complicit.)

In place of the 'wind from Europe' scene, Rhys substitutes the scenario of a suppressed letter to a father, a letter which would be the 'correct' explanation of the tragedy of the book.[20] 'I thought about the letter which should have been written to England a week ago. Dear Father ...' (p. 57). This is the first instance: the letter not written. Shortly afterward:

> Dear Father. The thirty thousand pounds have been paid to me without question or condition. No provision made for her (that must be seen to). ... I will never be a disgrace to you or to my dear brother the son you love. No begging letters, no mean requests. None of the furtive shabby manoeuvres of a younger son. I have sold my soul or

> you have sold it, and after all is it such a bad bargain? The girl is thought to be beautiful, she is beautiful. And yet ...
>
> (p. 59)

This is the second instance: the letter not sent. The formal letter is uninteresting; I will quote only a part of it:

> Dear Father, we have arrived from Jamaica after an uncomfortable few days. This little estate in the Windward Islands is part of the family property and Antoinette is much attached to it. ... All is well and has gone according to your plans and wishes. I dealt of course with Richard Mason. ... He seemed to become attached to me and trusted me completely. This place is very beautiful but my illness has left me too exhausted to appreciate it fully. I will write again in a few days' time.
>
> (p. 63)

And so on.

Rhys' version of the Oedipal exchange is ironic, not a closed circle. We cannot know if the letter actually reaches its destination. 'I wondered how they got their letters posted', the Rochester figure muses. 'I folded mine and put it into a drawer of the desk. ... There are blanks in my mind that cannot be filled up' (p. 64). It is as if the text presses us to note the analogy between letter and mind.

Rhys denies to Brontë's Rochester the one thing that is supposed to be secured in the Oedipal relay: the Name of the Father, or the patronymic. In *Wide Sargasso Sea*, the character corresponding to Rochester has no name. His writing of the final version of the letter to his father is supervised, in fact, by an image of the *loss* of the patronymic: 'There was a crude bookshelf made of three shingles strung together over the desk and I looked at the books, Byron's poems, novels by Sir Walter Scott, *Confessions of an Opium Eater* ... and on the last shelf, *Life and Letters of* ... The rest was eaten away' (p. 63).

Wide Sargasso Sea marks with uncanny clarity the limits of its own discourse in Christophine, Antoinette's black nurse. We may perhaps surmise the distance between *Jane Eyre* and *Wide Sargasso Sea* by remarking that Christophine's unfinished story is the tangent to the latter narrative, as St John Rivers' story is to the former. Christophine is not a native of Jamaica; she is from Martinique. Taxnomically, she belongs to the category of the good servant rather than that of the pure native. But within these borders, Rhys creates a powerfully suggestive figure.

Christophine is the first interpreter and named speaking subject in the text. 'The Jamaican ladies had never approved of my mother, "because she pretty like pretty self" Christophine said', we read in the book's opening paragraph (p. 15). I have taught this book five times, once in France, once to students who had worked on the book with the well-known Caribbean novelist Wilson Harris, and once at a prestigious institute where the majority of the students were faculty from other universities. It is part of the political argument I am making that all these students blithely stepped over this paragraph without asking or knowing what Christophine's patois, so-called incorrect English, might mean.

Christophine is, of course, a commodified person. '"She was your father's wedding present to me"' explains Antoinette's mother, '"one of his presents"' (p. 18). Yet Rhys assigns her some crucial functions in the text. It is Christophine who judges that black ritual practices are culture-specific and cannot be used by whites as cheap remedies for social evils, such as Rochester's lack of love for Antoinette. Most important, it is Christophine alone whom Rhys allows to offer a hard analysis of Rochester's actions, to challenge him in a face-to-face encounter. The entire extended passage is worthy of comment. I quote a brief extract:

> 'She is Creole girl, and she have the sun in her. Tell the truth now. She don't come to your house in this place England they tell me about, she don't come to your beautiful house to beg you to marry with her. No, it's you come all the long way to her house – it's you beg her to marry. And she love you and she give you all she have. Now you say you don't love her and you break her up. What you do with her money, eh?' [And then Rochester, the white man, comments silently to himself] Her voice was still quiet but with a hiss in it when she said 'money'.
>
> (p. 130)

Her analysis is powerful enough for the white man to be afraid: 'I no longer felt dazed, tired, half hypnotised, but alert and wary, ready to defend myself' (p. 130).

Rhys does not, however, romanticise individual heroics on the part of the oppressed. When the Man refers to the forces of Law and Order, Christophine recognises their power. This exposure of civil inequality is emphasised by the fact that, just before the Man's successful threat, Christophine had invoked the emancipation of slaves in Jamaica by proclaiming: 'No chain gang, no tread machine, no dark jail either. This is free country and I am free woman' (p. 131).

As I mentioned above, Christophine is tangential to this narrative. She cannot be contained by a novel which rewrites a canonical English text within the European novelistic tradition in the interest of the white Creole rather than the native. No perspective *critical* of imperialism can turn the Other into a self, because the project of imperialism has always already historically refracted what might have been the absolutely Other into a domesticated Other that consolidates the imperialist self.[21] The Caliban of Retamar, caught between Europe and Latin America, reflects this predicament. We can read Rhys' reinscription of Narcissus as a thematisation of the same problematic.

Of course, we cannot know Jean Rhys' feelings in the matter. We can, however, look at the scene of Christophine's inscription in the text. Immediately after the exchange between her and the Man, well before the conclusion, she is simply driven out of the story, with neither narrative nor characterological explanation or justice. '"Read and write I don't know. Other things I know". She walked away without looking back' (p. 133).

Indeed, if Rhys rewrites the madwoman's attack on the Man by underlining of the misuse of 'legality', she cannot deal with the passage that corresponds to St John Rivers' own justification of his martyrdom, for it has been displaced into the current idiom of modernisation and development. Attempts to construct the 'Third World Woman' as a signifier remind us that the hegemonic definition of literature is itself caught within the history of imperialism. A full literary reinscription cannot easily flourish in the imperialist fracture or discontinuity, covered over by an alien legal system masquerading as Law as such, an alien ideology established as only Truth, and a set of human sciences busy establishing the 'native' as self-consolidating Other.

In the Indian case at least, it would be difficult to find an ideological clue to the planned epistemic violence of imperialism merely by rearranging curricula or syllabi within existing norms of literary pedagogy. For a later period of imperialism – when the constituted colonial subject has firmly taken hold – straightforward experiments of comparison can be undertaken, say, between the functionally witless India of *Mrs Dalloway*, on the one hand, and literary texts produced in India in the 1920s, on the other. But the first half of the nineteenth century resists questioning through literature or literary criticism in the narrow sense, because both are implicated in the project of producing Ariel. To reopen the fracture without succumbing to a nostalgia for lost origins, the literary critic must turn to the archives of imperial governance.

In conclusion, I shall look briefly at Mary Shelley's *Frankenstein*, a text of nascent feminism that remains cryptic, I think, simply because it does not speak the language of feminist individualism which we have come to hail as the language of high feminism within English literature. It is interesting that Barbara Johnson's brief study tries to rescue this recalcitrant text for the service of feminist autobiography.[22] Alternatively, George Levine reads *Frankenstein* in the context of the creative imagination and the nature of the hero. He sees the novel as a book about its own writing and about writing itself, a Romantic allegory of reading within which Jane Eyre as unself-conscious critic would fit quite nicely.[23]

I propose to take *Frankenstein* out of this arena and focus on it in terms of that sense of English cultural identity which I invoked at the opening of this essay. Within that focus we are obliged to admit that, although *Frankenstein* is ostensibly about the origin and evolution of man in society, it does not deploy the axiomatics of imperialism.

Let me say at once that there is plenty of incidental imperialist sentiment in *Frankenstein*. My point, within the argument of this essay, is that the discursive field of imperialism does not produce unquestioned ideological correlatives for the narrative structuring of the book. The discourse of imperialism surfaces in a curiously powerful way in Shelley's novel, and I will later discuss the moment at which it emerges.

Frankenstein is not a battleground of male and female individualism articulated in terms of sexual reproduction (family and female) and social subject-production (race and male). That binary opposition is undone in Victor Frankenstein's laboratory – an artificial womb where both projects are undertaken simultaneously, though the terms are never openly spelled out. Frankenstein's apparent antagonist is God himself as Maker of Man, but his real competitor is also woman as the maker of children. It is not just that his dream of the death of mother and bride and the actual death of his bride are associated with the visit of his monstrous homoerotic 'son' to his bed. On a much more overt level, the monster is a bodied 'corpse', unnatural because bereft of a determinable childhood: 'No father had watched my infant days, no mother had blessed me with smiles and caresses; or if they had, all my past was now a blot, a blind vacancy in which I distinguished nothing' (pp. 57, 115). It is Frankenstein's own ambiguous and miscued understanding of the real motive for the monster's vengefulness that reveals his own competition with woman as maker:

> I created a rational creature and was bound towards him to assure, as far as was in my power, his happiness and well-being. This was my duty, but there was another still paramount to that. My duties towards the beings of my own species had greater claims to my attention because they included a greater proportion of happiness or misery. Urged by this view, I refused, and I did right in refusing, to create a companion for the first creature.
>
> (p. 206)

It is impossible not to notice the accents of transgression inflecting Frankenstein's demolition of his experiment to create the future Eve. Even in the laboratory, the woman-in-the-making is not a bodied corpse but 'a human being'. The (il)logic of the metaphor bestows on her a prior existence which Frankenstein aborts, rather than an anterior death which he re-embodies: 'The remains of the half-finished creature, whom I had destroyed, lay scattered on the floor, and I almost felt as if I had mangled the living flesh of a human being' (p. 163).

In Shelley's view, man's hubris as soul maker both usurps the place of God and attempts – vainly – to sublate woman's physiological prerogative.[24] Indeed, indulging a Freudian fantasy here, I could urge that, if to give and withhold to/from the mother a phallus is *the* male fetish, then to give and withhold to/from the man a womb might be the female fetish.[25] The icon of the sublimated womb in man is surely his productive brain, the box in the head.

In the judgment of classical psychoanalysis, the phallic mother exists only by virtue of the castration-anxious son; in *Frankenstein*'s judgment, the hysteric father (Victor Frankenstein gifted with his laboratory – the womb of theoretical reason) cannot produce a daughter. Here the language of racism – the dark side of imperialism understood as social mission – combines with the hysteria of masculism into the idiom of (the withdrawal of) sexual reproduction rather than subject-constitution. The roles of masculine and feminine individualists are hence reversed and displaced. Frankenstein cannot produce a 'daughter' because 'she might become ten thousand times more malignant than her mate ... [and because] one of the first results of those sympathies for which the demon thirsted would be children, and a race of devils would be propagated upon the earth who might make the very existence of the species of man a condition precarious and full of terror' (p. 158). This particular narrative strand also launches a thoroughgoing critique of the eighteenth-century European discourses on the origin of society through (Western Christian) man. Should I mention that, much like Jean-Jacques Rousseau's remark in his *Confessions*, Frankenstein declares himself to be 'by birth a Genevese' (p. 31)?

In this overly didactic text, Shelley's point is that social engineering should not be based on pure, theoretical, or natural-scientific reason alone, which is her implicit critique of the utilitarian vision of an engineered society. To this end, she presents in the first part of her deliberately schematic story three characters, childhood friends, who seem to represent Kant's three-part conception of the human subject: Victor Frankenstein, the forces of theoretical reason or 'natural philosophy'; Henry Clerval, the forces of practical reason or 'the moral relations of things'; and Elizabeth Lavenza, that aesthetic judgment – 'the aerial creation of the poets' – which, according to Kant, is 'a suitable mediating link connecting the realm of the concept of nature and that of the concept of freedom ... (which) promotes ... *moral* feeling' (pp. 37, 36).[26]

This three-part subject does not operate harmoniously in *Frankenstein*. That Henry Clerval, associated as he is with practical reason, should have as his 'design ... to visit India, in the belief that he had in his knowledge of its various languages, and in the views he had taken of its society, the means of materially assisting the progress of European colonisation and trade' is proof of this, as well as part of the incidental imperialist sentiment that I speak of above (pp. 151–2). I should perhaps point out that the language here is entrepreneurial rather than missionary:

> He came to the university with the design of making himself complete master of the Oriental languages, as thus he should open a field for the plan of life he had marked out for himself. Resolved to pursue no inglorious career, he turned his eyes towards the East as affording scope for his spirit of enterprise. The Persian, Arabic, and Sanskrit languages engaged his attention.
>
> (pp. 66–7)

But it is of course Victor Frankenstein, with his strange itinerary of obsession with natural philosophy, who offers the strongest demonstration that the multiple perspectives of the three-part Kantian subject cannot co-operate harmoniously. Frankenstein creates a putative human subject out of natural philosophy alone. According to his own miscued summation: 'In a fit of enthusiastic madness I created a rational creature' (p. 206). It is not at all far-fetched to say that Kant's categorical imperative can most easily be mistaken for the hypothetical imperative – a command to ground in cognitive comprehension what can be apprehended only by moral will – by putting natural philosophy in the place of practical reason.

I should hasten to add here that just as readings such as this one do not necessarily accuse Charlotte Brontë the named individual of harbouring imperialist sentiments, so also they do not necessarily commend Mary Shelley the named individual for writing a successful Kantian allegory. The most I can say is that it is possible to read these texts, within the frame of imperialism and the Kantian ethical moment, in a politically useful way. Such an approach presupposes that a 'disinterested' reading attempts to render transparent the interests of the hegemonic readership. (Other 'political' readings – for instance, that the monster is the nascent working class – can also be advanced.)

Frankenstein is built in the established epistolary tradition of multiple frames. At the heart of the multiple frames, the narrative of the monster (as reported by Frankenstein to Robert Walton, who then recounts it in a letter to his sister) is of his almost learning, clandestinely, to be human. It is invariably noticed that the monster reads *Paradise Lost* as true history. What is not so often noticed is that he also reads Plutarch's *Lives*, 'the histories of the first founders of the ancient republics', which he compares to 'the patriarchal lives of my protectors' (pp. 123, 124). And his *education* comes through 'Volney's *Ruins of Empires*', which purported to be a prefiguration of the French Revolution, published after the event and after the author had rounded off his theory with practice (p. 113). It is an attempt at an enlightened universal secular, rather than a Eurocentric Christian, history, written from the perspective of a narrator 'from below', somewhat like the attempts of Eric Wolf or Peter Worsley in our own time.[27]

This Caliban's education in (universal secular) humanity takes place through the monster's eavesdropping on the instruction of an Ariel – Safie, the Christianised 'Arabian' to whom 'a residence in Turkey was abhorrent' (p. 121). In depicting Safie, Shelley uses some commonplaces of eighteenth-century liberalism that are shared by many today: Safie's Muslim father was a victim of (bad) Christian religious prejudice and yet was himself a wily and ungrateful man not as morally refined as her (good) Christian mother. Having tasted the emancipation of woman, Safie could not go home. The confusion between 'Turk' and 'Arab' has its counterpart in present-day confusion about Turkey and Iran as 'Middle Eastern' but not 'Arab'.

Although we are a far cry here from the unexamined and covert axiomatics of imperialism in *Jane Eyre*, we will gain nothing by celebrating the time-bound pieties that Shelley, as the daughter of two anti-evangelicals, produces. It is more interesting for us that Shelley differentiates the Other, works at the Caliban/Ariel distinction, and *cannot* make the monster identical with the proper recipient of these lessons. Although he had 'heard of the discovery of the American hemisphere and *wept with Safie* over the helpless fate of its original inhabitants', Safie cannot reciprocate his attachment. When she first catches sight of him, 'Safie, unable to attend to her friend [Agatha], rushed out of the cottage' (pp. 114 [my emphasis], 129).

In the taxonomy of characters, the Muslim-Christian Safie belongs with Rhys' Antoinette/Bertha. And indeed, like Christophine the good servant, the subject created by the fiat of natural philosophy is the tangential unresolved moment in *Frankenstein*. The simple suggestion that the monster is human inside but monstrous outside and only provoked into vengefulness is clearly not enough to bear the burden of so great a historical dilemma.

At one moment, in fact, Shelley's Frankenstein does try to tame the monster, to humanise him by bringing him within the circuit of the Law. He 'repair[s] to a criminal judge in the town and ... relate[s his] history briefly but with firmness' – the first and disinterested version of the narrative of Frankenstein – 'marking the dates with accuracy and never deviating into invective or exclamation. ... When I had concluded my narration I said, "This is the being whom I accuse and for whose seizure and punishment I call upon you to exert your whole power. It is your duty as a magisrate"' (pp. 189, 190). The sheer social reasonableness of the mundane voice of Shelley's 'Genevan magistrate' reminds us that the absolutely Other cannot be selfed, that the monster has 'properties' which will not be contained by 'proper' measures:

> 'I will exert myself [he says], and if it is in my power to seize the monster, be assured that he shall suffer punishment proportionate to his crimes. But I fear, from what you have yourself described to be his properties, that this will prove impracticable; and thus, while every proper measure is pursued, you should make up your mind to disappointment.'
>
> (p. 190)

In the end, as is obvious to most readers, distinctions of human individuality themselves seem to fall away from the novel. Monster, Frankenstein, and Walton seem to become each others' relays. Frankenstein's story comes to an end in death; Walton concludes his own story within the frame of his function as letter writer. In the *narrative* conclusion, he is the natural philosopher who learns from Frankenstein's example. At the end of the *text*, the monster, having confessed his guilt toward his maker and ostensibly intending to immolate himself, is borne away on an ice raft. We do not see the conflagration of his funeral pile – the self-immolation is not consummated in the text: he too cannot be contained by the text. In terms of narrative logic, he is 'lost in darkness and distance' (p. 211) – these are the last words of the novel – into an existential temporality that is coherent with neither the territorialising individual imagination (as in the opening of *Jane Eyre*) nor the authoritative scenario of Christian psychobiography (as at the end of Brontë's work). The very relationship between sexual reproduction and social subject-production – the dynamic nineteenth-century topos of feminism-in-imperialism – remains problematic within the limits of Shelley's text and, paradoxically, constitutes its strength.

Earlier, I offered a reading of woman as womb holder in *Frankenstein*. I would now suggest that there is a framing woman in the book who is neither tangential, nor encircled, nor yet encircling. 'Mrs Saville', 'excellent Margaret', 'beloved Sister' are her address and kinship inscriptions (pp. 15, 17, 22). She is the occasion, though not the protagonist, of the novel. She is the feminine *subject* rather than the female individualist: she is the irreducible *recipient*-function of the letters that constitute *Frankenstein*. I have commented on the singular appropriative hermeneutics of the reader reading with Jane in the opening pages of *Jane Eyre*. Here the reader must read with Margaret Saville in the crucial sense that she must *intercept* the recipient-function, read the letters *as* recipient, in order for the novel to exist.[28] Margaret Saville does not repond to close the text as frame. The frame is thus simultaneously not a frame, and the monster can step 'beyond the text' and be 'lost in darkness'. Within the allegory of our reading, the place of both the English lady and the unnamable monster are left open by this great flawed text. It is satisfying for a post-colonial reader to consider this a noble resolution for a nineteenth-century English novel. This is all the more striking because, on the anecdotal level, Shelley herself abundantly 'identifies' with Victor Frankenstein.[29]

I must myself close with an idea that I cannot establish within the limits of this essay. Earlier I contended that *Wide Sargasso Sea* is necessarily bound by the reach of the European novel. I suggested that, in contradistinction, to reopen the epistemic fracture of imperialism without succumbing to a nostalgia for lost origins, the critic must turn to the archives of imperialist governance. I have not turned to those archives in these pages. In my current work, by way of a modest and inexpert 'reading' of 'archives', I try to extend, outside of the reach of the European novelistic tradition, the most powerful suggestion in *Wide Sargasso Sea*: that *Jane Eyre* can be read as the orchestration and staging of the self-immolation of Bertha Mason as 'good wife'. The power of that suggestion remains unclear if we remain insufficiently knowledgeable about the history of the legal manipulation of widow-sacrifice in the entitlement of the British government in India. I would hope that an informed critique of imperialism, granted some attention from readers in the First World, will at least expand the frontiers of the politics of reading.

POSTSCRIPT[30]

I 'chose' to study English Literature at University because I was not good enough in Science. I must confess I rather like the so-called English classics – shamefacedly in the way of a Kipling Bengali – and I don't want to stop liking them. Over the years I have developed, without stopping much to think about it, a new way of ranking them: in terms of how they accommodate(d) conquest.

Making public this private shift, I wrote an essay called 'Three Women's Texts and A Critique of Imperialism' a little over ten years ago. In it I wrote in praise of Mary Shelley's *Frankenstein* because, in my estimation, Shelley had attempted to come to terms with the making of the colonial subject. Sympathetic yet monstrous, clandestinely reared on sacred and profane histories of salvation and empire, shunned by the civilisation which produced his subjectivity, this creature's destructive rage propels him out of the novel into an indefinite future. But what of his history? The feminist dimension of the novel provides a frame that is critical of the effort to construct a creature without womb-life and infancy. But when it comes to the colonial subject's pre-history, Shelley's political imagination fails. (We have seen that in post-coloniality, the subject mourns the unlamented death of this previous history.)

Thus Shelley's emancipatory vision cannot extend beyond the speculary situation of the colonial enterprise, where the master alone has a history, master and subject locked up in the cracked mirror of the present, and the subject's future, although indefinite, is vectored specifically toward and away from the master. Within this restricted vision, Shelley gives to the monster the right to refuse the withholding of the master's returned gaze – to refuse an *apartheid* of speculation, as it were:

> 'I will not be tempted to set myself in opposition to thee. ... How can I move thee?' ... [He] placed his hated hands before my [Frankenstein's] eyes, which I flung from me with violence; 'thus I take from thee a sight which you abhor. Still thou canst listen to me ...'[31]

His request, not granted, is for a gendered future, for the colonial female subject.

I want now to advance the argument just a bit further, and make a contrastive point. The task of the post-colonial writer, the descendant of the colonial female subject that history did in fact produce, cannot be restrained within the specular master-slave enclosure so powerfully staged in *Frankenstein*. I turn to Mahasweta Devi's 'Pterodactyl, Pirtha, and Puran Sahay' to measure out some of the differences between the sympathetic and supportive colonial staging of the situation of the refusal of the withholding of specular exchange in favour of the monstrous colonial subject; and the post-colonial performance of the construction of the constitutional subject of the new nation.[32]

Devi stages the workings of the post-colonial state with minute knowledge, anger, and loving despair. There are suppressed dissident radicals, there is the national government seeking electoral publicity, there are systemic bureaucrats beneath good and evil, subaltern state functionaries to whom the so-called Enlightenment principles of democracy are counter-intuitive. Then there is the worst product of post-coloniality, the Indian who uses the alibis of Development to exploit the tribals and destroy their life-system. Over against him is the handful of conscientious and understanding government workers who operate through a system of official sabotage and small compromises. The central figure is Puran Sahay, a journalist. (Devi herself, in addition to being an ecology-health-literacy activist and a fiction writer, is also an indefatigable interventionist journalist.)

The post-colonial state gives the frame-narrative. At the heart of the novella is an act of mourning. A tribal boy has drawn the picture of a pterodactyl on the cave-wall. Puran and a 'good' government officer do not allow this to become public. Through his unintentionally successful 'prediction' of rain, Puran becomes part of the tribe's ongoing historical record. He sees the pterodactyl.

If the exchange between the nameless monster (without history) and Victor Frankenstein is a finally futile refusal of withheld specularity, the situation of the gaze between pterodactyl (before history) and a 'national' history that holds tribal and non-tribal together, is somewhat different.[33] There can be no speculation here; in a textual space rhetorically separated from the counter-factural funeral, the tribal and the non-tribal must pull together, both modern:

> You are moveless with your wings folded, I do not wish to touch you, you are outside my wisdom, reason, and feelings, who can place his hand on the axial moment of the end of the third phase of the Mesozoic and the beginnings of the Kenozoic geological ages? ... What do its eyes want to tell Puran? ... There is no communication between eyes. Only a dusky waiting, without end. What does it want to tell? We are extinct by the inevitable natural geological evolution. You too are endangered. You too will become extinct in nuclear explosions, or in war, or in the aggressive advance of the strong as it obliterates the weak, ... think if you are going forward or back. ... What will you finally grow in the soil, having murdered nature in the application of man-imposed substitutes? ... The dusky lidless eyes remain unresponsive.

For the modern Indian the pterodactyl is an empirical impossibility. For the modern tribal Indian the pterodactyl is the soul of the ancestors. The fiction does not judge between the registers of truth and exactitude, simply stages them in separate spaces. This is not science fiction. And the pterodactyl is not a symbol.

To read *Frankenstein* and 'Pterodactyl' together is an act of supplementation that leads us into the history of the present.

From *Critical Inquiry*, 12 (1985), 243–61.

NOTES

[The post-colonial criticism advanced in Gayatri Spivak's essay moves beyond the frameworks of feminism and deconstruction which it adapts and reassesses. Feminist criticism and women's writing are seen to be dependent on notions of individualism which are Western constructs and as such associated with imperialism. While *Jane Eyre* and *The Wide Sargasso Sea* similarly employ the language of individualism, *Frankenstein*, though full of imperialist sentiments, undoes the oppositions on which Western individualism is based. Such individualism, crystallised in Kant's three-part subject and represented by different figures in the novel, is presented as a disunified entity riven with the territorialising aspirations of the individual imagination. In contrast, the monster offers a different version of humanity and the 'framing woman', Mrs Saville, the occasion and recipient of the letters, occupies a feminine subject position that does not, individualistically, serve to close or assimilate the text in an imperialist manner. The novel's refusal of closure opens on to other questions. In the 'Postscript' to the essay, Spivak reflects on the critical strategy employed in 1985 and goes beyond the critique of imperialism to argue for a practice of reading and writing in which the post-colonial writer's relationship to history and the future is assessed in very different terms from the 'specular master-slave enclosure' staged in *Frankenstein*. Ed.]

1. My notion of the 'worlding of a world' upon what must be assumed to be uninscribed earth is a vulgarisation of Martin Heidegger's idea; see 'The Origin of the Work of Art', *Poetry, Language, Thought*, trans. Albert Hofstadter (New York, 1977), pp. 17–87.

2. See Charlotte Brontë, *Jane Eyre* (New York, 1960); all further references to this work will be included in the text.

3. See Jean Rhys, *Wide Sargasso Sea* (Harmondsworth, 1966); all further references to this work will be included in the text. And see Mary Shelley, *Frankenstein; or, The Modern Prometheus* (New York, 1965); all further references to this work will be included in the text.

4. I have tried to do this in my essay 'Unmaking and Making in *To the Lighthouse*', in *Women and Language in Literature and Society*, ed. Sally McConnell-Ginet, Ruth Borker, and Nelly Furman (New York, 1980), pp. 310–27.

5. As always, I take my formula from Louis Althusser, 'Ideology and Ideological State Apparatuses (Notes towards an Investigation)', *'Lenin and Philosophy' and Other Essays*, trans. Ben Brewster (New York, 1971), pp. 127–86. For an acute differentiation between the individual and individualism, see V. N. Vološinov, *Marxism and the Philosophy of Language*, trans. Ladislav Matejka and I. R. Titunik, Studies in Language, vol. 1 (New York, 1973), pp. 93–4 and 152–3. For a 'straight' analysis of the roots and ramifications of English 'individualism', see C. B. MacPherson, *The Political Theory of Possessive*

Individualism: Hobbes to Locke (Oxford, 1962). I am grateful to Jonathan Rée for bringing this book to my attention and for giving a careful reading of all but the very end of the present essay.

6. I am constructing an analogy with Homi Bhabha's powerful notion of 'not-quite/not-white' in his 'Of Mimicry and Man: The Ambiguity of Colonial Discourse', *October*, 28 (Spring 1984), 132. I should also add that I use the word 'native' here in reaction to the term 'Third World Woman'. It cannot, of course, apply with equal historical justice to both the West Indian and the Indian contexts nor to contexts of imperialism by transportation.

7. See Roberto Fernández Retamar, 'Caliban: Notes towards a Discussion of Culture in Our America', trans. Lynn Garafola, David Arthur McMurray, and Robert Márquez, *Massachusetts Review*, 15 (Winter–Spring 1974), 7–72; all further references to this work will be included in the text.

8. See José Enrique Rodó, *Ariel*, ed. Gordon Brotherston (Cambridge, 1967).

9. For an elaboration of 'an inaccessible blankness circumscribed by an interpretable text', see my 'Can the Subaltern Speak?' *Marxist Interpretations of Culture*, ed. Cary Nelson (Urbana, Ill., 1988), pp. 271–313.

10. See Elizabeth Fox-Genovese, 'Placing Women's History in History', *New Left Review*, 13 (May–June 1982), 5–29.

11. Rudolph Ackerman, *The Repository of Arts, Literature, Commerce, Manufactures, Fashions, and Politics* (London, 1823), p. 310.

12. See Terry Eagleton, *Myths of Power: A Marxist Study of the Brontës* (London, 1975); this is one of the general presuppositions of his book.

13. See Sandra M. Gilbert and Susan Gubar, *The Madwoman in the Attic: The Woman Writer and the Nineteenth-Century Literary Imagination* (New Haven, Conn., 1979), pp. 360–2.

14. Immanuel Kant, *Critique of Practical Reason, The 'Critique of Pure Reason', the 'Critique of Practical Reason' and Other Ethical Treatises, the 'Critique of Judgement'*, trans. J. M. D. Meiklejohn et al. (Chicago, 1952), pp. 328, 326.

15. I have tried to justify the reduction of sociohistorical problems to formulas or propositions in my essay 'Can the Subaltern Speak?' The 'travesty' I speak of does not befall the Kantian ethic in its purity as an accident but rather exists within its lineaments as a possible supplement. On the register of the human being as child rather than heathen, my formula can be found, for example, in 'What Is Enlightenment? in Kant, *'Foundations of the Metaphysics of Morals', 'What Is Enlightenment?' and a Passage from 'The Metaphysics of Morals'*,

trans. and ed. Lewis White Beck (Chicago, 1950). I have profited from discussing Kant with Jonathan Rée.

16. Jean Rhys, in an interview with Elizabeth Vreeland, quoted in Nancy R. Harrison, *Jean Rhys and The Novel as Women's Text* (Chapel Hill, 1988). This is an excellent, detailed study of Rhys.

17. See Louise Vinge, *The Narcissus Theme in Western European Literature Up to the Early Nineteenth Century*, trans. Robert Dewsnap et al. (Lund, 1967), ch. 5.

18. For a detailed study of this text, see John Brenkman, 'Narcissus in the Text', *Georgia Review*, 30 (Summer 1976), 293–327.

19. See, e.g. Thomas F. Staley, *Jean Rhys: A Critical Study* (Austin, Tex. 1979), pp. 108–16; it is interesting to note Staley's masculist discomfort with this and his consequent dissatisfaction with Rhys' novel.

20. I have tried to relate castration and suppressed letters in my 'The Letter As Cutting Edge', in *Literature and Psychoanalysis; The Question of Reading: Otherwise*, ed. Shoshana Felman (New Haven, Conn., 1981) pp. 208–26.

21. This is the main argument of my 'Can the Subaltern Speak?'

22. See Barbara Johnson, 'My Monster/My Self', *Diacritics*, 12 (Summer 1982), 2–10.

23. See George Levine, *The Realistic Imagination: English Fiction from Frankenstein to Lady Chatterley* (Chicago, 1981), pp. 23–35.

24. Consult the publications of the Feminist International Network for the best overview of the current debate on reproductive technology.

25. For the male fetish, see Sigmund Freud, 'Fetishism', *The Standard Edition of the Complete Psychological Works of Sigmund Freud*, ed. and trans. James Strachey et al., 24 vols (London, 1953–74), 21:152–7. For a more 'serious' Freudian study of *Frankenstein*, see Mary Jacobus, 'Is There a Woman in This Text?' *New Literary History*, 14 (Autumn 1982), 117–41. My 'fantasy' would of course be disproved by the 'fact' that it is more difficult for a woman to assume the position of fetishist than for a man; see Mary Ann Doane, 'Film and the Masquerade: Theorising the Female Spectator', *Screen*, 23 (Sept.–Oct. 1982), 74–87.

26. Kant, *Critique of Judgement*, trans. J. H. Bernard (New York, 1951), p. 39.

27. See [Constantin François Chasseboeuf de Volney], *The Ruins; or, Meditations on the Revolutions of Empires*, trans. pub. (London, 1811). Johannes Fabian has shown us the manipulation of time in 'new' secular histories of a similar kind; see *Time and the Other: How Anthropology Makes Its Object* (New York, 1983). See also Eric R.

Wolf, *Europe and the People without History* (Berkeley and Los Angeles, 1982), and Peter Worsley, *The Third World*, 2d edn (Chicago, 1973); I am grateful to Dennis Dworkin for bringing the latter book to my attention. The most striking ignoring of the monster's education through Volney is in Gilbert's otherwise brilliant 'Horror's Twin: Mary Shelley's Monstrous Eve', *Feminist Studies*, 4 (June 1980), 48–73. Gilbert's essay reflects the absence of race-determinations in a certain sort of feminism. Her present work has most convincingly filled in this gap; see, e.g. her recent piece on H. Rider Haggard's *She* ('Rider Haggard's Heart of Darkness', *Partisan Review*, 50, no. 3 [1983], 444–53).

28. 'A letter is always and *a priori* intercepted, ... the "subjects" are neither the senders nor the receivers of messages. ... The letter is constituted ... by its interception' (Jacques Derrida, 'Discussion', after Claude Rabant, 'Il n'a aucune chance de l'entendre', in *Affranchissement: Du transfert et de la lettre*, ed. René Major [Paris, 1981], p. 106; my translation). Margaret Saville is not made to appropriate the reader's 'subject' into the signature of her own 'individuality'.

29. The most striking 'internal evidence' is the admission in the 'Author's Introduction' that, after dreaming of the yet-unnamed Victor Frankenstein figure and being terrified (through, yet not quite through, him) by the monster in a scene she later reproduced in Frankenstein's story, Shelley began her tale 'on the morrow ... with the words "It was on a dreary night of November"' (p. xi). Those are the opening words of ch. 5 of the finished book, where Frankenstein begins to recount the actual making of his monster (see p. 56).

30. The following is a slightly revised extract from Spivak, *Thinking Academic Freedom in Gendered Post-Coloniality* (Cape Town, 1992), pp. 28–32.

31. Mary Wollstonecraft Shelley, *Frankenstein, or the Modern Prometheus (the 1818 text)*, ed. James Rieger (Chicago, 1974), pp. 95, 96.

32. Mahasweta Devi, 'Pterodactyl, Pirtha, and Puran Sahay', in *Imaginary Maps*, trans. Gayatri Chakravorty Spivak (New York, forthcoming).

33. This is of course rigorously to be distinguished from a romanticisation of the *tribal* as pre-history (or the 'unconscious') that Kuman Sangari correctly deplores in 'Figures of the Unconscious', *Journal of Arts and Ideas* (1991).

Further Reading

The section headings are broad guidelines to critical approaches.

EDITIONS OF THE NOVEL

Mary Shelley, *Frankenstein: or, The Modern Prometheus,* ed. M. K. Joseph (Oxford: OUP, 1969). [1831 edition]

—, *Frankenstein: or, The Modern Prometheus* (the 1818 Text), ed. James Rieger (Chicago and London: Chicago UP, 1982).

—, *Frankenstein: or, The Modern Prometheus,* ed. Maurice Hindle (Harmondsworth: Penguin, 1985). [1831 edition]

—, *Frankenstein: or, The Modern Prometheus* (the 1818 Text), ed. Paddy Lyons (London: Dent, 1992).

—, *Frankenstein: or, The Modern Prometheus* (the 1818 Text), ed. Marilyn Butler (London: Pickering, 1993).

BIBLIOGRAPHIES

Frank, Frederick S., 'Mary Shelley's *Frankenstein*: a Register of Research', *Bulletin in Bibliography*, 4 (1983), 163–87.

Lyles, W. H., *Mary Shelley: An Annotated Bibliography* (New York and London: Garland, 1975).

Spector, Robert D., *The English Gothic: A Bibliographic Guide to Writers from Horace Walpole to Mary Shelley* (Westport, Conn: Greenwood Press, 1984).

GENERIC STUDIES

Aldiss, Brian, 'The Origin of the Species', *Extrapolation*, 14 (1973), 167–91.

Butler, Marilyn, *Romantics, Rebels and Reactionaries: English Literature and its Background 1760–1830* (Oxford: OUP, 1981).

Hume, Robert D., 'Gothic versus Romantic: a Re-evaluation of the Gothic Novel', *PMLA*, 84 (1969), 282–90.

Jackson, Rosemary, *Fantasy: The Literature of Subversion* (London and New York: Methuen, 1981).

Kiely, Robert, *The Romantic Novel in England* (Cambridge, Mass: Harvard UP, 1972).
Levine, George, *The Realistic Imagination: English Fiction from Frankenstein to Lady Chatterley* (Chicago and London: Chicago UP, 1981).
Levine, George and Knoepflmacher, U. C., *The Endurance of Frankenstein: Essays on Mary Shelley's Novel* (Berkeley, Cal.: U. of California Press, 1979).
Platzner, Robert L., 'Gothic versus Romantic: a Rejoinder', *PMLA*, 86 (1971), 266–74.
Punter, David, *The Literature of Terror: A History of Gothic Fiction from 1765 to the Present Day* (London: Longman, 1980).
Schug, Charles, 'The Romantic Form of Mary Shelley's *Frankenstein*', *Studies in English Literature 1500–1900,* 17 (1977), 607–19.
Swingle, L. J., 'Frankenstein's Monster and its Romantic Relatives: Problems of Knowledge in English Romanticism', *Texas Studies in Literature and Language,* 15 (1973), 51–66.

BIOGRAPHICAL CRITICISM

Carson, James P., 'Bringing the Author Forward: *Frankenstein* through Mary Shelley's Letters', *Criticism*, 30 (1988), 431–53.
Clubbe, John, 'Mary Shelley as Autobiographer: the Evidence of the 1831 Introduction to *Frankenstein*', *Wordsworth Circle,* 12 (1981), 102–6.
Dunn, Jane, *Moon in Eclipse: A Life of Mary Shelley* (New York: St. Martin's Press, 1978).
Lovell, Ernest J. Jr, 'Byron and Mary Shelley', *Keats–Shelley Journal,* 2 (1953), 35–49.
Murray, E. B., 'Shelley's Contribution to Mary Shelley's *Frankenstein*', *Keats-Shelley Memorial Bulletin*, 29 (1978), 50–68.
Spark, Muriel, *Child of Light: A Reassessment of Mary Wollstonecraft Shelley* (Hadleigh, Essex: Tower Bridge Publications, 1951) [reprinted in revised form as *Mary Shelley* (London: Constable, 1988)].
Sunstein, Emily W., *Mary Shelley: Romance and Reality* (Boston: Little, Brown, 1989).

LITERARY-HISTORICAL APPROACHES

Callahan, Patrick J., '*Frankenstein,* Bacon, and the "Two Truths" ', *Extrapolation,* 14 (1972), 39–48.
Clifford, Gay, '*Caleb Williams* and *Frankenstein:* First-Person Narratives and "Things as They are" ', *Genre*, 10 (1977), 601–17.
Crawford, Iain, 'Wading through Slaughter: John Hampden, Thomas Gray, and Mary Shelley's *Frankenstein*', *Studies in the Novel,* 20 (1988), 249–61.
Crouch, Laura E., 'Davy's *A Discourse Introductory to a Course of Lectures on Chemistry:* a Possible Source for *Frankenstein*', *Keats–Shelley Journal*, 27 (1971), 35–44.

Florescu, Radu, *In Search of Frankenstein* (Boston: Graphic Society, 1975).
O'Rourke, James, '"Nothing More Unnatural": Mary Shelley's Revision of Rousseau', *English Literary History*, 56 (1989), 103–12.
Pollin, Burton R., 'Philosophical and Literary Sources of *Frankenstein*', *Comparative Literature*, 17 (1965), 97–108.
Rieger, James, 'Dr Polidori and the Genesis of *Frankenstein*', *Studies in English Literature 1500–1900*, 3 (1963), 460–72.
Tannenbaum, Leslie, 'From Filthy Type to Truth: Miltonic Myth in *Frankenstein*', *Keats–Shelley Journal*, 26 (1977), 101–13.
Todd, Janet M., 'Frankenstein's Daughter: Mary Shelley and Mary Wollstonecraft', *Women and Literature*, 4 (1976), 18–27.
Vasbinder, Samuel Holmes, *Scientific Attitudes in Mary Shelley's Frankenstein* (Ann Arbor: UMI Research Press, 1984).
Young, Arlene, 'The Monster Within: the Alien Self in *Jane Eyre* and *Frankenstein*', *Studies in the Novel*, 25 (1991), 325–38.
Ziolkowski, Theodore J., 'Science, *Frankenstein* and Myth', *Sewanee Review*, 89 (1981), 34–56.

NEW CRITICISM

Bloom, Harold, '*Frankenstein*, or the New Prometheus', *Partisan Review*, 32 (1965), 611–18.
Dunn, Richard J., 'Narrative Distance in *Frankenstein*', *Studies in the Novel*, 6 (1974), 408–17.
Ketterer, David, *Frankenstein's Creation: the Book, the Monster and Human Reality* (Victoria, BC: Victoria UP, 1979).
McInerney, Peter, '*Frankenstein* and the Godlike Science of Letters', *Genre*, 13 (1980), 455–75.
Rao, E. Nagaswara, 'The Significance of *Frankenstein*', *Triveni*, 37 (1968), 20–6.
Seed, David, '*Frankenstein*: Parable of Spectacle?' *Criticism*, 24 (1982), 327–40.
Wexelblatt, Robert, 'The Ambivalence of *Frankenstein*', *Arizona Quarterly*, 36 (1980), 101–17.

PSYCHOANALYTIC CRITICISM

Hill, J. M., '*Frankenstein* and the Physiognomy of Desire', *American Imago*, 332 (1975), 335–58.
Joseph, Gerhard, 'Frankenstein's Dream: the Child as Father of the Monster', *Hartford Studies in Literature*, 7 (1975), 97–115.
Rubenstein, Marc A., ' "My Accursed Origin": the Search for the Mother in *Frankenstein*', *Studies in Romanticism*, 15 (1976), 165–94.
Twitchell, James B., '*Frankenstein* and the Anatomy of Horror', *Georgia Review*, 37 (1983), 47–78.
Veeder, William, 'The Negative Oedipus: Father, *Frankenstein* and the Shelleys', *Critical Inquiry*, 12 (1986), 265–90.

MARXIST–HISTORICIST–POSTCOLONIAL CRITICISM

Lew, Joseph W., 'The Deceptive Other: Mary Shelley's Critique of Orientalism in *Frankenstein*', *Studies in Romanticism,* 30 (1991), 255–83.

Moretti, Franco, *Signs Taken for Wonders: Essays in the Sociology of Literary Forms,* trans. Susan Fischer, David Forgacs and David Miller (London: Verso, 1983).

Paulson, Ronald, 'Gothic Fiction and the French Revolution', *English Literary History*, 48 (1981), 532–54.

Vlasopolous, Anca, '*Frankenstein's* Hidden Skeleton: the Psycho-Politics of Oppression', *Science Fiction Studies,* 10 (1983), 125–36.

FEMINIST AND GENDER CRITICISM

Gilbert, Sandra M. and Gubar, Susan, *The Madwoman in the Attic: the Woman Writer and the Nineteenth-century Literary Imagination* (New Haven and London: Yale UP, 1979).

Hatlen, Burton, 'Milton, Mary Shelley and Patriarchy', in *Rhetoric, Literature and Interpretation,* ed. Harry R. Garvin (London and Toronto: Associated University Presses, 1983).

Hodges, Devon, '*Frankenstein* and the Feminine Subversion of the Novel', *Tulsa Studies in Women's Literature,* 2 (1983), 155–64.

London, Bette, 'Mary Shelley, *Frankenstein*, and the Spectacle of Masculinity', *PMLA*, 108 (1993), 253–67.

Moers, Ellen, *Literary Women* (London: Women's Press, 1978).

Oates, Joyce Carol, '*Frankenstein's* Fallen Angel', *Critical Inquiry,* 10 (1984), 543–54.

Poovey, Mary, '"My Hideous Progeny": Mary Shelley and the Feminisation of Romanticism', *PMLA*, 95 (1980), 332–47.

Randel, Fred V., '*Frankenstein,* Feminism and the Intertextuality of Mountains', *Studies in Romanticism,* 24 (1985), 515–32.

Smith, Susan Harris, '*Frankenstein:* Mary Shelley's Psychic Divisiveness', *Women and Literature*, 5 (1977), 42–53.

Tillotson, Marcia, '"A Forced Solitude": Mary Shelley and the Creation of Frankenstein's Monster', in *The Female Gothic,* ed. Juliann E. Fleenor (Montreal and London: Eden Press, 1983), pp. 167–75.

POSTSTRUCTURALIST CRITICISM

Botting, Fred, *Making Monstrous: Frankenstein, Criticism, Theory* (Manchester: Manchester UP, 1991).

Cottom, Daniel, '*Frankenstein* and the Monster of Representation', *Substance*, 28 (1980), 60–71.

Ferguson, Frances, 'The Nuclear Sublime', *Diacritics,* 14 (1984), 4–9.

Jacobus, Mary, 'Is There a Woman in this Text?', *New Literary History,* 14 (1982), 119–41.

Johnson, Barbara, 'My Monster/My Self', *Diacritics,* 12 (1982), 2–10.

Musselwhite, David, E., *Partings Welded Together: Politics and Desire in the Nineteenth-century English Novel* (London and New York: Methuen, 1987).
Sherwin, Paul, '*Frankenstein*: Creation as Catastrophe', *PMLA*, 96 (1981), 883–902.

Notes on Contributors

Chris Baldick is Professor of English at Goldsmiths' College, University of London. His publications include *The Social Mission of English Criticism, 1843–1932* (Oxford, 1983), *In Frankenstein's Shadow: Myth, Monstrosity and Nineteenth-century Writing* (Oxford, 1987), *The Concise Oxford Dictionary of Literary Terms* (Oxford, 1990) and, as editor, *The Oxford Book of Gothic Tales* (Oxford, 1993).

Peter Brooks is Tripp Professor of Humanities at Yale University. His publications include *The Melodramatic Imagination: Balzac, Henry James, Melodrama and the Mode of the Excess* (New Haven, 1976), *Reading for the Plot: Design and Intention in Narrative* (Oxford, 1984) and *Body Work: Objects of Desire in Modern Narrative* (Harvard, 1993).

Barbara Claire Freeman is Assistant Professor of English and American Literature at Harvard University. She has published articles in *The Yale Journal of Criticism, Cahiers du Grif, Paragraph* and *Oxford Literary Review* and is preparing for publication a book entitled *Representing Excess: Gender and the Sublime in Women's Fiction.*

Jerrold E. Hogle is Professor of English at the University of Arizona. His publications include articles on Romantic poetry and Gothic fiction and a book, *Shelley's Process: Radical Transference and the Development of his Major Works* (Oxford, 1988).

Margaret Homans is Professor of English at Yale University. Her publications include *Women Writers and Poetic Identity: Dorothy Wordsworth, Emily Brontë, and Emily Dickinson* (Princeton, 1980) and *Bearing the Word: Language and Female Experience in Nineteenth-century Women's Writing* (Chicago, 1986).

Joseph A. Kestner is McFarlin Professor of English at the University of Tulsa. His publications include *The Spatiality of the Novel* (Detriot, 1978), *Protest and Reform* (Madison, 1985), and *Mythology and Misogyny* (Madison, 1989).

Anne K. Mellor is Professor of English and Women's Studies at the University of California, Los Angeles. Her publications include *Blake's*

Human Form Divine (Berkeley, 1974), *English Romantic Irony* (Cambridge, Mass., 1980), *Mary Shelley: Her Life, Her Fiction, Her Monsters* (London and New York, 1988), *Romanticism and Gender* (London and New York, 1993) and, as editor, *Romanticism and Feminism* (Bloomington, 1988) and *The Other Mary Shelley: Beyond Frankenstein* (Oxford, 1993).

Beth Newman is Associate Professor of English at Southern Methodist University, Dallas. She has published articles in *PMLA* and *Novel* and is completing a book, *The Fictive Gaze: Sexual Politics and Visual Relations in Nineteenth-century British Fiction*.

Paul O'Flinn is Principal Lecturer in English at Oxford Brookes University. His publications include *Them and Us in Literature* (London, 1975) and *How to Study Romantic Poetry* (Basingstoke, 1988).

Gayatri Chakravorty Spivak is Professor of English and Comparative Literature and Adjunct Professor of Philosophy at Columbia University. Her publications include the translation of Jacques Derrida's *Of Grammatology* (Baltimore, 1976), *In Other Worlds: Essays in Cultural Politics* (London and New York, 1987), *The Post-Colonial Critic: Interviews, Strategies, Dialogues* (London and New York, 1990) and *Outside in the Teaching Machine* (London and New York, 1993).

Index